BUDDHISM IN TAIWAN

BUDDHISM IN TAIWAN

Religion and the State, 1660–1990

Charles Brewer Jones

University of Hawai'i Press
Honolulu

Library of Congress Cataloging-in-Publication Data
Jones, Charles Brewer, 1957–
    Buddhism in Taiwan: religion and the state, 1660–1990 /
Charles Brewer Jones.
        p.   cm.
    Includes bibliographical references and index.
    ISBN 0–8248–2061–4 (alk. paper)
    1. Buddhism—Taiwan—History.   2. Religion and state—
Taiwan.   I. Title.
BQ649.T32J65   1999   98–31740
294.3'095124'9—dc21   CIP

Printed by The Maple-Vail Book Manufacturing Group.

CONTENTS

**Part III
From Retrocession to the
Modern Period (1945–1990)**

ACKNOWLEDGMENTS

Although I cannot list all of the people whose time and assistance made this study possible, a few stand out as having given crucial help at several points. I wish to thank Prof. Chu Hai-yüan of the Ethnology Institute of the Academia Sinica, whose sponsorship enabled me to reside in Taiwan from 1993 to 1994. Two of my classmates at the University of Virginia, Miss Yang Yih-feng and Miss Huang Yi-hsün, opened doors and helped with perplexities on several occasions. I also wish to thank the monks and nuns of the Xilian Temple in Sanhsia, especially the vice-abbot, Dr. Huimin, and the guest prefect, Huiqian, for their hospitality and willingness to answer my endless questions. Special thanks go also to the teachers and staff of the Fa Kuang Institute of Buddhist Studies and the Chung-Hwa Institute of Buddhist Studies for their help and compassion, especially the Chung-Hwa for allowing me to spend days on end in their storage facilities, rooting through back issues of various Buddhist journals. Dr. Heng Ch'ing of the National Taiwan University Philosophy Department provided much-needed guidance, as did Profs. Lin Meirong and Lu Huixin of the Ethnology Institute of the Academia Sinica, the former for help in understanding *zhaijiao,* and the latter for pointers in approaching the Buddhist Compassion Relief Tz'u-Chi Association. The monks and nuns of the Nongchan Temple in Peitou also deserve mention, especially Guogu and the abbot, Dr. Shengyan, for their patience with me when I was struggling most with the language. And I could not have hoped to complete this study had it not been for the expert language instruction offered by the Inter-University Program for Chinese Language Study in Taipei. *Xiexie laoshimen!*

I also benefited from interaction with other Western scholars of religion in Taiwan; and I wish to express my gratitude to Dr. Philip Clart and Dr. Paul Katz, and especially to Dr. Marcus Günzel of Göttingen University for his many timely cautions. Dr. John Shepherd of the University of Virginia Anthropology Department also steered me to many sources that helped enormously in contextualizing my study in terms of modern Western scholarship.

Financial assistance came from several quarters during the research and writing phases. Funding for fieldwork came in the form of a Dupont Fellowship from the University of Virginia for the 1993–1994 academic session, and a grant (no. SC6811) from the Pacific Cultural Foundation. During the writing phase I was supported by a Skinner Scholarship administered through St. Paul's Memorial Church, Charlottesville, and a University of Virginia Graduate Arts and Sciences Dissertation Year Fellowship.

I cannot begin to put into words the incalculable debt of gratitude that I owe to my advisor, Dr. Paul Groner, who has helped me in more ways than I can number. His discipline, academic rigor, and high standards of scholarship set an example that I will spend the rest of my professional career emulating; I am also grateful that his patience, good humor, and friendship made the graduate school process enjoyable and rewarding.

I would be less than filial if I omitted to mention my deep thankfulness to my parents and my in-laws for their unstinting support, both material and moral, through the whole graduate school experience.

And, finally, there is my dear wife, Brenda. Although dedications to spouses might seem de rigueur in works such as this, there are probably few partners who would have allowed themselves and their children to be dragged halfway around the world and back in pursuit of a dream; and so it is with all my love that I dedicate this work to her.

NOTES ON ROMANIZATION AND PRONUNCIATION

The scholar whose research area is Taiwan faces a real dilemma when choosing a romanization system. For the past several decades, Western sinologists have cut their linguistic teeth on the pinyin system that is the standard on the mainland and in international journalism. However, the ROC government on Taiwan has only recently acknowledged that this system is the international standard, and English materials produced there still make a very inconsistent use of the older Wade–Giles system. Religious studies as a discipline has also been very slow in accepting pinyin as the standard.

However, when the 1992 edition of the *Far East Chinese–English Dictionary* came out in Taiwan, it dropped Wade–Giles altogether and adopted pinyin romanization and indexing.[1] Thus, I have decided to utilize pinyin as my primary system. (The reader should note, however, that both systems ignore the fact that many of the personages discussed in the following pages spoke only Hokkien, and may have lived their entire lives without ever hearing their own names pronounced in Mandarin!) I have made exceptions in two cases: (1) geographical names that are already well-known under a certain non-pinyin spelling (e.g., Taipei instead of Taibei, Kaohsiung instead of Gaoxiong, etc.), and (2) Chinese authors who have published in English under their own romanizations of their names (e.g., Chu Hai-yüan instead of Qu Haiyuan).

With Sanskrit words and names, I have made every effort to ensure that they are romanized with the correct diacritical marks. There are, however, a few words that I deem to have become English words and so have presented them without diacritics. These words are "samsara," "nirvana," "Mahayana," "Hinayana," and "sutra."

Most letters in Hanyu Pinyin are pronounced as they are written. However, a few letters require explanation:

j: j with the tip of the tongue touching the back of the lower front teeth, as the *dg* in "judge";

zh: also a *j,* but much harder and more explosive, with the tongue curled back so the tip is pointing directly at the roof of the mouth;

x: A *sh* sound, but with the tongue positioned as for *j;*

q: a *ch* sound, but with the tongue positioned as for *j* and *x;*

z: a soft *dz* sound;

c: a hard, aspirated *ts* sound, as at the end of the word *suits;*

e: by itself, like the *oo* in "book." Followed by *n* or *ng,* like the short *u* in English. Example: *leng* would be pronounced like the English word *lung.* When following another vowel, pronounced like the English short *e;*

ui: pronounced "way." Thus, the word *shui* (water) would be pronounced "shway";

i: by itself at the end of a word beginning with *sh, ch,* or *zh,* pronounced like an *r* sound. Example: *shi* is pronounced "shr," *chi* is pronounced "chr." At all other times, pronounced like a long *e.* Example: *qi* is pronounced "chee";

ü: as an umlauted *u* in German. However, the letter *u* is pronounced as if it had an umlaut after *y, x, q,* and *j,* even though it is not normally so marked;

ong: pronounced as if written "oong."

ABBREVIATIONS

FG   *Foguang Dacidian* (Buddha's Light Dictionary) 1988

T   *Taishō Shinshū Daizokyō* (Great Collection of Scriptures Newly Edited in the Taishō Emperor's Reign)

1971 Gazetteer *Taiwan Sheng Tongzhi* (General Gazetteer of Taiwan Province), Taiwan Provincial Historical Commission, 1971

1992 Gazetteer *Chongxiu Taiwan Sheng Tongzhi* (Revised General Gazetteer of Taiwan Province), Taiwan Provincial Historical Commission, 1992

INTRODUCTION

This book primarily concerns the institutional and political aspects of the history of Chinese Buddhism in Taiwan from the mid-1600s to the late 1980s. Because the study of religion in Taiwan has been the province of anthropology and sociology in the past, it is important to state that this study is not based on either of these two disciplines, although it certainly makes occasional use of their results, particularly those drawing on historical source materials. As a study of *Chinese* Buddhism in Taiwan, this book also omits a few recent developments such as the small but growing presence of Theravāda Buddhism, and the current popularity of Tibetan esoteric Buddhism with its concomitant influx of Tibetan masters. More significantly than either of these two omissions, however, this study does not purport to examine in any depth the activities of Japanese Buddhists during the fifty-year period when Taiwan was a part of the Japanese empire, except as these activities affected the lives of the Chinese Buddhist population.

Stated positively, the primary focus of this study is the history of Chinese Buddhism as an organized religion in Taiwan; and consequently it deals with the following: The transmission of Buddhism and its cousin *zhaijiao* (vegetarian religion) to the island; the development of institutions that were or are islandwide in scope and function; biographies of significant figures; doctrinal negotiations that have helped shape the identity of Taiwan Buddhism; Buddhism's interactions with government authorities under the three regimes that have ruled the island during the period under discussion; and the legal environment that Buddhism often had to contend with.

This study came into being in the wider academic context of the acceptance of Taiwan studies as a separate field of inquiry. From 1949 to the mid-1980s, the Nationalist government actively discouraged scholarship that concentrated on Taiwan as a discrete politico-cultural entity, fearing that "Taiwan studies" might be a code word for Taiwan separatism.[1] Western researchers, who depended upon the government's good graces for visas and access to materials, felt constrained to adopt this viewpoint. Not only that, but during periods of severe anti-Nationalist criticism in the West, scholars who wished to concentrate on Taiwan were suspected by their Western colleagues of being Nationalist sympathizers or apologists.[2] Furthermore, because, prior to America's diplomatic recognition of the Beijing government in 1979, researchers had no access to sites or materials located on the mainland, they were forced to go to Taiwan for language training and field research on the subject of "greater China" as defined by both the Nationalist regime and their own academic communities. As a result, many scholars went to Taiwan to pursue the goal of understanding "Chinese society," "Chinese culture," or "late imperial Chinese history," an approach subject to severe criticism.[3]

Religious studies were not immune to the exigencies imposed by these conditions. The most massive study of Chinese Buddhism ever undertaken in Taiwan to date was that of Holmes Welch in the early 1960s. Although he did much of the research for his books *The Practice of Chinese Buddhism* and *The Buddhist Revival in China* on the island, his overall aim was not to understand Taiwan Buddhism as such, but to gather oral histories from mainland refugee monks so as to reconstruct what Chinese Buddhism had looked like *there* prior to the Communist takeover.[4] As far as I can determine, he never once interviewed a native Taiwanese cleric, nor did he address any issues peculiar to Buddhism in Taiwan, such as the lingering effects of the Japanese occupation, or the conflicts that ensued between native clergy and the very mainland monks upon whom he depended for his research.

A few scholars from Japan, notably Nakamura Hajime, Kubo Noritada, Yoshioka Yoshitoyo, and Kamata Shigeo, did write on

Buddhism in Taiwan during this period; but their scholarship is largely unsatisfying on two counts. Studies such as Kubo's are overly dependent upon Nationalist government sources, such as the 1956 *Draft
Gazetteer of Taiwan Province* or the 1971 *Gazetteer of Taiwan Province,*
which he uses uncritically and often simply quotes verbatim.[5] Others,
such as Yoshioka's, are impressionistic and lack documentation.[6] Perhaps
the best of the Japanese accounts are those by Nakamura, who commissioned a Taiwan scholar, Zhang Mantao, to write the basic text that
Nakamura then arranged to have translated into Japanese;[7] and
Kamata's, since he has worked in the field for a long time and has come
to a deep understanding of Taiwan Buddhism.[8]

Many things have changed since the publication of these studies. The
lifting of the Bamboo Curtain after 1979 meant that scholars interested
in mainland China now had direct access to their sources and no longer
needed to rely on Taiwan as the sole supplier of information on China
as a whole. The lifting of martial law in 1987 did much to alleviate the
threat of government sanctions should the scholar appear too much a
partisan of Taiwan culture and possibly Taiwan independence. The
Nationalist government itself has initiated widescale democratization,
allowing local culture to find its own voice and make its presence felt.
Notably, the official government school curriculum now includes large
sections on local history and culture, topics once rigorously excluded
from school textbooks.[9] Scholars in Taiwan itself, particularly those of
Taiwanese heritage, are beginning to turn their attention to the study of
Taiwan as a separate cultural and historical unit and, at the same time, are
involving themselves more with the international academic community, making their findings available to a wider circle of colleagues.

The academy in the West has responded to these changes. In 1992,
the John King Fairbank Center at Harvard University set up its Taiwan
Studies Workshop.[10] The Association for Asian Studies now has a
Taiwan Studies Group, and the American Political Science Association
has a Conference Group on Taiwan Studies.[11] Many academics, even if
they consider themselves China specialists, are still paying more attention to Taiwan as a source of pressure and influence on the mainland.
The government in Taiwan has further encouraged scholarly inquiry
by opening up academic resources and funding. The result has been an
explosion of publications in Taiwan area studies.

All of the above indicates a growing scholarly concensus that Taiwan is distinct enough from the whole of China to merit the consolidation of its own special study. At this point, in order to press the necessity of the study of Taiwan Buddhist history, I want to say a few words about those aspects that make it distinctive.

Taiwan has been part of "greater China" for only four of the last hundred years (1945–1949). From 1895 to 1945, it was part of the Japanese empire, and Chinese Buddhism had to plot its course cautiously. It had to make itself acceptable to the Japanese government in order to survive the backlash against religious groups that resulted from local rebellions early in the colonial period, and it accomplished this by forming Buddhist associations with Japanese Buddhism under the aegis of the viceregal government. The most important of these associations was the South Seas Buddhist Association, founded in 1922. The same circumstances forced *zhaijiao* and Buddhism to make common cause for mutual protection, and their institutional affiliation during this time constitutes the only instance in Chinese history where the "orthodox" Buddhist establishment recognized and worked together with a form of White Lotus-style folk Buddhism.

Later, when the "Japanization Movement" *(kominka undō)* and its concomitant "temple reformation" *(jibyō seiri)* measures took effect, most lineages of Taiwan Buddhism put themselves directly under the administrative control of Japanese Buddhist schools. All through this period, however, one finds the countervailing sentiment that Japanese Buddhism, in which priests drink wine, eat meat, and marry, was decadent and that its influence was to be resisted. Thus, at the same time that Taiwan's ethnic Chinese Buddhists were joining Japanese associations and subordinating themselves to Japanese lineages, they also brought "orthodox" Chinese Buddhist ordinations to the island for the first time and tried very hard to keep the Chinese *saṁgha* ideal alive.

When, in the face of the Communist victory on the mainland, the Nationalist government fled to Taiwan in 1949, it was accompanied by two kinds of Buddhist clergy. One was clergy who came to Taiwan as refugees or as soldiers in the Nationalist army. These monks and nuns struggled for bare subsistence in a strange land that viewed them with great suspicion. The other kind consisted of eminent monks, men who had been high functionaries in the Buddhist Association of the

Republic of China (*Zhongguo Fojiao Hui,* hereafter BAROC) on the mainland and who readily found government patronage through pre-existing connections. These monks gained quick ownership of government-confiscated Japanese temples, and were able to set themselves up as the governing body administering the Buddhist establishment in Taiwan. Local clergy found themselves underrepresented in a legislative body that claimed to house representatives from all over China, just as the population at large found itself outnumbered by mainland representatives in the Legislative Yuan. The consequent imposition of mainlander rule has occasionally been a source of tension within the Buddhist community. The need to cope with ill-feeling and resistance on the part of the local culture also colored the BAROC's mission and effectiveness, and probably contributed to the extreme cliquishness that hampered its effectiveness in subsequent decades.

The above remarks should make it clear that Buddhism in Taiwan has a unique history derived from a unique set of historical and environmental circumstances. I hope that the present study will fill a need yet to be addressed in the current boom in Taiwan studies: an examination of Buddhism as an organized, institutional religion on the island of Taiwan.

PART I

THE MING AND QING DYNASTY

(1660–1895)

CHAPTER 1

———*⁓*———

THE QING-DYNASTY PERIOD

THE ARRIVAL AND DEVELOPMENT OF BUDDHISM IN TAIWAN

The history of Buddhism in Taiwan begins with the arrival of the Chinese people. There is no way to tell exactly when the first Han Chinese settlers migrated to Taiwan, but government records indicate that there was a Chinese presence on the island well before the Dutch colonists arrived in 1624. The *1971 Gazetteer* goes on to state that there were Buddhist monks among the Chinese inhabitants. However, these monks maintained only the most minimal forms of Buddhist practice and were, in effect, mere caretakers of small temples built by the local Chinese people. The monks' main function was to provide funeral and memorial services for the Chinese population (Kubo 1984:49–50). Whatever Buddhism existed in 1624 suffered from the Dutch law prohibiting the practice of any religion other than Christianity; the penalty for "idol worship" was a public flogging followed by banishment

(Zhang 1979b:59). Thus, a more substantial level of Buddhist presence and practice had to wait for the first large-scale wave of Chinese immigrants, who arrived with the Ming loyalist Zheng Chenggong (also known as "Koxinga") in 1661 following the downfall of the Ming dynasty.

Zheng Chenggong (1624–1662) had been carrying out a protracted rebellion against the Qing dynasty forces for many years when he decided to force the hand of the Manchu court by beseiging Nanjing. After his defeat at the hands of the Qing army on September 8 and 9, 1659, he grew less confident of his ability to maintain control over his base of operations along the southeastern coast of Fujian and Guangdong provinces, and decided to move his forces to Taiwan. He arrived toward the end of April 1661, accompanied by a fleet of warships carrying several thousand trained and battle-seasoned troops, and made landfall near the poorly manned and provisioned Dutch installation at Fort Provintia in what is now the town of Tamsui *(danshui)*. By February of the next year, he had succeeded in taking the southern Dutch installation of Fort Zeelandia (in modern Tainan city), thus expelling the Dutch and putting the entire island under his control. However, it quickly became clear that his plans for retaking the mainland from the Qing court were unrealizable; and in his frustration he began to commit acts of madness and brutality against his own people, even his own family. Consequently, he soon lost the loyalty of his followers. He died in June 1662 at the age of thirty-eight (Mote and Twitchett 1988,7:717–724).

The vast majority of those who followed Zheng Chenggong to Taiwan came from the provinces of Fujian and Guangdong; even after Zheng arrived with several thousand followers in 1661, people from these areas continued to migrate across the Taiwan Strait (Kubo 1984:51–52). Because all of the Chinese inhabitants of Taiwan were recent immigrants, Buddhism, and indeed all of the religions that they brought with them, exhibited both continuities and discontinuities. Migration involves tearing oneself away from home and family, and moving to a new environment in which one may feel quite isolated and vulnerable. Under these circumstances, immigrants will attempt to recreate as much of the life to which they are accustomed as possible, thus creating strands of continuity. (The existence of "Chinatowns" and

"Little Italies" in many major American cities attests to this process.) However, immigrants must also adapt themselves and their lifestyles to their new situation, so discontinuities also result.

Continuities and Discontinuities

First, let us look at the continuities. During the early Qing period, the bodhisattva Guanyin was the most worshipped Buddhist figure in Fujian province among the common people (Hsing 1981:11). This has remained so in Taiwan to the present day. A 1959 government survey found that Guanyin was the second most popular deity on the island, with 441 temples dedicated to her (Lin 1976:42). (The first most popular was Wangye, a folk/Daoist divinity.) In the same survey, Śākyamuni Buddha came in fifth, with 306 temples.

Another source of continuity lies in the connection between temples in Taiwan and their counterparts on the mainland. Frequently, immigrants to Taiwan brought with them either an image of a deity from their temple back home or some incense ashes to enshrine in new temples they built in Taiwan. Very often, these new temples simply took on the names of their mainland counterparts. For example, the Longshan Temple in Taipei, founded in 1738, is named for a Longshan Temple in Quanzhou prefecture, Fujian province (*Buddhism in Taiwan* n.d.:19). This temple was founded by immigrants from three counties *(xian or yi)* in this prefecture (Jinjiang, Huian, and Nan'an) who established Guanyin, the primary deity of the mainland temple, as the main object of worship in the new temple. (Editorial Committee for the Complete Annals of the Longshan Temple 1951:10). So closely were these links maintained that the devotees of the Longshan Temple in Taipei periodically organized trips to the original Longshan Temple in Fujian province, taking the Guanyin image with them in order to "renew her power" (*Buddhism in Taiwan* n.d.:19–20). Sometimes, a more direct link was established when Taiwan temples recruited their abbots from mainland temples (Hsing 1981:11), as a result of which the southern lineages of Buddhism predominated at this time.

During this early period, temples in Taiwan met operating expenses by the traditional method: they owned farmlands and rented them to tenant farmers. Some of the larger temples owned fairly extensive tracts of land. A Qing government gazetteer published in 1743 states that the Haihui Temple in Tainan owned 50 *jia* of pastureland in back and six *jia* of garden space out front (a *jia* equals 0.97 hectares, or about 2.396 acres). The Mituo Temple owned land in Fengshan County from which it received 72 *shi* of rice paddy annually (a *shi*, literally a "stone," is an ancient measure of weight equal to about 182.6 pounds). The Fahua Temple owned about two *jia* of uncultivated land as well as an entire lake. The Zhuxi Temple received rice and paddy from 12 *jia* of land (*Chongxiu Fujian Taiwan Fuzhi* [1743] 1983:1112–1113). These landholdings were generally sufficient to provide for the temples' financial needs until the cession of Taiwan to Japan in 1895, when the new government confiscated these lands, forcing temples to look for other ways to support themselves (Lin Hengdao 1976:42).

One other factor of continuity deserves mention. The fortunes of Buddhism in Taiwan, as on the mainland, tended to rise and fall in dependence upon its relationship with the government and with the wealthy and intellectual classes. Many temples were founded on land donated by government officials and intellectuals, or built with funds they provided (Hsing 1981:10), following a pattern that has held since Buddhism first arrived in China. It is thus no accident that the earliest Buddhist temples flourished in the capital city of Tainan, although the constant military pressure from the Qing court during the period of Zheng rule must have made temple construction difficult.

When the Qing court finally took Taiwan in 1683, the political situation settled down, and other temples went up in the years following. The first of these, the Fahua Temple in Tainan, also shows the dependence of Buddhism on the governing and intellectual classes. The intellectual in this case is one Li Maochun, who came to Taiwan in 1664 in response to Zheng Chenggong's son Jing's call for all Ming loyalists who wished to avoid the disturbances on the mainland to come to Taiwan. Li owned a hermitage *(an)* called the "Dream Butterfly Garden" *(Mengdie yuan),* which he donated to the monk Jiuzhong for the construction of the temple (*Chongxiu Fujian Taiwan Fuzhi* [1743] 1983:1113). In 1708, Song Yongqing, the magistrate of Fengshan County, donated the funds for the new Front Hall and the Bell and Drum Towers of the Fahua Temple (ibid.). The Haihui Temple (predecessor of the present-day Kaiyuan Temple, Tainan), is another example, having been built in 1692 on a plot of land behind a villa belonging to the Zheng family itself (ibid:1112).

Despite the fact that Buddhism in Taiwan grew out of and continued to be an integral part of Chinese Buddhism, some very striking discontinuities appeared from the very beginning. First, on the mainland during that period, the Qing bureaucracy proscribed the construction of temples built by the common people *(minjian chuangjian)*. These restrictions stemmed from the government's wariness of revolutionary secret societies that tended to congregate around temples. However, the government was much weaker and its ability to enforce imperial decrees much more limited on Taiwan than elsewhere in China, and so privately built temples were probably more numerous. Many of these were simply set up at first in the largest room of a private residence until circumstances allowed the construction of a more suitable building (Chen Ruitang 1974:2).

This development produced some interesting results. Because so many temples in Taiwan were founded by private citizens with sometimes minimal knowledge of their religious traditions, many anomalies ensued. We have just seen how the immigrants from Fujian and Guangdong brought images from their home districts and enshrined them in their houses or in temporary huts until they could build proper temples. One result was that occasionally, in the intervening years, the people forgot which deities the images represented and how they ought to be worshipped. So, for example, an immigrant group might bring an image of Tianshang Shengmu, a Daoist divinity, and worship her as Guanyin, a Buddhist figure. Alternately, they might take an image of Guanyin and worship her using Daoist rituals. A Japanese colonial government report issued in June of 1943 revealed the existence of 304 temples dedicated to Guanyin where she was worshipped as a completely Daoist divinity under the appellation "Mother Guanyin" *(Guanyin Ma)*. The report goes on to say, "Pigs are butchered and chickens slaughtered in front of her image in sacrifice, and so she has completely lost all of her original Buddhist significance" (Taiwan Sōtokufu Bunkyōkyoku 1943).

Lin Hengdao, a historian of Taiwan, believes that this "homegrown" quality gives Taiwan temples a special character that one does not encounter on the mainland. In several temples in Taiwan that have

been active since the late-Ming/early-Qing period, one can see a pro-
fusion of altars dedicated to a substantial number of divinities. Lin
asserts that for the most part, temples on the mainland are dedicated to
one divinity only (Lin Hengdao 1976:41). This, however, is a very
broad, unsupported generalization that stands in need of verification.

Some temples in Taiwan during the Qing dynasty fulfilled functions far beyond the religious sphere. Large temples might also serve as
community gathering places, meeting-halls for trade guilds and other
groups, and loci of political power (Chen Ruitang 1974:3). I will
quote Lin Hengdao's account of the role of the famous Longshan
Temple in Taipei as an example.

> During the Qing, Taipei's Longshan Temple was a central meeting place
> for trade guilds from the three *yi* of Jinjiang, Huian, and Nan'an in
> Quanzhou prefecture [in Fujian]. It had a great deal of economic muscle
> and military strength. It collected a five percent sales tax on anything
> imported from Quanzhou. At that time, the Longshan Temple not only
> took responsibility for Mengjia's municipal government, self-defense,
> and external relations, it also provided a center for socializing, education,
> and entertainment. In this respect its power was second only to the
> medieval European trade guilds. It could bring a lot of influence to bear
> on government policy. Once, during the Guangxu reign period
> [1875–1908], the Taiwan provincial governor planned to build a railroad,
> putting a large bridge across Mengjia. But because the authorities at the
> Longshan Temple opposed it, it was moved to another site across a rice
> paddy as a compromise. From this one can see the government's weak-
> ness relative to the large temples (Lin Hengdao 1976:42).

As Lin explains, the reason for this lies in the weakening of lineage ties
that followed upon immigration into Taiwan (see also Shepherd
1993:512, n. 26). In Fujian and Guangdong at the end of the Ming and
the early Qing, villages tended to be dominated by a single family; and
so the locus of political power at the village temple was the ancestral
hall. However, people migrating to Taiwan left their families behind and
typically settled in villages with émigrés from other towns and families.
In addition, the Qing government banned the emigration of women
and children, with the result that most of the immigrants were men
travelling alone. The communities of Taiwan tended to be multi-sur-
name and largely composed of men bereft of their familial support net-
works. Thus, temples founded on ties other than lineage affiliation

took over the political and social functions previously belonging to ancestral halls (Lin Hengdao 1976:42).[1]

The State of Taiwan Buddhism Under the Qing

Chinese and Japanese scholars are unanimous in their negative assessment of the state of Buddhism in Taiwan in the period between the brief reign of Zheng Chenggong and the cession of Taiwan to Japan in 1895. The modern Taiwan jurist and legal historian Chen Ruitang speaks for many other historians in attributing the weak condition of Buddhism in Taiwan during this period to Taiwan's status as an untamed frontier.

> Taiwan at this time was a land of rain and miasmas, and the soil was undependable and inconsistent. Plague was rampant, and natural disasters followed upon one another. In addition, during the Qing dynasty, the ability and virtue of government officials constantly declined, the quality of government was poor, and those above competed with those below. The strong raised the banner of revolt, the weak merely swallowed their anger, and everyone lived out their days in fear (Chen Ruitang 1974:2).

Under these conditions, the common people were not interested in learning meditation or in arguing the finer points of doctrine. Instead, they built temples for other purposes: divine protection; ethnic, common-surname, and common-hometown solidarity; trade-guild association and mutual aid; and local territorial community-building (Wang Shih-ch'ing 1974:71–82; Feuchtwang 1974:263–264).

This was also not a situation attractive to the finest monks and nuns on the mainland, although some did come at the invitation of the laypeople who provided the funds and land to build temples. One of these monks was the Ven. Canche, who came over from Fujian province in response to a request from Chen Yonghua, a military staff officer who served under Zheng Jing. Chen was the moving force behind the construction of the Dragon Lake Grotto *(Longhu Yan)* in Chishan, Kaihua Settlement *(li),* and he invited Canche to serve as abbot. Canche arrived in 1675 but later moved on to found the Blue Cloud Temple *(Biyun Si)* on Fire Mountain *(Huoshan)* near present-day Chiayi. He was the first fully ordained monk known to have come over to Taiwan from the mainland.

The witness of history speaks very highly of Canche and his disciples. He was known for keeping the precepts, reciting sutras morning and evening, and worshipping the Buddha. When he first moved to Fire Mountain, he built a thatched hut in which to practice. He soon won the hearts of the local villagers with his piety and discipline, and they came and built a more suitable structure for him. When he passed away, the local people buried him in front of the temple and built a pagoda for him (*1971 Gazetteer*:49b).

The *1971 Gazetteer* states that, during the Zheng era, Canche and his disciples were the only legitimate monks in Taiwan (p. 49b). Further evidence of the paucity of properly ordained monks comes from looking at tax revenue figures from the Zheng era. The government collected two taels in tax for each Buddhist ordination certificate, and five taels per Daoist ordination. For one year, the Zheng government collected a total of 200 taels in ordination taxes from both Daoists and Buddhists, which shows how few monks there must have been in Taiwan at that time (*1971 Gazetteer*:48b).

There were somewhat more monks in the more-settled situation of the mid- and late-Qing dynasty. However, because of the widespread destruction and restructuring of temples during the period of Japanese rule, there is very little documentary evidence regarding other monks. Only a few names of the more eminent of Taiwan's monks appear in the *1971 Gazetter*. There is the Ven. Zhengsheng, also called Shi'an, one of the abbots of the Haihui Temple. He was known for his abilities in painting, singing, and playing go (a board game), and for his success in praying for rain during times of drought. Another is the Ven. Lianfang, also known as Ouchuan, who was the abbot of the Sanguan Tang. He was widely acclaimed for his singing, painting, and skill in the medical arts. A third is the Ven. Zhaoming, whose paintings of orchids and chrysanthemums were unrivalled, and who wrote a collection of poetry called *Songs Sung in Huanhua* (*1971 Gazetteer*:51a).

The *1971 Gazetteer,* while praising the achievements of monks such as these, laments that legitimate monks at this time were the minority. Chen Ruitang explains that one of the reasons for the dearth of properly ordained monks was the simple lack of any ordination platform in Taiwan during the Qing dynasty. Monks could and did accept disciples in Taiwan, shave their heads, and assign them monastic names; but if these disciples wished to take full ordination, they had to go to the mainland at their own expense, something only a very few were willing to do. So, Chen writes, the "monks" that one found in Taiwan during this time were usually only novices who had not undergone full ordination and the training in temple procedures that went with it. "They had shaved heads, wore robes, and lived in temples, and they thought that being able to recite a few scrolls of scripture was sufficient" (Chen Ruitang 1974:11). The result is that the only legitimate monks in Taiwan at that time were those such as Canche, who had come from the mainland, and the few who had made the journey to the mainland and back.

Chen also notes that there were very few nuns in Taiwan at the beginning of the Qing era, and none at the end. This is because the government actually put a stop to women's ordinations because of the confused and disorderly atmosphere that reigned at that time. The government also proscribed the ordination of Daoist priestesses for the same reason (Chen Ruitang 1974:11).

Taiwan, being a frontier area away from the centers of civilization and the reach of the law, came to be a haven for many fugitives. Some of these came into Taiwan wearing monk's robes and shaved heads, and the *1971 Gazetteer* offers a selection of tales of these "dubious monks" *(guaiseng).* Here is one such story, taken from the *Overview of Qing Dynasty Folk History (Qingchao Yeshi Daguan):*

At the time when Zheng Chenggong occupied Taiwan, there was an extraordinary monk in Guangdong who took up his robe and bowl and crossed the sea to visit him. He claimed to be familiar with the arts of disappearing into the earth and predicting the future by observing the wind, which gave him the key to the martial arts, and he said that Zheng should test him and see. Zheng did as he suggested, and in discussing strategy with him found he went with certainty straight to the crux of each question, and that he was able to draw together the general outline [of the present situation] with [the ways of] antiquity. Zheng marvelled at him, honored him as a "national teacher" [*guoshi*], and accorded him special treatment, which the monk accepted with equanimity.

This monk was by nature proud and haughty, even with his fellow monks. At first his peers treated him with deference because of the esteem in which Zheng held him, but over a long period of time, his presumptuousness even began to bother Zheng, who came to suspect him of being a Qing court spy. The disgruntled monks, seeing their opening, fanned up Zheng's animosity until he came to regard this monk as a bandit. His heart became burdened with the problem of how to get rid of him, but he also was afraid of the monk's prowess in *qigong,* and feared that if his plans went awry, he might bring disaster upon himself.

Now there was a man named Liu Guoxuan, a hoodlum who used to hang around on the coast. Once he had gotten drunk and killed someone, and had joined Zheng's forces for fear of being caught and punished. Zheng admired his courage, and had given him a high post. Upon hearing Zheng's complaint, he arched his back and vowed to stake his own life against that of this troublesome monk to repay Zheng for his patronage. Zheng was afraid that the venture would fail, but while he hesitated, Liu read his thoughts, went down on his knees before him and declared, "The success or failure of this matter is your servant's responsibility. Let your majesty not give it another thought."

So Liu proceeded to strike up a friendly relationship with this monk. A little over a month later, Liu called the monk over to bathe with him in a pond fed by hot springs, and engaged the monk in friendly banter, saying, "The National Teacher has matched the Buddha's own original nature. You have a clear mind that seeks the Way, and your prowess in *gongfu* is perfect. Suppose that you encountered Mataṅgī herself, could you maintain your composure?" The monk smiled and said, "The Venerable Canliao used to say that the plaster and wadding of Chan [practice] do not drive away the spring breezes [a Chinese idiom for sexual desire], but this old monk has engaged in long and thorough application, and the vow that I took to remain aloof from the female form is yet enough to obstruct the tempter!" Liu feigned admiration at this, and the two arranged to meet another day.

Soon afterward, [Liu] gave a feast for the monk in an official reception hall for those who had offered significant public service. It was a real "red lantern and green wine" [i.e., debauched] affair, with fine dancing and excellent singing, and all the guests got dead drunk. Liu began to speak of his past and present erotic adventures, and pressed the monk to drink some more. The monk remained cheerful and composed, and kept his attention fixed on Liu. At last, the wine gave out, and Liu said, "The night is old and the evening quiet, and it is hard to find amusement. But in a back room here there is some secret sport that is very lively. Would you care to come and have a look?" The monk thought, "This is an even more interesting bit of business. What would it hurt to play along?"

So, casting aside discretion, the monk followed Liu to the secret room. Once there, he looked around a few times and saw [Liu's] pallets with their red woollen blankets covered with brocaded cushions and embroidered pillows. On top of these he saw rows of handsome young boys and fine women, most of them without a stitch of clothing on, each one of them in turn displaying their sensuality up [at him]. The brightly flickering lamplight made their lustiness appear more vividly, and their flowery faces and jadelike skin became all the more sexually beguiling.

Now there was one particularly enchanting young girl who crouched down by his side and signalled him with her finger. Would not her tender feeling and lithe bearing [be enough to] send the mind of the beholder into disorder? The monk at first appeared to ignore her, and then to regard her only lightly. But in an instant he felt his vitality give out, and he called for a servant to arrange a seat, as if he had no more strength to stand. Then Liu, as soon as he saw that this monk was unable to maintain his composure, came up from behind, took up his sword, and swung it. Little flowers of blood spattered the ground, and the monk's head fell with a cracking sound (*1971 Gazetteer*:49a, 49b).

This is an extreme example from a source of questionable reliability, and probably has more to say about popular views on monastic life and the power of spiritual practice than it does about history. Be that as it may, most monks of this period were not quite this "dubious," and their number may have included, in addition to criminals, former officials in the Ming state bureaucracy. Timothy Brook, in his study of gentry–monastic relations during the Qing dynasty, produces evidence that a number of scholar-officials who remained loyal to the deposed Ming court hid themselves by shaving their heads, donning Buddhist robes, and living in temples. They did not, however, take even the most basic of lay Buddhist precepts, and so cannot be considered genuine Buddhist monks (Brook 1993:50). Li Maochun, mentioned above in connection with the Fahua Temple in Tainan, may have been one of these; and others might have followed. As further circumstantial evidence of this possibility, we may note that the three eminent monks named in the *1971 Gazetteer* achieved their distinction in such pursuits as the scholar-dilettante of late Ming gentry society would have valued: art, poetry, games, and so on.

So much for the monks, dubious or otherwise. As we have observed, they were few in number and for the most part not of high quality. However, predominance in the Taiwan Buddhist scene throughout the Qing dynasty lay not with them, but with another strain of Buddhism altogether, a form variously called *zhaijiao* (vegetarian religion), *baiyi fojiao* (white-clad Buddhism[2]), or *zaijia fojiao* (lay Buddhism).

This form of Buddhism has been largely ignored by Western-language scholarship on Buddhism in Taiwan; but it is important that the reader understand its place and significance, because its fate under the Japanese colonial period has had repercussions in the emergence of the modern Buddhist scene.

ZHAIJIAO DURING THE QING DYNASTY

Overview

The *1971 Gazetteer* contains the following definition of *zhaijiao:*

> *Zhaijiao* means to adhere to a vegetarian diet and worship the Buddha within the householder's life. One does not leave human society, but while earning one's living in the city and village, adheres to the Buddhist precepts as a layperson (73b).

This form of Buddhism exists outside the traditional and orthodox structure of Chinese Buddhism, with its relationships of mutual aid and support between clergy and laity. *Zhaijiao* represents a strain of lay Buddhism that is completely independent of the Buddhist monastic *saṅgha,* does not look to it for teaching, and does not support it with contributions. During times of political instability it has sometimes been suspected of alignment with rebellious White Lotus societies and been subject to persecution (for example, see Murano 1934:10). For these reasons *zhaijiao,* like other forms of folk Buddhism, has been held in suspicion and contempt by the government and the orthodox Buddhist world.

Zhaijiao's *Status vis-à-vis Buddhism*

To set the scene briefly, *zhaijiao* in Taiwan distributes itself into three dominant sects: the Longhua (Dragon Flower), Jinchuang (Gold Pennant), and Xiantian (Prior Heaven) sects. The *1971 Gazetteer* mentions a fourth sect that is sometimes listed alongside these three, called the Kongmen (Gate of Emptiness) sect *(kongmen pai);* but this "sect" has no patriarchate and no organizational structure, and so should not really be counted (1971 Gazetteer:73b).[3] All three sects claim descent not only from their own founders, but also from China's ancient cultural heroes and sages, the Buddha, and the Indian and Chinese Chan patriarchs; but in reality, they are the direct or indirect descendants of the Luo Teaching *(luojiao),* founded by Luo Qing (1442–1527) (*1971 Gazetteer*:74a).

That all of these sects were identified primarily by the term *zhaijiao* indicates that they and others saw vegetarianism as their most distinguishing characteristic. The word *zhai,* still used today to indicate the ideal Buddhist diet that eschews meat, fish, wine, and the five "pungent herbs" (onions, garlic, leeks, scallions, and chives), was originally a Confucian term. Within imperial circles, it indicated a set of purificatory practices that all participants in the Sacrifice at the Round Altar (i.e, sacrifices offered to heaven by the emperor) were to engage in for the three days prior to the event (*1971 Gazetteer*:73b; E-tu Zen Sun 1961:188, 190). Because of the connotations of purification and special discipline, Buddhism borrowed the term to designate its special dietary proscriptions. *Zhaijiao* took this as its special defining quality, even though in actual practice members might observe the proscription on meat only at certain times (see Lin and Zu 1994:5 for a description of the practice in contemporary Taiwan *zhaijiao*). This style of lay Buddhism was also sometimes known as *caijiao* (lit., vegetable religion) or *chicaijiao* (religion of eating vegetables), thus reinforcing the impression that this was its most essential characteristic (Zheng 1984:39).

Besides vegetarianism, members of *zhaijiao* also vow to observe other rules of conduct. During the initiation ceremony, members take refuge in the Three Jewels of Buddhism (the Buddha, the teachings, and the monastic community), take the traditional Five Lay Precepts *(wujie)* (not to kill, steal, indulge in illicit sex, lie, or drink alcohol), and vow to engage in the Ten Virtues *(shishan)* (i.e., to refrain from the Ten Demeritorious Acts *(shi'e),* viz., killing, stealing, illicit sex, lying, double speech, malicious speech, salacious talk, greed, anger, and false views). Members also vow not to engage in other antisocial behavior: eat meat, smoke opium, smoke cigarettes, chew betel nut, gamble, or set firecrackers (Murano 1934:9).

Given that *zhaijiao* initiates take refuge in the Three Jewels of Buddhism, the third of which is the monastic community, an interesting question arises: how do they reconcile this vow with the sect's explicit rejection of the clergy's traditional supervisory role over laity? The translation of the Longhua initiation text given in J.J.M. de Groot's *Sectarianism and Religious Persecution in China* includes this revealing section:

> The Third Refuge! Bow down your heads to the earth and take refuge in the *saṅgha!* This *saṅgha* is not the tonsured clergy, nor the clergy who collect subscriptions from house to house; it is composed of all disciples who offer incense and keep temples in the country-hills, and to whose care our Old Patriarch [i.e., Luo Qing] has entrusted the religious books he left (de Groot [1903–04] 1970:206).

Modern researchers have found that contemporary adherents maintain a similar pride in their independence from the "tonsured clergy," even going so far as to assert superiority over them (Lin and Zu 1994:16).

Members of these sects consider themselves to be pure Buddhists; indeed, they believe their credentials on this score to be more valid than even the clergy's. However, in actual practice, at least four distinct sources of *zhaijiao* identity are discernible. The first is Buddhism, in particular the typically Buddhist emphasis on reciting scriptures and the Chan teaching of Sudden Enlightenment. The second is Daoism, from which *zhaijiao* derived the reciting of spells, and emphasis on practices for "nourishing life" *(yangsheng)* and Inner Alchemy *(neidan)*. The third is Confucianism, from which it drew the content of its ethical teaching and the concept of the "Way of Heaven" *(tiandao),* and from whose offshoot Neo-Confucianism it drew its cosmology. The last is folk religion, from which it derived its customs and its style of teaching and evangelization (Zheng 1990:73).

The specific mixture of these elements varied with each sect, each new generation of leadership, and each new "precious scroll" (*baojuan,* the name given to folk scriptures frequently written by means of spirit mediumship). For example, an examination of Xiantian Sect *baojuan* from a period of over two centuries reveals a doctrinal development from an almost purely Buddhist style at the end of the Ming Dynasty to a more overtly Daoist emphasis on *neidan* during the mid-Qing, to a balance of Buddhism, Daoism, and Confucianism with the latter predominating during the late Qing period (Zheng Zhiming 1989:49).

Marui Keijirō, an official of the Japanese government charged with investigating religion in Taiwan during the early period of Japanese rule, also noticed a Confucian bias in the Xiantian Sect, as well as a slant towards Daoism in the Jinchuang Sect (Marui 1919:82).

Outside observers were never as certain of *zhaijiao*'s Buddhist identity as believers were. Although the Japanese government officials responsible for managing religious affairs during the colonial period referred to *zhaijiao* as "lay Buddhism" *(zaike bukkyō),* they consistently classed it separately for statistical purposes, and used characteristic *zhaijiao* terminology to refer to their places of worship (*zhaitang*, "vegetarian hall") and their adherents (*zhaiyou*, "friend in vegetarianism"). Recently, scholars in Taiwan have begun exploring the phenomenon of *zhaijiao* in a more rigorous way, and as the picture of these sects' actual doctrines and beliefs becomes more clear, their differences with more established Buddhist doctrines appear more starkly.

Zhaijiao *Doctrine*

I do not propose here to present a detailed description of *zhaijiao*'s cosmology, soteriology, pantheon, and practices; such a study would be a book in itself, given the fluidity of these things even within a single lineage. However, a general picture drawn in very broad strokes of just the Xiantian Sect's beliefs reveals a doctrinal framework that is both gnostic and millenarian. According to Xiantian cosmology, behind all reality and all sages and buddhas stands a creator-deity, frequently conceived as a goddess called the "Unborn Venerable Mother" *(Wusheng Laomu)* who also goes by many other names as well (Zheng 1989:40–43, 45–46). This mother created all living beings, 9.6 billion altogether, who subsequently strayed from her, found their way to the *Sahā* world (present realm of delusion and suffering) and forgot the way home. In her mercy, the Mother sent a series of emissaries to call her children back. The identities of these savior-figures vary from one document to the next. In one scheme, the first emissary was Dīpaṁkara Buddha, whose preaching brought 200 million suffering children back home; the second was Śākyamuni Buddha, who saved another 200 million. This leaves 9.2 billion beings still entrapped and in need of a savior. For some this future savior will be Maitreya, while for others he has already come in the person of Luojiao founder Luo Qing (de Groot [1903–04] 1970:180). In another scheme, the first 200 million are saved by Daoism and the next 200 million by Buddhism; the last 9.2 billion will be saved by Confucianism (Zheng 1989:43, 50–51).

As these examples, all drawn from Xiantian literature, show, belief in the Unborn Venerable Mother was strongest in that sect, although there are scattered references to her in the writings of the other two sects as well (Zheng 1990:82). Zheng also explains why Japanese investigators often took the buddhas and sages of the past as the objects of *zhaijiao* veneration: the Unborn Venerable Mother, being ineffable, was never portrayed in paint, wood, or stone and enshrined on an altar as the others were. Rather, her presence was most often represented by a lamp on the central altar (Zheng 1990:82).

As is readily apparent, this scheme combines a Daoist or Neo-Confucian cosmology with a Pure Land Buddhist soteriology. In fact, in one Xiantian precious scroll, the entire content of religious practice prescribed by the three saviors during their periods of preaching (called the "three Dragon-flower Assemblies" [*Longhua San Hui*]) consists of progressively longer invocations of Amitābha Buddha's name: a four-character, then six-character, then ten-character invocation. In another scheme, however, the soteriology is based more on Daoist concepts of Inner Alchemy; and what the saviors teach are methods for generating the "Inner Alchemy" *(neidan)*. This particular scheme was especially popular in Jinchuang as well as Xiantian teachings (Wang Jianchuan 1993:38–40). Still others mix the two, claiming that the soteriology proclaimed at the first Dragon-flower Assembly focused on generating the Inner Alchemy, that of the second meeting revolved around Chan-style meditation, whereas the third will preach the "Principle of the True Scripture Without Words" *(wu zi zhen jing li)* (Zheng 1989:42, 48–50). One may thus see the extreme volatility of *zhaijiao* soteriological concepts. This mutability, along with the fact that the sects have remained secret societies to the present day and researchers do not know what practices members undertake, should encourage caution against overly hasty generalizations about *zhaijiao* doctrines.

It is also apparent that the cosmology implicit in the Xiantian Sect's creation-fall-redemption story, which it shares with the other *zhaijiao* sects, reflects concepts regarding the generation of the cosmos that go all the way back to the *Laozi,* which contains descriptions of an ineffable source from which all created things derive and to which they seek to revert (see, for example, sections 25, 40, and 42 of the *Laozi*). Some terminology derives from Neo-Confucianism, especially the identification of this primal source as the *wuji,* the "limitless" or the "Extremity of Non-being," a term coined by the Neo-Confucian scholar Zhou Dunyi (1017–1073) during the Song dynasty in his *Commentary on the Diagram of the Great Ultimate (Taiji Tu Shuo).* However, in *zhaijiao* soteriology, the return to this source is not a reversion of created things to their primal state, but a return of sentient beings to a personified creator-deity. This indicates the influence of Buddhist Pure Land soteriology, and the folk conception of the Pure Land as a palpable place to which one could go after death.

This short presentation of *zhaijiao* beliefs should also shed some light on the question of how Buddhist these sects really were. Their soteriology sometimes coincided with more traditional Chinese-Buddhist schemes of salvation, especially in recommending the invocation of Amitābha's name and seated Chan meditation to "see one's nature" directly. However, it should be apparent that their conception of the predicament from which living beings need salvation differs radically from the traditional Buddhist exposition. In contrast to the latter's assertion that beings have been caught in the cycle of birth-and-death since beginningless time, *zhaijiao* posits a well-defined etiology of human existence; and salvation comes as a reunion with one's long-lost mother, a concept that must have appealed powerfully to Chinese culture with its strong view of family and quasi-worship of parents.

The Longhua Sect

Of the three generally recognized sects, the Longhua is the largest and has the most detailed records and elaborate sectarian ramifications. Its mainland source is a Luojiao sect known as Laoguan Zhaijiao, whose name marks the first appearance of the term *"zhaijiao."* This term is properly applied only to the Laoguan Sect and the Longhua sect that issued from it. The application of this name to the other two sects originated with the Japanese colonial government in Taiwan after 1895, for convenience in compiling statistics (Zheng 1989:31; Overmyer 1978:292).

The founder of the Laoguan Zhaijiao sect was one Yao Wenyu (1578–1646), although he himself claimed to be the third patriarch of the sect. The first was, of course, Luo Qing himself. The second is Yin Jinan (1540–1582), a native of Chuzhou Prefecture, Zhejiang Province. As the dates indicate, Yin was born several years after Luo Qing's death in 1527, which precludes any possibility of a direct master–disciple relationship between the two men. At the age of eleven, Yin went to the Jinshan Temple for ordination into the Buddhist novitiate, but was turned away by the abbot. Four years later, Yin converted to Luojiao and took the religious name Puneng. He quickly made progress in religious austerities and gathered a large number of followers. He soon began claiming that he was a direct reincarnation of Luo Qing and calling himself the "Holy Patriarch of the Limitless" (wuji shengzu), a name that would lead believers to associate him with Wusheng Laomu, the highest goddess of the religion. In 1582, his activities attracted official attention, and he was arrested and executed at the age of forty-two on charges of inciting the masses (Zheng 1984:40). He left behind a number of writings, and his "Limitless Orthodox Sect" (wuji zhengpai) went through alternating periods of growth and decline. The Laoguan Zhaijiao sect came into being sometime after Yin's death, and his Limitless Orthodox Sect merged with it before its transmission into Taiwan (Zheng 1990:74).

Yao Wenyu was born in the same prefecture in Zhejiang as Yin four years before the latter's death. Legend has it that Yao did not open his mouth to speak until the age of four. Sometime in his early adulthood he took refuge in Yin's Limitless Orthodox Sect and took the religious name Pushan. At the age of thirty-six he achieved initial enlightenment and undertook a tour of the tombs of his two predecessors, after which he called three meetings in order to declare himself the Third Patriarch of Laoguan Zhaijiao. He called these meetings "Longhua Hui" (Dragon-flower Assemblies); this name and the number of these meetings were highly symbolic, calling to mind the soteriological scheme outlined above in connection with Xiantian doctrines. At each meeting thousands of followers came to take refuge under him (Zheng 1990:75).

These meetings mark the real beginning of the Longhua Sect, which derived its name from them.

From the third patriarch Pushan (i.e., Yao Wenyu) to the thirteenth patriarch Pucong, the Longhua sect had a unified lineage of leaders that gave it a point of focus, despite subsequent brachiation. The lineage, called the "dharma-burden system" *(fadan xitong),* became the object of controversy after the passing of the eleventh and twelfth patriarchs, two brothers named Pule (lay name: Zhang Jiayi), who died in 1779; and Puying (lay name: Zhang Lang), who died in 1788. Unfortunately, they deceased without having named a successor; and as the Longhua Sect searched for a new patriarch, a great deal of factional infighting ensued.

At last, sect members held a general election, with the result that a relatively senior member of the sect named Pucong attained the office. Pucong was evidently a very humble man who did not aspire to high office, and so he immediately passed the dharma-burden on to Puyou, a younger man. However, the general membership of the sect, angry at having their wishes thwarted, forced Pucong to resume the office of patriarch. Puyou, a man of quite different temperament and ambitions, refused to accept that he was no longer patriarch after the dharma-burden had been legitimately passed on to him; and so he absconded with the official seal of *zongchi* (the title of the leader of the sect) and fled to White Horn Ridge *(baijiaoling)* in Xianyou county. There he set up his own *zhaitang* called the Hanyang Hall *(hanyang tang),* thus forming a new subsect and ending forever the unified patriarchate of the Longhua Sect. At this point, the history of the Longhua Sect centers around the fortunes of its three main subsects.

Yishi Hall Branch. The Yishi Hall Branch *(yishi tangpai)* was the earliest subsect to emerge, simply by virtue of being the center from which the other two branches split off. Its headquarters *(benshan)* was the Yishi Hall in Fuzhou, Fujian Province, the hall founded around 1696 by the tenth patriarch Puyue and developed by the next two patriarchs. It is not clear when this branch entered Taiwan, but it seems to have been somewhere around the time of Pucong's election

as thirteenth patriarch, or somewhere during the Qianlong Reign
period (1736–1796). The earliest Yishi Hall on record is the Shenzhai
Hall *(shenzhai tang)*, established in Taichung city in 1797 (Zheng
1984:40–41). According to a manuscript written around 1900 by an
Yishi Branch devotee named Zheng Langsong of Taichung:

> During the time of [twelfth patriarch] Puying, [thirteenth patriarch]
> Pucong, and [fourteenth patriarch] Puyao, of the lineage of Pubai of the
> Right Branch, those who came to Taiwan included Purong, who found-
> ed the Dadun *daochang* [i.e., the Shenzhai Hall in Taichung], and Puci of
> Zhunan [a township south of Hsinchu]. Furthermore, Puci's disciple
> Pumiao was the founder of the Shande Hall in Jiasheng (*1971
> Gazetteer*:75b).

According to the records of the Shenzhai Hall, Purong came from
Fujian province, and founded the hall in 1797. He expanded the hall
in 1804; and after his death in 1841, leadership passed on to his disciple Pujie.

The Yishi Hall Branch focused its missionary activities on the area
north of Taichung, and at its peak had twenty-five halls in what was
then Taichung *zhou* (province) (now Taichung city and Taichung,
Nantou, and Changhua counties), and forty-three in Hsinchu *zhou*
(now Hsinchu, Taoyuan, and Miaoli counties). It acted independently
of the headquarters in Fujian until 1914, when one Xu Lin went to
Fujian to receive the title *taikong* (the second highest rank in the Yishi
Hall Branch) from the *kongkong* (the highest rank), twenty-eighth
patriarch Pumei. There was a *kongkong* of the Longhua Sect in Taiwan
at the time, but he was a member of the Hanyang Hall Branch, and Xu
wanted to receive the conferral from the leader of his own branch.
After Xu's return, he went ahead and promoted others to the rank of
taikong as Pumei's proxy, primarily because of the increasing difficulty
of travel to the mainland as the Japanese occupation progressed (*1971
Gazetteer*:75b). In addition to this, the thirtieth patriarch Pujing's visit
to Taiwan in 1929 further reinforced contact with the home temple
(Zheng 1990:76).

Hanyang Hall Branch. We have already seen how this branch was
founded as a direct result of the break between the thirteenth patriarch

Pucong and his putative successor Puyou. Not long after his defection, Puyou, now the *zongchi* of his own subsect, sent his *fuchi* (the second highest rank in this sect) Putao to Taiwan to establish the branch there. Putao arrived somewhere around 1797 and went directly to Tainan, where he remained for eight years. What happened after this is difficult to determine, because the *1971 Gazetteer* and the researchers who rely upon it for their information are all ultimately dependent upon the garbled chronology in the manuscript left by Xu Lin. According to him, the earliest hall to have been constructed was the Huashan Hall, which was said to have been built in 1765, at least twenty years before the schisms that divided the Longhua Sect.

However, the *1971 Gazetteer* goes on to state that Putao, assisted by his follower Pujue, built the Huashan Hall in 1799 and then the Deshan Hall in 1814. This statement presents another problem. This date is well beyond the eight years that Putao is supposed to have remained in Taiwan; and indeed only two lines after stating this fact, the *1971 Gazetteer* tells us that Putao boarded a ship to go back to Fujian Province in 1804 but unfortunately died on the way (*1971 Gazetteer*:75a). I believe that this is simply a typographical error, either in the *1971 Gazetteer* or in its manuscript sources. The date given for the founding of the Deshan Hall is "Jiaqing 19"; but if the character *shi* (ten) is omitted, then the date becomes 1804 and the discrepancy is resolved.

Fuxin Hall Branch. The Fuxin Hall Branch *(fuxin tangpai)* was the last of the three subsects to form. The initial force behind its formation was the fourteenth patriarch Puyao. His lay name was Lu Bing, and he had a strong religious bent and had maintained a vegetarian diet since childhood. At the age of twenty-four he joined the Yishi Hall and threw himself into its religous life but left in disgust after the controversy surrounding the election of the thirteenth patriarch, in spite of his having been chosen as the fourteenth patriarch. He lived for a while in the Hanyang Hall but eventually left and founded the Fuxin Hall in Fuzhou city. It went on for a while as a part of the Hanyang Hall Branch; but because of Puyao's energy and charisma, it grew until it was in a position to act independently and establish its own lineage.

This branch entered Taiwan at about the same time as the Hanyang Hall Branch and operated mainly in the central region, eventually establishing twelve halls around Taichung and Changhua (*1971 Gazetteer*:75b, 76b; Zheng 1984:42).

The Jinchuang Sect

The Jinchuang (Gold Pennant) Sect claims to be a direct offshoot of Luojiao by virtue of the putative connection between its founder, Wang Zuotang (1538–1620) and the fourth patriarch of Luojiao, Sun Zhenkong. According to a pair of sectarian chronicles quoted in the *1971 Gazetteer*, Wang Zuotang was born in 1564 (the reasons for the discrepancy with the dates given above will become apparent shortly). In 1578, his niece was accepted as an empress in the central palace, giving him the title of "outer uncle" *(waishu)*. However, Wang Zuotang had already been ordained as a monk with the name Guangming, so he received no special ceremonies or treatment. By this time, Longhua Sect founder Luo Qing had passed away; and his son Fo Zheng and daughter Fo Guang (also named Jiliunü) had taken over their father's work of upholding lay Buddhism but had changed their sectarian affiliation to Longhua. Wang Zuotang wanted to marry Jiliunü; but she refused his requests, so he married a daughter of the Zheng family instead. He took leave of Master Luo and went to Guanlin Prefecture to follow the Patriarch Sun, who was a follower of the Longhua Sect.

In 1582, Sun ceded his leadership position to Wang, then only eighteen years old. Eventually, Wang's talent and success made it possible for him to break free of the Longhua Sect altogether; and by 1612 he took a grand tour of Anhui and Zhejiang provinces, where he proselytized openly in the streets. (Other sources give his itinerary at this time as Jiangnan, Henan, Guangdong, and Guangxi provinces [Wang Jianchuan 1993:25].) His procedure was to beat a gong to attract an audience and raise a golden banner, which accounts for the name of the sect he founded. Enough people took refuge in his new teaching to worry the imperial court, and he was arrested. However, because of his niece's position, the court pardoned him in 1619. There were apparently no further incidents; and he passed away quietly ten years later, leaving his sect in the care of his disciple and second patriarch Dong Yingliang (1582–1637) (*1971 Gazetteer*:81a–b).

This biography provides many important bases for the Jinchuang Sect's self-understanding. It provides Wang with two different connections with Luo Qing, first in his failed attempts to marry Luo's daughter, and second in his alignment with Luo's fourth-generation disciple Sun Zhenkong. Furthermore, his 1612 tour gives the halls in those areas the cachet of the founder's presence. However, in 1993, Academia Sinica scholar Wang Jianchuan made a systematic survey of a broad range of sect documents and collated the results in order to determine the real course of Wang Zuotang's life, and discovered that much of the traditional account did not stand up to scrutiny. Finally, Wang Jianchuan shows that Wang Zuotang never personally made the grand tour attributed to him late in life but instead deputed his chief disciple Dong Yingliang to go on a preaching mission (Wang Jianchuan 1993:15–27).

The second patriarch of the sect, Dong Yingliang (1582–1637), has a fascinating biography. He was born outside Beijing in a district called Yongping in 1582, but lost his father at an early age and was sent to live with his uncle. His uncle changed the boy's name to Qingcao, dressed him in female clothing, and sold him as a serving-girl to a family named Li. There he came under the influence of the Li's daughter Yuying, who was a Longhua devotee. At the suggestion of a friend named Chang Shaosong, however, he soon switched his allegiance to Wang Zuotang's Jinchuang teaching. Through his connection with Chang, who held a very high position within the sect, Dong made the acquaintance of Wang himself, who came to think very highly of the young man. When Wang was arrested, Dong was sent southward on a tour of the countryside to spread the teachings (the very trip officially misattributed to Wang himself). During this trip, he converted his three most important followers, one of whom was named Cai Wenju (1584–1634). After he returned, Wang Zuotang made Dong his successor. Things did not go smoothly from there, however; in 1635 a White Lotus rebellion broke out, and the Jinchuang Sect was implicated in it. Twenty of its leaders were executed, six banished, and another hundred or so imprisoned. Dong Yingliang himself was executed by dismemberment in the sixteenth day of the sixth month,

1637. His followers had all been executed or had fled. Only Cai Wenju remained alive (*1971 Gazetteer*:81b; Zheng 1990:79).

Cai, like Dong, was originally a Longhua devotee but converted to the Jinchuang teachings under Dong's influence. He quickly attained a leading role in the sect and went to Fujian to found the Shude Hall (*shude tangpai*) in 1622. He was among those imprisoned after the 1635 uprising; but fortunately for the sect, he was pardoned and lived to propagate the sect's teachings and practices. He lived out the rest of his life peacefully and died at an old age (Zheng 1990:79).

It was Cai's grandson, Cai Quan, who first brought the Jinchuang sect into Taiwan sometime after the Qing court captured and subdued the island in 1683 (although Jinchuang tradition asserts that they were present prior to this; see Huang Mei 1984:748). Cai Quan established two halls in Tainan (one of which, the Shende Hall, is still standing). At the same time, another Jinchuang missionary named Weng Wenfeng established another hall, also in Tainan. Other missionaries came; and the Jinchuang sect flourished primarily in the belt connecting Tainan, Kaohsiung, and Pingtung, although Jinchuang *zhaitang* were established in other parts of the island as well. The sect recruited most of its members from among the laboring, mercantile, and farming classes, establishing twenty-seven halls in all (*1971 Gazetteer*:82a–b).

The Xiantian Sect

By all accounts, the Xiantian Sect was the strictest in observing a vegetarian diet, and it did not allow its members to marry (Zheng 1990:82). Japanese field investigators noted that its entry requirements were the most difficult to fulfill (Suzuki 1989:35). For this reason, it was always the smallest of the three sects in Taiwan, having only twenty-one halls across the island, according to the results of field investigations conducted by the Japanese in 1919 (Marui 1919). It has also been one of the most secretive and ill-documented. De Groot was able to find out almost nothing of the sect, even though he had the acquaintance of a number of sect members (de Groot [1903–04] 1970:176–196); the *1971 Gazetteer* was forced to rely entirely on the Taiwan sect leader's oral testimony collected early in this century.

As with the other two sects, the patriarchal lineage includes several figures prior to the actual historical founder, in this case Huang Dehui (1624–1690), a native of Jiangxi province. Xiantian lineages are unanimous in naming him as the ninth patriarch, but the names of the first eight are quite mutable. Regardless of the actual persons who make up the patriarchate of this sect, it is clear that the transmission of its teachings did not depend upon a physical meeting between master and disciple; several of the figures who appear on patriarchal lists lived several centuries apart. How, then, did the sect legitimate this succession? According to sect lore, Huang was in Lushan, a famous Buddhist site in Jiangxi Province, when he received Patriarch Luo's "hidden mind-dharma" by telepathy. With this transmission from afar, he was authorized to re-establish the Luo teachings and to assume the role of ninth patriarch. He worked thereafter with great vigor and success in his own home territory (Zheng 1990:80).

After his death, the sect suffered a gradual decline for about half a century, after which Wu Ziyang was named tenth patriarch at the Youyuan Temple, although it is unclear who commissioned him. After his death in 1784, the patriarchate passed to He Liaoku. Eleven years later, He was exiled into military service in Guizhou, thus bringing the teachings to the southwest. In 1802, Yuan Zhiqian assumed the mantle as the twelfth patriarch, and in 1823 he founded the Xigang Hall in Chengdu. From there he worked actively to spread the teachings in the Yangtze River valley. In 1826, the patriarchate passed to a new generation and was shared between two men, Yang Shouyi and Xu Jinan. The fact that these men both gained recognition as the thirteenth patriarch seems symptomatic of a general decentralization that prevailed during this time; history shows that several new subsects started then: Yuanming Dao; Guiyi Dao; Tongshan She; and, most importantly for Taiwan religious history after 1945, Yiguandao.

After this, the sect lost any semblance of a unified patriarchate; but Xiantian records in Taiwan list two more patriachs, Peng Shuide as the fourteenth and Lin Jinmi as the fifteenth. After their passing, the Xigang Hall in Chengdu split into two other halls with separate lineages, the Sanhua Hall and the Xihua Hall, the former of which was led by three men whom the subsect remembers collectively as the sixteenth patriarch. After these men passed from the scene, the Sanhua Hall itself underwent a further schism into no less than four more halls under four separate leaders. Two of these are important for the history of Xiantian in Taiwan. The first is the Wanquan Hall, founded by Xia Daohong, the man who was, from the Taiwan perspective, the seventeenth patriarch. Around 1861, two missionaries, Li Changjin and Huang Changcheng, came to Taiwan all the way from Chengdu in Sichuan Province in order to bring the teachings into a new region. Later, sometime during the Guangxu reign period (1875–1907), another missionary named Chen Yunrong came from the second sub-subsect, based in the Ganyuan Hall in Chengdu (Zheng 1990:80–82).

According to tradition, when the first pair of missionaries arrived in Taiwan, they decided to draw lots in order to determine who would work which territory. As it turned out, Li went to the northern end of the island, while Huang went south. They both worked very hard and enjoyed some measure of success, although, as noted, the strictness of the sect's rules and the requirement of celibacy kept it from ever rivalling Longhua in popularity (Huang Mei 1985:616). Altogether, the two founded some twenty halls (Zheng 1984:45). In the north, Li personally inducted Huang Yujie (185?–1918), the man who would dominate the sect in Taiwan through the early Japanese period and who would provide most of the oral testimony that Japanese researchers depended on for their information.

Huang Yujie was a native of Taipei, but he received his consecration from Li in the Chongfo Hall in Taichung in 1867 (Lin Wanchuan 1984:I–232). Five years later, another missionary named Cai Yunchang arrived from the mainland, and Huang traveled with him on his preaching tours. Cai saw the young man's potential and later gave him the mission of taking the teachings back to his native Taipei, equipping him with books and a sum of money before sending him on his way.

At that time, Li Changjin was still active there and toured his territory annually. During the first year that Huang was in Taipei, Li gave him a hall to cultivate. Huang worked assiduously, and in 1892 he founded the Xingshan Hall. As the 1890s progressed, all of the original missionary-leaders of the Xiantian sect passed away; and Huang gained recognition as the general leader of Xiantian in Taiwan. His leadership became official in 1908, when the leader of the sect in the Fujian–Zhejiang area visited Taiwan and formally charged Huang with responsibility for the entire island. Again, two years later, another sect leader from the mainland came and reaffirmed Huang's status, conferring upon him the formal title of *dinghang* (first navigator) (Lin Wanchuan 1984:I–232–234). Huang remained very active in religious affairs for the few years that remained to him, and we will see a few of the tasks he undertook on behalf of the wider religious community in Taiwan in the next chapter, as well as the further vicissitudes of the sect. Suffice it here to say that, in a lecture delivered toward the end of his life, Huang lamented the fact that the sect was then in decline (*1971 Gazetteer*:83b). He passed away in 1918.

CONCLUSION

As should now be evident, Buddhism and *zhaijiao* differ significantly in terms of self-concept, doctrine, and organization; so the question naturally arises: Why should they be considered together in a study of Buddhism in Taiwan? The answer is partly phenomenological and partly historical.

Despite their differences, Buddhism and *zhaijiao* during this period represented two manifestations of a single phenomenon. Many observers of East Asian religion have noted the difference between the religion that constitutes ordinary Chinese people's inherited beliefs and practices, and the religion that they consciously choose to believe and join. C.K. Yang called the first "diffuse religion" and the second "institutional religion" (Yang 1994:20–21), while more recently, Winston Davis called the first "locative religion" and the second "adventitious religion" (Davis 1992:30–32). Stated briefly, the former type consists of the religion in which people become involved by virtue of their family, place of birth, trade, or—in the case of Taiwan—common subethnic group or hometown provenance. This type of religion, and the temples in which it finds expression, constitutes the bulk of religious praxis in Taiwan during this period (cf. Feuchtwang 1974:275).

The second type, on the other hand, is comprised of those religions that are consciously chosen and which have an organized, institutional infrastructure that crosses familial, geographic, vocational, or other boundaries. During the Late Ming and Qing periods, Buddhism and *zhaijiao* were the two major forms of institutional or adventitious religion in Taiwan. As we shall see in the next two chapters, this similarity in style led to extensive cross-pollination as devotees moved from one group to the other, or even in both simultaneously.

Historically, Buddhist and *zhaijiao* history came to be tightly intertwined during the Japanese period, a fact of enormous significance. Throughout most Chinese religious history, "orthodox" (that is, clergy-supervised) Buddhism has joined the government in criticizing and seeking to undermine any kind of folk Buddhism, particularly any that followed the patterns of White Lotus religion. However, during the Japanese period, both orthodox Buddhism and *zhaijiao* subordinated themselves to Japanese Buddhist lineages and organizations as a matter of survival; and both joined to found islandwide Buddhist associations in order to represent their common interests before the government. This is the only time that I am aware of in Chinese history where monastic Buddhism has entered into an alliance with any form of folk Buddhism, or that any Luojiao-derived form of folk Buddhism has cooperated with Buddhist clergy.

Such, then, was the state of Buddhism in Taiwan during the Qing era. Taiwan was a wild frontier, and attracted people of all sorts. The monastic establishment contained a few virtuous monks and not a few charlatans, but for the most part consisted of unlearned temple caretakers and funeral specialists who lived quietly and did their jobs for the surrounding community without benefit of full ordination. Most of the laity was ignorant of Buddhist doctrines and scriptures, resulting in such anomalies as animal sacrifices before images of Guanyin and so forth; and some members broke free of the clergy and forged their own faith in the form of *zhaijiao*. Many too turned Buddhist temples into guild-halls and bases for political power. But the whole scene was to change drastically in 1895, at the end of the Sino-Japanese war, when Taiwan was ceded to Japan. It is to these changes and to the interactions between Chinese and Japanese Buddhism, as well as between Chinese Buddhism and the Japanese government, that we will turn our attention next.

PART II

THE JAPANESE
COLONIAL
PERIOD
(1895–1945)

CHAPTER 2

—≈≈≈—

THE EARLY JAPANESE PERIOD

When China ceded Taiwan to Japan at the end of the Sino-Japanese War in 1895, its government evidently did not feel that it was losing anything valuable. Li Hongzhang (1823–1901), the Qing official who signed the Treaty of Shimonoseki on behalf of the Chinese court and gave Taiwan away, later wrote in his *Memoirs:*

> Formosans are neither of us nor with us, and we praise all the ancestors that this is so! In all Asia, in all the world, I believe there are no tribes of animals called men more degraded and filthy than these people of Taiwan. ... They are cut-throats, all of them, along the coasts and back into the jungles. And so they have been from the days of Chia-Ch'ing to the present time (Li Hongzhang 1913:268).

While we must not put too much stock in his assessment of the people of Taiwan, his harsh words still reflect to some extent the societal and environmental realities that contributed to the difficulties of life at that time. We have already seen the extent to which these realities helped give shape to the Buddhism found in Taiwan during the Qing; now we shall examine what happened after the treaty went into effect and Taiwan became part of the Japanese Empire.

THE ADVENT OF JAPANESE BUDDHISM

The ethnic Chinese and aboriginal peoples of Taiwan did not agree with the Qing court that their territory should be so lightly given away. In the years following 1895, many Taiwanese people formed rebel armies and rose up to fight the Japanese, several of them under the banner of a hoped-for independent Republic of Taiwan. The Japanese responded quickly and forcefully, sending in troops to put down the rebels and restore order (Kerr 1974:28–34). Like many armies, the Japanese army came equipped with chaplains to minister to the spiritual needs of its soldiers, and in this way Japanese Buddhism entered Taiwan (*1971 Gazetteer*:53a).

These chaplain-missionaries came from many schools *(shū)* and sects *(ha)* of Japanese Buddhism. At first, their primary task was to provide spiritual service only to the troops and to Japanese citizens who had migrated into Taiwan. It was because the latter people had prior affiliations with particular lines of Japanese Buddhism that so many schools were represented among the influx of clergy; this way, most Japanese citizens could participate in the kind and style of religious activities to which they had previously been accustomed. Among the first arrivals, the Sōtō School of Zen, the Shinshū Honganji Sect, the Shinshū Ōtani Sect, the Jōdo School, and the Shingon School sent in the largest contingents (*1971 Gazetteer*:53a).

During the period of turmoil in which the Japanese had to expend the most effort to pacify the island, not many Japanese civilians came to Taiwan. As a result, the clergy sought ways to gain influence among the Chinese population and began to establish missionary preaching stations. However, it soon became apparent that the language barrier had to be overcome before they could make any headway, and so they got funds from their headquarters in Japan to set up Japanese language schools and charity hospitals. These efforts, however, were short-lived; during the years 1899–1900, the home temples were experiencing financial difficulties of their own due to the withdrawal of government support from Buddhism in favor of State Shintō (see Hardacre 1989:3–41); and they in turn reduced or cut off funds for activities that did not directly benefit Japanese citizens. Thus Japanese Buddhist organizations in Taiwan had to rely on their own resources for survival. They sought to increase revenues through performing funerals and directly appealing to the local wealthy Japanese citizenry for donations, and to decrease expenditures, in part by suspending mission programs aimed at the Chinese population (*1971 Gazetteer*:53b).

Meanwhile, the government was also taking action within the religious world. As part of an effort to consolidate political power and limit the influence of such extragovernmental bodies as temples, the viceregal authorities quickly expropriated temple land and moved to limit the economic and military functions of places such as Taipei's Longshan Temple. As Lin Hengdao explains:

> Under the Japanese, [the temples'] lands were declared either "unowned" or "ownership unclear," and confiscated for public use. Thus, [the temples] were thrown back into dependence on religious services *(foshi)* or seeking contributions. So temples were forced to collude with spirit channelers [Taiwanese: *dangki*], sandboard readers, dharma masters *(fashi)*, matchmakers *(hongyi)*, and that ilk to make a living by inciting the masses with superstitious beliefs. Other temples simply became commercialized (Lin Hengdao 1976:42).

As time went on and affairs settled down, other sects and schools of Japanese Buddhism sent monks to open up the new territory. Among these were the Shinshū Kibe Sect, the Rinzai School of Zen, the Jōdo School's Seizan Sect, the Nichiren School, the Tendai School, the Hokke School, and the Kegon School. The total number of Buddhist groups represented eventually rose to eight schools and twelve sects, and many of the members of these groups came to Taiwan determined to carry out missionary and educational activities among the Chinese, financial difficulties notwithstanding (*1971 Gazetteer*:53b).

As one might expect, the earliest offices of these groups were not full temples as such, but simply "branch offices" *(shutchōjō)* or "branch temples" *(betsuin)* organized and run under the direct supervision of the head temple *(honzan)* in Japan. Such establishments were usually referred to within each school or sect as a "missionary station" *(fukyōjō)*. In the event that a station's operations grew large enough to warrant the establishment of a full temple, the monks in charge would apply to their home temples for both concurrence and whatever

SCHOOL	TEMPLES	ABBOTS		MISSIONARIES		DEVOTEES		
		JAPANESE	CHINESE	JAPANESE	CHINESE	JAPANESE	CHINESE	KOREAN
Tendai	1	1	0	0	0	138	0	0
Shingon	4	4	0	4	1	7,487	1,040	21
Jōdo (Pure Land)	6	6	0	9	2	7,897	1,764	109
Jōdo (Seizan Sect)	1	1	0	1	2	1,500	150	0
Rinzai	15	9	5	16	43	7,913	9,334	0
Sōtō	14	9	5	11	35	9,578	10,247	1
Shinshū Honganji (Sect)	16	15	0	17	15	21,204	5,184	22
Shinshū Ōtani (Sect)	5	5	0	16	21	9,487	369	0
Nichiren	3	3	0	5	3	2,543	315	0

financial backing was available, as well as to the local viceregal authorities for permission (Chen Lingrong 1992:117).

What was the rate at which such temples were constructed? A Japanese government survey of 1941 reveals the information in the table at left.

As is readily apparent, the Sōtō and Rinzai Schools of Zen were by far the most active. They deployed the greatest number of missionaries, and they were the only schools whose native Chinese missionaries outnumbered the Japanese missionaries (although the tiny Seizan Sect had one Japanese and two Chinese missionaries). The Shinshū Honganji Sect was the most numerous in terms of devotees (Chen Lingrong 1992:121). However, it must be borne in mind that these are all very small numbers indeed. The grand total of all the devotees of Japanese Buddhism after almost fifty years of proselytizing comes only to 96,205, of whom only 28,303 were Chinese. This is at a time when the population of the island was about six million (Chen Lingrong 1992:119).

Who were the Chinese who involved themselves with Japanese Buddhism? For the most part they were people who needed good relations with the government. Most of them were from the wealthier classes of society, presumably because the exigencies of their business enterprises put them in official contact with government agencies more often than the average citizen. They might patronize Japanese Buddhist temples in order to maintain closer personal ties with the officials whose good will they needed. Others joined officially sponsored religious associations to avoid the charge of using religion as a cover for seditious activities. Finally, there were some very highly placed Chinese monks who needed a good relationship with the government in order for their temples to thrive and develop, and we shall look at the careers of four of the most important of these monks next.

THE FOUR GREAT LINEAGES OF TAIWAN BUDDHISM DURING THE JAPANESE PERIOD

Overview

Occasionally, in looking over materials on Buddhism in Taiwan issued within the island, one sees reference to the "Four Great Ancestral *Daochang*" *(si da zushi daochang)* of Taiwan (for instance, see Chu Ch'i-lin

1988, vol. 1, "Introduction"). These consist of the following four temples: (1) the Lingquan Chan Temple *(Lingquan Chansi)* in Keelung, (2) the Fayun Chan Temple *(Fayun Chansi)* in Miaoli County, (3) the Chaofeng Temple in Kaohsiung County, and (4) the Lingyun Chan Temple *(Lingyun Chansi)* on Guanyin Mountain in Taipei County.[1] What do these four temples signify for Taiwan Buddhist history?

Briefly, they represent the arrival in Taiwan of the lineages of Chinese Buddhism that would predominate during the Japanese occupation, as well as the beginning of full monastic ordinations in Taiwan. The reader will recall that, during the Qing dynasty period, Taiwan had no place for the conferral of the full monastic precepts; and anyone who wanted to receive full ordination had to travel to the mainland at his own expense. The monks who founded or revived these four temples rectified this situation. They not only received valid ordinations on the mainland, they also began taking on disciples and conferring the precepts in Taiwan. Thus they created large "tonsure families" whose personal loyalty would be to them, and whose members usually remained with them to receive the full ordination at their hands. These disciples would then go out and either assume the abbacy of other temples or found new ones of their own, and the result was the founding of the four major dharma lineages *(fapai)* in Taiwan (Jiang 1993a:49).

Welch reported on the significance of these relationships based on his interviews with Chinese monks during the early 1960s, and it is worth quoting him at length so that the reader will become familiar with the pattern and feeling of the "tonsure family."

> ... [T]hrough tonsure a monk entered a "family." The head of the "family" was his "father-master" *(shifu)* or his "grandfather-master" *(shigong)*. The rest of the family included members of various generations, who were called "older-brother-masters" and "younger-brother-masters" *(shixiong, shidi)*, "uncle-masters" *(shibo, shishu)*, "nephew-disciples" *(tuzhi)*, "grandson-disciples" *(tusun)*, and so on. Before any of these terms the word "tonsure" *(tidu)* would be prefixed to show that this, rather than ordination or transmission of the dharma, was the basis of the kinship in question.
>
> The tonsure family was a private organism within the public body of the sangha. Just as there was supposed to be a clear distinction between public and the private in lay life, so monks attempted to keep the "family matters" of the private temple separate from the public operation of large monasteries. This was one reason for the rule that disciples could

have their heads shaved and receive their training *only* at private hereditary temples. … [I]f a large public monastery allowed tonsure families
to take root there, the selection of abbots and officers would come to
depend increasingly on kinship and less and less on qualifications to
serve. …

Tonsure was not the only basis for religious kinship. The elders who
presided at a monk's ordination were considered his "ordination masters"
[*jie shifu*] and his fellow ordinees were his "ordination brothers" [*jie
xiongdi*]. Later in his career, he might enter into a series of master–disciple relationships with those from whom he received the dharma. Each
time he did so, he acquired a new set of dharma relatives. But, except
where the dharma involved the right to an abbotship, both ordination and
dharma types of kinship were largely nominal (Welch 1967:276–279;
romanization adapted for consistency).

While this quotation explains the close-knit relationships engendered
by receiving the tonsure and entering the Buddhist *saṅgha* at the hands
of a particular master, it also raises a question. If as Welch says, the
Chinese system was strict about keeping "tonsure family" relationships
out of the process of conferring and receiving full ordination, to the
extent that tonsure and ordination had to be done at different temples,
then why did these four temples in Taiwan allow their abbots to perform both functions?

The answer lies in the fact that each abbot received his ordination
at the Yongquan Temple in Fuzhou, across the straits in Fujian Province.
According to Welch (who refers to this temple in his works as Ku Shan
(gushan) after the mountain upon which it sits), Yongquan was unique
in ignoring this rule; at this temple, a prospective ordinand could
indeed receive both tonsure and full ordination in the same place
from the same master (Welch 1967:138–141). This was the model that
these four monks, along with all the others who went to the mainland
to receive the precepts, brought with them to Taiwan, where it subsequently became the norm.

Shanhui (1881–1945) and the Lingquan Temple Lineage[2]

Ven. Shanhui was a native of the Keelung area of northern Taiwan. He
was born in 1881, and his lay name was Jiang Qingjun (*1992
Gazetteer*:208). He spent his earliest childhood during a period of

constant turmoil, one that lasted until the Japanese pacified the island shortly after 1895. At the age of nine he entered into a privately run school (sishu) and managed to keep up his studies for a number of years. In 1896, at the age of fifteen, he went with his mother to take refuge in the Longhua sect of zhaijiao, and received the religious name Pujie.

Shanhui might well have spent the rest of his life as a follower of zhaijiao had it not been for the arrival of two missionary monks, Shanzhi and Miaomi, from Fujian Province in 1900. The two came to Keelung, which by this time had eclipsed Tamsui as the most important port city in the north, and lodged in a building behind a Daoist temple. With this temple as their provisional base of operations, they began preaching, lecturing on the sutras, and holding dharma-meetings for averting natural calamities, all in very popular and accessible language. As a result, they attracted bigger and bigger audiences, among whom was young Qingjun.

They quickly noticed that this was a young man of good education, a quick mind, and sincere religious feeling; and they took special interest in his religious training. Under their influence, he gradually made up his mind to leave home and become an orthodox Buddhist monk. His mother, who desired that he remain with her in zhaijiao, objected strenuously. In spite of this, in 1902 he accompanied Shanzhi back to Fujian and to the temple of Shanzhi's master Jingfeng under the pretext of going sightseeing. (Miaomi had passed away in Taiwan prior to their departure.) This was the Yongquan Temple; and Shanhui resided there for six months, during which time he received both the tonsure and full ordination. When he and Shanzhi returned to Taiwan, his mother was very upset; but, as Jiang Canteng notes, "Once raw rice is boiled, then it is cooked and there's nothing you can do about it."

Upon landing in Keelung once again, the two monks, now tonsure "brothers" under the same "master-father," set to work propagating the dharma. One of their first projects was to found a temple in Keelung as a base of operations for educating local clergy. Shanzhi, as the elder brother, took on the responsibility of working among the people to raise the funds and find the land. Shanhui looked after the day-to-day construction.

A plot of land was obtained from a Lin Laifa, who donated one *jia* from his tea plantation on Yuemei (Moonbrow) Mountain. Then, another difficulty arose from military considerations: This land sits in a pass in the ring of mountains surrounding Taipei and was crucial in the city's defenses. At that time, one needed the permission of the Japanese authorities just to photograph the area—so one may imagine the difficulties in obtaining permission to build a temple there! The monks first submitted their application in 1903; and in the temple records, it is noted that Shanzhi died in 1906 "without having completed that business."

Jiang Canteng is of the opinion that Shanzhi's death helped speed up the application process, because it left Shanhui, a native son of Keelung, free to pursue the application on his own. He quickly won the support of several local officials, and the Great Hall was finally completed in 1908. A delegate from the Yongquan Temple, the Ven. Xingjin, came to conduct the opening ceremony for the temple and to install Shanhui as abbot; and it was Xingjin who decided upon the name of the temple, based upon the mountain's natural topography and abundant water supply.

The Japanese authorities had their own reasons for wanting a large temple in Keelung. For one thing, Keelung was now the major port city and point of entry for visiting Japanese dignitaries, and the location of the Lingquan Chan Temple made it a perfect lodging for them. Also, as Welch reminds us, the Japanese were very interested in cultivating Buddhist contacts with the Chinese as a means of preparing the ground for their eventual takeover of the rest of China (Welch 1968:160–173). Thus, we see that Shanhui was able to build a base of three very important kinds of support: (1) the Japanese authorities, who trusted him to be loyal and needed him as a bridge to the mainland; (2) the Chinese authorities, who liked him because he was a local citizen known to them and because their Japanese supervisors trusted him; and (3) the moneyed class of Chinese merchants and industrialists who needed a religious outlet that would not offend the Japanese authorities.

Shanhui now found himself in a web of obligations that extended both to mainland China and to Japan. First, he was the channel by which the Yongquan Temple lineage entered into Taiwan from Fujian province. At the same time, the Sōtō line was still trying to establish its own mission in Taiwan. They considered Keelung a key mission area, but they had not yet been able to raise the money needed to build a proper temple of their own. Therefore, it was in their interest to claim Shanhui as a member of their lineage in order to get a foothold in his temple for use as a future base of operations. Immediately upon installation as abbot of the Lingquan Chan Temple, Shanhui was adopted into the Sōtō Zen lineage; and a representative of the Sōtōshū attended the ceremony.

With all this support, the temple grew rapidly. The year after its opening, Shanhui applied for permission to expand its property; and some new buildings were completed by 1910. This time, over twelve hundred people from the spheres of government, commerce, industry, and religion attended the opening celebration. That same year, on the Buddha's birthday in the fourth lunar month, Shanhui held the first transmission of lay precepts ever given in Taiwan (at least outside of *zhaijiao*). Over thirty people took the precepts, laying a foundation for the development of modern Buddhism on the island. Shanhui was not yet thirty years old at the time.

With his temple firmly established, Shanhui put his energy into helping build Buddhist organizations on the island. At other times he took care to keep his contacts fresh in mainland China, Japan, and Taiwan. For example, in 1911, he and a disciple went to the mainland and made a grand tour of Buddhist sites in Shanghai, Tiantong, Hangzhou, and Putuo Island. He also visited every temple and *zhaijiao* hall in Taiwan, working to build relationships for future cooperative ventures. He made many trips to Japan throughout the rest of his life. In 1912 he brought a copy of the Tripiṭaka back to Taiwan. Also, since the leadership of the Sōtō order rotated every year, he was obliged to go to the main Sōtō temple annually to pay his respects to the new head.

Through Shanhui's efforts, Buddhism in Taiwan was able to remain informed about currents of thought on the mainland. For example, in 1931, he prevailed upon Yuanying, the president of the BAROC, to spend two weeks in Taiwan lecturing on the sutras. In 1917, Shanhui invited no less a personage than the Ven. Taixu himself to come and deliver a series of lectures, which Shanhui translated into Hokkien. The two then embarked on a long tour around Taiwan, and later visited Japan. They found each other's company congenial, especially because they shared similar views on monastic education. Shanhui once went to visit Taixu during his time in Lushan, Jiangxi province, in the early 1920s. In 1925, when Taixu organized the first East Asian Buddhist Conference in Tokyo, Shanhui was one of three representatives from Taiwan to attend, delivering a short talk in which he showed how the monastic system fulfilled the Marxist ideal of a classless society without resorting to violence and thus could help bring about world peace (Sengcan 1981:2. For more information on the conference itself, see Welch 1968:56, 166–167).

However, it was Shanhui's educational efforts that brought about the most lasting effect. After bringing back the Tripiṭaka, he inaugurated a short course of lectures on the sutras and Buddhist doctrine, given by monks from both Japan and the mainland and attended by over forty people. This was the first time a temple had ever held a large-scale educational conference in Taiwan, and Shanhui was very clear about its purpose: "To nurture talent for spreading the dharma, and to instill a spirit of respect for the emperor and reverence for the Buddha in all people." From this the reader may see why, when other Buddhists and the devotees of *zhaijiao* were scrambling for refuge after the Xilai Hermitage Incident of 1915 (to which we will come presently), Shanhui was in Tokyo receiving a gold medal from the Taishō emperor.

In the course of his work with the Sōtō organization in Taiwan, Shanhui became close to the fifth Missioner General, Ōishi Kendō. Ōishi later returned as the seventh Missioner General and expended great efforts in founding a Sōtō-run high school in Taipei in order to augment the number of Japanese-speaking scholars in Taiwan for the benefit of the government. The school was to be called the "Taiwan Buddhist Middle School" *(Taiwan Bukkyō Chūgakurin)*. During this period of organizing (1913–1920), he asked Shanhui to be the dean of studies. Shanhui accepted, and held this position from its first year when it took in twenty-five students for its three-year curriculum, through 1935 when it adopted a full five-year curriculum, to 1937 when it expanded to include both men's and women's campuses.

Shanhui continued in this vein for the rest of his life, remaining active in organizing Buddhist associations, in education, and as abbot of the Lingquan Chan Temple. One of his disciples, Derong, was the first Taiwan cleric to go to Japan for study and later worked at the Taiwan

Buddhist Middle School as a teacher, encouraging many of its graduates to follow his example and study in Japan. He later succeeded Shanhui as abbot of the Lingquan Chan Temple (FG 6017c). Shanhui himself died in 1945, the year Taiwan was returned to Chinese rule.

Because of Shanhui's willingness to collaborate with the Japanese, much of what he accomplished came to nothing after Retrocession (*guangfu*) and the subsequent backlash against Japanese influence. The Lingquan Chan Temple went into a decline with the loss of official support; the Taiwan Buddhist Middle School changed hands and lost its religious character; all the associations that Shanhui had helped organize evaporated. However, during his life, he gave the tonsure to many disciples, who spread out all over Taiwan and founded temples of their own; the *1992 Gazetteer* lists forty-seven of these temples in all, most of which were founded by clergy who stand in the second generation after Shanhui (*1992 Gazetteer*:128–131). Therefore, he is still important as the channel through which a great number of monks, nuns, and temples trace their lineage back to the Yongquan Temple, and thus he is still revered as a patriarch in the "family tree."

Benyuan (1883–1946) and the Lingyun Temple Lineage

Like Shanhui, the Ven. Benyuan was a native of Keelung who received the tonsure and the full precepts at the Yongquan Temple in Fujian, returned to Taiwan, and then spent the remainder of his monastic career working with the Japanese viceregal government. He was born in 1883 to a family named Chen, and, also like Shanhui, received a good basic education in the classics of Chinese literature. Sometime during his early childhood he entered into the Buddhist novitiate under a monk named Yuanjing. After studying at Yuanjing's temple for a few years, he departed for the mainland, going to the Yongquan Temple in Fujian for ordination. He arrived there in 1900, and remained eleven years, returning only at the request of the Ven. Baohai, who needed help to establish a new temple in northern Taiwan.

Baohai, whose lay name was Lin Huoyan, was a native of Sanchung (now a suburb of Taipei). After taking formal refuge in Buddhism in

1896, he also traveled to the Yongquan Temple for full ordination, returning to Taiwan in 1900, the year that Benyuan departed. He set up a temple of sorts in his own home and began teaching and preaching, while looking for a way to build a proper *daochang*. His chance finally came in 1909, when he received word that the Liu clan, a wealthy agricultural and commercial family in Taipei, had recently lost their grandfather, and wished to do something on a grand scale to gain religious merit on his behalf. Baohai went to see them, and convinced them to fund and build the temple of which he had been dreaming for nine years.

The Liu family's two senior brothers set aside the money and chose a committee of three to scout out a suitable place for the new temple. By November of 1910, they had located a site on Guanyin Mountain, in the modern Wugu area of Taipei County. However, Baohai's health was deteriorating rapidly, and he lacked the energy to pursue the project on his own. He therefore got in touch with Benyuan at the Yongquan Temple in Fujian and asked him to return and help out. Upon Baohai's death, Benyuan took over as abbot of the new temple.

This turn of events well suited Benyuan's personal ambitions. He had been on the mainland for a long time, and this had had two effects on his thought and career. First, he was in Fujian in the years leading up to the Wuchang incident in 1911, when the Manchu government fell and the ROC came into being. He followed the events around him closely and became just as conversant in modern currents of thought as in matters of temple decorum. By the time he returned to Taiwan, he had already developed many ideas about what he wanted to do, and what sort of temple structure and social connections he needed to do it.

The second effect was more negative: By staying so long on the mainland, he had lost valuable time while Shanhui built up a sphere of influence in Taiwan. As previously mentioned, Shanhui only stayed on the mainland for six months, and returned in 1902. By 1908 the Lingquan Chan Temple was already completed, and rapidly rose in eminence so that by the time Benyuan returned in 1910, it was already the premier Buddhist temple in the Keelung area. Had Benyuan remained in his home town of Keelung he would have had a difficult time garnering support for his efforts, as all the moneyed people who were disposed towards Buddhism had already cast their lot with Shanhui. Thus, when asked to take over the founding of a new temple in a site away from Keelung, he felt it was his best opportunity for remaining outside Shanhui's circle and building his own domain.

Benyuan's efforts to distance himself from Shanhui went beyond mere physical relocation. Shanhui had submitted his temple and its operations to the Sōtō school of Zen Buddhism; therefore, Benyuan aligned himself with the Rinzai school. Even while the Lingyun Chan Temple was under renovation, Benyuan collaborated with the Rinzai missionary Nagatani Jien in organizational and educational activities. With Benyuan's help, the Rinzai school set up the "Taiwan Friends of the Buddha Way Association" (Taiwan Fojiao Daoyou Hui) and helped organize and administer the Chinnan Academy (Chinnan Gakurin). In 1920, he formally submitted his temple and its organizations to the Rinzai school's administrative oversight.

Even before Baohai passed away, Benyuan decided that the temple as originally planned was going to be unsuitable for what he had in mind. The design was too traditional and steeped in popular superstitions for his modernist outlook, and the scale was too small. He wanted something with a more spacious feeling, similar to the temples he had visited and lived in on the mainland. Therefore, almost as soon as the Lingyun Chan Temple was completed, he met with Baohai and the Liu family to talk about possible renovations. He also gained approval for several reforms in religious practice to steer the life of the temple's resident clergy away from the Japanese model and towards the Chinese model. For example, among other reforms he forbade the resident clergy to have wives or eat meat.

There were other problems Benyuan had to solve in order to adjust the facilities to his activities and goals. He wanted a temple that would attract large numbers of people from all over Taiwan, but the location on Guanyin Mountain was not easily accessible to visitors. Therefore, although the Lingyun Chan Temple complex was largely finished and functional at the end of its reconstruction, Benyuan constantly added new buildings all the way to 1933. He built new guest quarters, reception rooms, terraces for gazing at the moon, refectories, and side chapels one after the other. He also put in a road so that visitors could reach the temple by car. In these ways he hoped to create a facility that would lure people with its grand scale and excellent vista over the Taipei basin and the sea.

These efforts, he knew, would bring sightseers to the temple, but he also knew that sightseers only donate money once and then go home; they do not constitute a dependable source of long-term support. So Benyuan also devised ways to give people a feeling of lasting connection with the temple: He continued cultivating official contacts for the rest of his life. Also, like Shanhui, he began early administering refuges and precepts at the temple, an activity that instills in its participants a sense of ongoing commitment, and involvement in the life of the temple. He held the first large-scale precepts ceremony in the Lingyun Temple on November 11, 1923; and, although the ordination of the monks and nuns only lasted one week (today it can last three months), over seven hundred people came for both lay and monastic ordinations. The roster of officials in attendance was a veritable *Who's Who* of Taiwan Buddhism at that time. Benyuan himself was the preceptor; Shanhui acted as *daojie* master; and the "catechist" (Welch's translation for *jiaoshoushi*) was none other than Yuanying, like Benyuan and Shanhui an ordinand of the Yongquan Temple, and who in later years, as president of the BAROC would be preoccupied with staving off government confiscation of temple properties back on the mainland. The list of ordaining masters also included other representatives of the Yongquan Temple and Japanese Buddhism, showing that Benyuan, like Shanhui, also stood in the nexus of Taiwanese, Japanese, and mainland Buddhist relations.

Concerning Benyuan's activities in helping the Buddhists and government officials of Taiwan set up religious organizations, more will be said below. Once Benyuan had established himself as a major figure in Taiwan Buddhist circles, like Shanhui, he continued in this vein for the remainder of his life. When he died in 1946, the abbacy passed to the Ven. Juejing, another Taiwanese who had received ordination at the Yongquan Temple during Benyuan's stay there, returned with him to Taiwan, and worked with him from then on. Besides Juejing, Benyuan left behind a number of other capable and devoted disciples, and a network of temples that either the disciples or Benyuan himself had founded, establishing the Lingyun Chan Temple as the second of the "Four Great Ancestral *Daochang*" of Taiwan.

However, like the Lingquan Chan Temple in Keelung, this temple went into a decline with the end of Japanese rule in 1945. The massive loss of financial support meant that Juejing was unable to do anything beyond minor repairs and routine maintenance; and by the time he died in 1963, the temple was in a sad state of disrepair. The third abbot, Zhiding, had better luck. Taiwan's economic development began accelerating in the mid 1970s, and he was able to raise two million New Taiwan Dollars (about U.S. $50,000 at that time) toward renovation, putting the Lingyun Chan Temple on a firmer financial footing. Today it is a solid and active monastery, although it never recovered the preeminence it enjoyed during the Japanese period (Zhu Qichang 1977:223).

Jueli (1881–1933), Miaoguo (1884–1964), and the Fayun Chan Temple Lineage

Of all the eminent monks and nuns whose lives form the substance of this chapter, Jueli is unique as the only non-native of the island. Also, although this temple came into being and prospered primarily through his efforts, it still would never have seen the light of day without the efforts of his first and most eminent Taiwan disciple, Miaoguo.[3]

Although Jueli was not born on Taiwan, his birthplace lay not too far away. He was the only son in a family surnamed Lin on the small island of Gubo (Drumwave) in Xiamen (or Amoy), Fujian province. As to his date of birth, sources vary between 1878 and 1881, but the editors of his *Annals* argue for the latter as according more firmly with his known chronology. His family was reasonably well-to-do and supported themselves by means of a saltworks in their living compound. Their son, whom they named Lin Jinshi, was able to go to school throughout his childhood (Shi Chanhui 1981:124). He was an exceptionally bright and talented child, with clear, penetrating eyes (*1992 Gazetteer*:198).

However, in 1896, when he was sixteen years old, he received word one day just as his class was dismissed that one of his schoolmates had suddenly sickened and died. He was instantly filled with repugnance for life's transitoriness, and decided then and there to run away to seek ordination. He left a note in his inkwell instructing his father not to come looking for him, and made straightaway for the Yongquan Temple in Fuzhou. When he got to Gushan, the site of the temple, he met a monk in the street who took him to see the abbot, Ven. Wanshan. Wanshan accepted him as a disciple and tonsured him shortly thereafter, giving him the clerical name of Jueli. However, the abbot also took care to notify the family of this new arrival, and they quickly came to plead for their son to return. Jueli was adamant in his resolve and ignored their protests that now they would have no one to care for the family's ancestral cult. Having failed to persuade him to come home, his parents returned to Xiamen and adopted another boy into the family.

As was the custom at the Yongquan Temple, Jueli received the full monastic precepts there from his tonsure-master (the temple's prior, Benzhong) later that year. He spent the next six years studying *vinaya* with Benzhong and, in 1901, accompanied him on a tour of the southeast Asian islands (Shi Chanhui 1981:129). Four years later, Jueli undertook a trip on his own to China's heartland and then to Japan in order to observe the state of Buddhism in various places. During this trip he passed through Taiwan and stayed for a time at the Lingquan Chan Temple founded by Shanhui. After completing his tour, he returned to the Yongquan Temple and accepted an appointment as senior instructor in the meditation hall *(shouzuo)*.[4] The following year, Wanshan promoted him to prior *(jianyuan)* (Shi Chanhui 1981:131).

During Jueli's tenure as prior, he received a visit from a young man named Ye Aming, a native of Taoyuan county, Taiwan. Born in 1884, Ye was the fourth of five sons and had proved himself very adept at traditional Confucian studies. His father had died when he was thirteen years old, and three brothers followed in quick succession. Badly shaken by these events, he turned to vegetarianism and began to think about seeking ordination. At this point, the various sources on his life become confused and present questionable information. Most, based on the records of the *Annals* themselves, say that he went to the Zhaiming Temple in 1901 to take the Three Refuges (Shi Chanhui 1981:157; *1992 Gazetteer*:209–210; Liang and Huang 1993:288–289). In the entry for 1911, the *Annals* portray Ye Aming as meeting Jueli for the first time at the Yongquan Temple rather than in Taiwan, and say that, at the time, he was a member of the Longhua Sect of *zhaijiao* with the high rank of *taikong*. Thus, it is likely that Ye Aming, the future Ven. Miaoguo, spent a few years as a *zhaiyou* before traveling to Fuzhou to seek ordination at the Yongquan Temple.

Whatever the truth of the matter, it is clear that from the beginning the two men felt a sense of intertwined fate. In relating their first meeting at the Yongquan Temple in 1911, the *Annals* say that Miaoguo questioned Jueli closely for three days and nights without sleep or rest, leaving his quarters only to attend chanting services. In the end, Miaoguo asked Jueli, only three years his senior, to take him as a disciple, which Jueli did. Later that year, Miaoguo received the full monastic precepts at the temple (Shi Chanhui 1981:133; *1992 Gazetteer*:210). Shortly thereafter, he received word that his mother had fallen ill, and he was compelled to return to Taiwan (*1992 Gazetteer*:210). Upon his return, he settled in the Lingyun Chan Temple, where he assumed the post of temple treasurer *(fusi)*.

Not long after his return, however, he began holding discussions with prominent laymen from the Miaoli area (then a part of Hsinchu *gun* [county]) about the possibility of building a new temple there. They chose a site and a name: the Fayun Chan Temple. Once the construction was underway, Miaoguo crossed the straits to Fujian once again to invite Jueli to return to Taiwan as the new temple's founding abbot. Jueli consented, but Wanshan, his abbot, disapproved. The *Annals* relate the following anecdote: When Jueli asked Wanshan for permission to return to Taiwan permanently, Wanshan refused, saying, "Taiwan is too superficial. If you go, you will surely end up returning to lay life." He picked up a short iron staff *(tiechi)* and made as if he were going to kill Jueli, saying it would be more merciful to end his life and save him the bad karma that would result from disrobing. Jueli, however, had some skill in martial arts, especially *qinggong* (the art of leaping to great heights); and he jumped out of the way. In the act of dodging the blow, he experienced a small enlightenment (Shi Chanhui 1981:135). His fellow disciples then helped him to escape from the monastery, packing his bags for him and carrying them down to the bottom of the mountain where he picked them up on his way out.

Arriving in Miaoli, Jueli took over supervision of the new temple's construction. In this endeavor, he had to rely on Miaoguo not only as a bridge to the local gentry, but as an interpreter as well: Jueli, a native of Fujian, spoke Hokkien, but Miaoli has a high Hakka population. It was also an area of intense warfare between the ethnic Chinese and the aborigines, but the *Annals* state that Jueli was ultimately instrumental in creating a lasting peace between these two sides. The Great Shrine Hall was formally inaugurated on November 17, 1914.

From this point until his death in 1933, Jueli was active in two primary areas: clerical education, and transmitting the precepts. As to the first, he cooperated with Shanhui and Xinyuan in founding the Taiwan Buddhist Middle School. In 1922 he was named a missionary for the Sōtōshū, an impressive accomplishment for a monk who could not speak Japanese. At this time he also received an invitation to return to the Yongquan Temple as abbot; but in his autobiographical statement, he says, "There was no way for me to be in two places at once, and so I decided to concentrate my efforts on the Fayun Chan Temple and the revival of Buddhism in Taiwan" (Shi Chanhui 1981:146).

Taking a special concern for the education of young monks, he opened the Fayun Buddhist Study Society *(Fayun Foxueshe)* at the temple in 1928, with an initial enrollment of about sixty (Shi Chanhui 1981:151–152). He put Zhenchang, recently returned from study on the mainland, in charge of its operations. One of his followers, Chanhui, explains that this enterprise was significant because it represented the first wave of real monastic education in Taiwan. Even though both the Taiwan Buddhist Middle School and the *Chinnan Gakurin* at the Rinzai Zen Temple preceded it, these two presented more of a Japanese-style, secularized education. The *Fayun Foxueshe*'s program of studies, on the other hand, was aimed solely at clerical education conducted in a purely traditional Chinese style. Its purpose was to raise up the next generation of clergy and equip them to spread the teachings (Shi Chanhui 1981:186).

Jueli took a special interest in the education of nuns, which, says Chanhui, shows that he foresaw how important nuns would be in the future of Buddhism in Taiwan (Shi Chanhui 1981:187).[5] His first effort in this direction was a special six-month course of lectures that he delivered at the Yishan Temple near Hsinchu. Later that year, having seen how uneducated the nuns of Taiwan were and sensing a need for an ongoing institution, he established the Fayun Female Seminary *(Fayun Nüzhong Yanjiuyuan)* on the grounds of the Fayun Chan Temple itself, with an initial enrollment of eleven nuns (Shi Chanhui 1981:148).

His educational program also included maintaining contact with eminent monks on the mainland and encouraging exchanges of students. In 1923, he provided funds to send two of his disciples, Miaoji and Zhenchang, to study on the mainland, the former at Taixu's Wuchang Buddhist Seminary, the latter at two schools in Nanjing. When Miaoji returned, Jueli asked him to take over editorial duties at his *Light of Asia (Yaguang)* magazine (Shi Chanhui 1981:147). In 1924, when Yuanying came to Taiwan at the invitation of Shanhui, Jueli invited him to come to the Fayun Chan Temple, where Yuanying delivered a two-week course of lectures on the *Śūraṃgama-sūtra* (Shi Chanhui 1981:147). Jueli himself also traveled abroad on two occasions, and he used these opportunities to invite other learned monks to come to Taiwan; in 1925 he headed the Taiwan delegation to Taixu's East Asian Buddhist Conference.

However, it is the transmission of precepts that turned the Fayun Chan Temple from a single active, successful temple into the root temple of a large dharma-lineage. During the Japanese colonial period, the temple hosted seven ordination sessions for both clergy and laity. The first four took place over four consecutive years: 1918, 1919, 1920, and 1921. Jueli and his temple were so popular with the Buddhists of Taiwan that by the end of the fourth of these sessions, the temple had accumulated over 250 resident clergy. The last three sessions took place five years later in 1926, 1927, and 1928 (Shi Chanhui 1981:143–144, 150–152).

In these sessions, Jueli imparted to his disciples a very high regard for the precepts. In the preface to the 1928 *Fayun Chan Temple Ordination Records (Fayun Chansi Tong Jie Lu),* he expressed his views this way:

> Of all those both ancient and modern who have studied and practiced Buddhism, there is none who has not viewed the virtue of precepts as important. The true *Śūraṃgama-samādhi* has the precepts for its root, and all forms of wisdom have the precepts for their first guide; such is the

importance of the effects of taking the precepts! In a word, they are the seed of all buddhas and sages, and a guiding star for all human beings (Shi Chanhui 1981:152).

Most Chinese sources agree that this maintenance of traditional Chinese monastic discipline was important because it provided a check against the Japanization of Buddhism in Taiwan. Jueli, although an official Sōtōshū missionary dressed in Japanese-style monastic robes, lived at a distance from the center of power in Taihoku (Taipei), and spread a purely Chinese dharma (Shi Chanhui 1981:146).[6]

He was one of the most successful of the Japanese-era monks in spreading this dharma. In these seven ordination sessions, he produced over two hundred first-generation disciples, who either remained at the Fayun Chan Temple to live and work, or went and founded other temples within that lineage. The *1992 Gazetteer* provides a chart that shows a total of 129 temples, 10 of which were established by first-generation disciples, and the rest by second-, third-, or fourth-generation disciples (*1992 Gazetteer*:133–141). Besides these, Jueli himself received invitations to take over other temples. In 1922, he accepted the abbacy of the famous Longshan Temple in the Mengjia area of Taipei (presently the Wanhua district); and he helped his disciples in the planning and establishment of their own temples (Shi Chanhui 1981:145, 151). The "Fayun Chan Temple Lineage" that sprang from his efforts is concentrated mostly in central Taiwan but has temples in all areas of the island.

In 1930, after returning from leading a visitation team to the mainland to tour Buddhist sites, Jueli had "a sudden realization of impermanence," and began a vigorous lecture series at the Fayun Chan Temple, concentrating on the regulations of the Yongquan Temple, the Lotus Sutra, and Tiantai philosophy. Later in the same year, at the age of fifty-two, Jueli began to feel unwell, and his disciples prevailed on him to go see a doctor, who diagnosed him with hepatitis, which later worsened into cirrhosis of the liver. As his condition deteriorated, he gave various instructions to his disciples: Miaoguo was to take over as abbot of the Fayun Chan Temple, and they were not to relax their efforts to further Buddhist education: "Take all the income from our mountain and forest lands, and devote it to running a

Buddhist seminary; do not appropriate it for the clergy's daily expenses." (Shi Chanhui 1981:156)[7]

Jueli died on June 13, 1933, at the age of fifty-three. The temple itself experienced difficulties almost immediately: In 1935, a massive earthquake in central Taiwan reduced almost all of its buildings to rubble, and Miaoguo was hard-pressed to rebuild it (Shi Chanhui 1981:121). Japan was already at war with China at this time, which made materials difficult to come by. In fact, towards the end of the war, the Japanese government began a program of recovering metal from citizens in order to get around an embargo that made it impossible to import it. One of the casualties of this program was the temple's bell. After 1945, when Taiwan was returned to China, the Nationalist government's economic policies caused massive inflation, which further weakened the temple. As a result of these impediments, the Great Shrine Hall was not rebuilt until 1951 (Shi Chanhui 1981:161).

The Fayun Chan Temple did eventually become a place for the transmission of the monastic precepts once again beginning in 1965; but this time, as we shall see, the program came under the control of the BAROC, whose dominance over the proceedings eclipsed the temple's own importance as the center of a dharma-lineage. Perhaps its most enduring legacy has been this lineage's special attention to women. The *1992 Gazetteer* reports that women constituted the majority of Jueli's disciples, and his care of them and concern for their education empowered them in an unprecedented way, and perhaps helped set the stage for the dominance of nuns in post-Retrocession Taiwan.

Yongding (1877–1939), Yimin (1875–1947), and the Chaofeng Temple Lineage

Of the Four Great Ancestral *Daochang,* the Chaofeng Temple is the only one in the southern half of Taiwan; it sits on the slopes of Dagang Mountain in the Alian Rural District of Kaohsiung County. Its other distinguishing feature is that, unlike the other three, it was not actually founded by the monk who is revered as having brought the dominant dharma-lineage to the temple. In fact, the temple may have been founded nearly two hundred years before the arrival of Yongding and his master Yimin in 1908.

I say "may have been," because the actual founding date is unclear. A Japanese travel guide published in 1937 states that the temple was founded by the monk Shaoguang sometime during the Yongzheng reign of the Qing dynasty (1723-1735). It is possible, according to the Taiwan scholar Lin Li, that Shaoguang was an official of the fallen Ming dynasty who joined the *saṅgha* in order to gain anonymity and escape political persecution, thus making it understandable that he would not have left behind many records. According to the story, he came to the mountain and built a thatched hut on the present site of the temple for solitary practice. Considering that the Ming court fell from power in 1644, and that the Qing dynasty gained control of Taiwan in 1683, Shaoguang would have been a very old man if he indeed founded the temple at this late date. However, there is no way to verify this story, and so we must leave it in the realm of speculation.

Be that as it may, many sources on the Chaofeng Temple simply give 1763 as the date of its official founding.[8] From that point on, the temple had a completely undistinguished history for the remainder of the Qing-dynasty era. It functioned in much the same way as any other Buddhist temple in Taiwan; it provided funeral services as well as a place where the public could come and worship at its many altars, particularly their famous image of Guanyin. There was another major renovation in 1880, initiated by one Li Jiancheng; but this was simply a physical renewal, not a major change of direction. The impetus for the temple's transformation into one of the Four Great Ancestral *Daochang* did not come until after the Japanese government took over Taiwan in 1895.

As we have seen before, there were anti-Japanese resistance groups active during the early years of the colonial period. One of these, led by Lin Shaomao, rose in the area around Dagang Mountain almost as soon as the Japanese arrived. He and his rebel army occupied the mountain, which the Japanese army immediately surrounded. Rebels and criminals seeking refuge on the mountain could usually hold out for a while, living off the food and water available naturally on the slopes; but because the mountain sits alone on the surrounding plain "like a capsized ship," there is no way to leave it or evade capture for long, and so Lin Shaomao's rebellion was quelled by 1898. However, the temple had been affected by the state of siege that obtained for the two or three years prior to Lin's capture. The Japanese army did not allow food and provisions to be delivered up the mountain to anyone, and so the temple experienced a severe loss of resources and went into a rapid and steep decline. After Lin's army was captured, the temple authorities needed to find someone to lead it to an equally rapid recovery. In their search, they looked to the abbot and rebuilder of the Kaiyuan Temple in Tainan, the Ven. Yongding.

Yongding was clearly a remarkable monk. A work by Zheng Chuoyun entitled *Taiwan Kaiyuansi Shamen Liezhuan* (Biographies of the monks of the Kaiyuan Temple in Taiwan) gives the following notice:

> Chan Master Yongding, style Hongjing, lay name Lin Fanshu: originally a native of Tainan *ting,* born in 1877. He had a very gentle and loyal disposition. In 1896, he joined the Longhua Sect of *zhaijiao.* In 1898, he became a monk at the Kaiyuan Temple under the Ven. Yimin, after which he continued to live at the temple and work very hard. For a time he was simultaneously prior [*jianyuan,* the head of the business office] and abbot. He resigned the abbotship in 1903 and began doing things on behalf of the Chaofeng Temple while at the same time helping the Ven. Xuanjing repair the Great Hall of the Three Jewels at the Kaiyuan Temple. In this his accomplishments were notable. After completing this project, he removed to the Chaofeng Temple and planned other monasteries. He also founded the Longhu Convent [a nunnery adjoined to the Chaofeng Temple] (Jiang Canteng 1993–1994, 38/1:30–31).

One can get an idea of Yongding's capabilities and outstanding qualities simply by calculating his age at various points. The quotation states that he resigned the abbotship of the Kaiyuan Temple in 1903; at this time he was only twenty-six years old. The reader should also bear in mind that this is not a small, insignificant temple; it was one of the major temples in what had been the capital of Taiwan prior to the Japanese period. However, Yongding was a very capable and energetic young monk, and perhaps in need of constant challenges to exercise his capabilities. The Kaiyuan Temple provided him with one opportunity to show what he could do when he supervised the rebuilding of the Great Shrine Hall; but the Kaiyuan Temple was still an old and established temple with most of its organization and procedures already in place, while the notice quoted above makes plain that Yongding had ambitions of setting up new monasteries according to his own plan. The invitation from the Chaofeng Temple, a temple in deep trouble that needed a more thoroughgoing renovation and reorganization, must have looked very attractive. For this reason, he began working with the temple from a distance while fulfilling his obligation to complete the rebuilding project at the Kaiyuan Temple; and as soon as this was finished in 1908, he moved, bringing with him his ordination lineage.

The lineage he inherited was that of his master, the Ven. Yimin. Yimin was actually only two years older than Yongding, but he entered into Buddhist monastic life much earlier, having received the tonsure under Miaodi at the Kaiyuan Temple while still a boy. Later, in 1896, he went to the Yongquan Temple on Gushan in Fujian and received full ordination. He returned to the Kaiyuan Temple shortly thereafter and busied himself with religious work, and it was during this period that Yongding came to him for tonsure and took him as his master. After this, Yimin and Yongding did most things together, and when Yongding relocated to the Chaofeng Temple, Yimin accompanied him.

Although it may appear from this that Yongding was a dominant personality who turned his own master into his follower, Yimin's role was actually very positive; indeed, without him, the Chaofeng Temple would never have become the center of a major Buddhist ordination lineage in Taiwan during the Japanese period. Yongding excelled in two areas: he was very competent in fundraising and construction, and he had a good sense of religious propriety. However, he spent the remainder of his life on Dagang Mountain pursuing the renovation of the Chaofeng Temple and the building of its sister institution for female disciples, the Longhu (Dragon Lake) Convent *(Longhu An)*. Even though he pursued these tasks with great skill and energy, he was not inclined toward outreach; and it was Yimin who served as the founding abbot for many of the temples within the Chaofeng Temple system. Thus, we will examine these two men's contributions separately.

Yongding had great ambitions for the Chaofeng Temple; he wanted to turn it into a an institution whose support network extended beyond its own environs and would serve as a pilgrimage site for all of Taiwan. Indeed, this was the only way the temple could thrive, because its remote location meant that there was no community within walking distance who might develop lifelong ties to it. If it was to survive, the temple had to draw people to it. He saw that before this goal could be reached, there were two prerequisites: First, visitors would need a way to reach the temple easily and conveniently, and would need food and lodging while there; second, they would need a reason to come. Thus, the building program that occupied him for the rest of his life consisted of building a road and guest quarters to fulfill the first prerequisite, while at the same time building a magnificent Great Hall of Guanyin that would not only play on her cult's island-wide popularity, but would also capitalize on the reputation of the mountain as a site where there had been many miraculous manifestations of the bodhisattva.

The costs of these projects were staggering. The road alone would cost 45,000 yen to construct, a figure that equals the entire combined road and bridge budgets for Kaohsiung city and county for 1930 (Jiang Canteng 1993–1994, 38/6:28–29). Construction of the other buildings and facilities cost about the same figure again; and so it is understandable that it took Yongding until 1926 to raise enough money to begin building the hall (the year he received permission from the government to expand his fundraising to the entire island), and that the project was not completed until shortly before his death in 1939. However, from the very beginning of Yongding's tenure at the Chaofeng Temple, another factor operated to further slow down the process of renovation: the necessity of constructing a new facility for his female disciples.

In 1908, a woman arrived seeking a place to practice religious austerities. Yongding was thirty-one years old, the woman twenty-seven, and he realized that cohabitation in the same temple would offend not only his own sensibilities, but in all likelihood those of his donors as well. Consequently, he ordered the construction of bamboo-and-thatch buildings at a respectable distance down the mountain, and he named them Longhu Convent. This establishment enjoyed even more success than the Chaofeng Temple itself; within two years it had ninety-four women in residence and outgrew its facilities. This forced Yongding, as abbot of both temples, to divide his fundraising activities in order to keep up with the rapid growth of the Longhu Convent while pursuing his original plans for renovating the Chaofeng Temple. However, he went at this additional task with his characteristic enthusiasm, and the building proceeded apace. The first tile-roofed buildings were completed in 1918; by 1926 the convent had a guest reception room, the refectory opened the following year, and by 1931 there was a guest dormitory. By 1935 the convent's resident population had grown to over 140 women (Jiang Canteng 1993–1994, 38/4:29; 38/7:32).

However, none of the women who lived at the Longhu Convent ever sought ordination as Buddhist nuns; apparently Yongding did not insist that they take this step. The full-time residents wore white tunics over long black pants, and tied their hair in topknots. Yongding's first female disciple, Kaihui, succeeded him as abbess of the convent after his death in 1939; but it was not until after Retrocession that she took the full nun's precepts. In 1953, at the first BAROC-sponsored ordination session at the Daxian Temple in Tainan county, she went with fifteen other residents of the convent. Fifteen of them took the full precepts of the *bhikṣuṇī*, while one took the novice's precepts. By this time, Kaihui was seventy-two years old (Jiang Canteng 1993–1994, 38/7:33).

Here, then, is a unique characteristic of the Chaofeng Temple system. There is no doubt that Yongding was a brilliant fundraiser and an able administrator, and that he had a vision of what the Chaofeng Temple and Longhu Convent could be that motivated him over the course of many years. However, this vision did not extend to a strict transmission of the monastic precepts. Unlike the other three temples already examined, the Chaofeng Temple never held monastic ordinations, and its residents rarely went to receive the precepts anywhere else, whether in Taiwan or on the Chinese mainland. Longhu, as we have seen, had no properly ordained residents until well after 1945, and only held one transmission of the Lay Bodhisattva Precepts in 1929 (Jiang Canteng 1993–1994, 38/7:32).

Another area in which Yongding's activities differed from those of the other great founding figures is education. The Chaofeng Temple never sponsored any educational events and only sent one or two clergy members abroad to study in Japan or the mainland. Yongding himself had only a minimal education in Buddhism and never contributed any articles to any Buddhist journal (Jiang Canteng 1993–1994, 38/7:34).

This is not to say that he was not concerned with the quality of religious life at his temples. On the contrary, in 1929, concerned that the "nuns" in the Longhu Convent seemed to know nothing of the decorum expected of Buddhist clergy, he invited the Ven. Huiquan of Nanputuo Temple to come and give a series of lectures on monastic etiquette (Jiang Canteng 1993–1994, 38/7:32). Also, contemporary sources praised the solemn atmosphere of the two temples, where the residents lived lives of strict seclusion from the world and practiced rigorous austerities. Thus, Yongding's priorities appear to have been more practical than theoretical: He wanted to build a place of serious religious practice and a major pilgrimage site, but did not believe that monastic precepts or Buddhist education were strictly necessary for either of these.

However, with no tradition of transmitting the precepts, one is led to wonder on what basis it is possible to speak of a "Chaofeng Temple lineage," a question whose answer necessitates an examination of the activities of Yimin, Yongding's tonsure-master. While Yongding was occupied with the enormous task of construction and renovation on Dagang Mountain itself, Yimin accepted an invitation in 1911 to take over a former *zhaitang* in Chiayi, the Deyuan Chan Temple. After making the necessary renovations, he remained there as abbot from 1911 to 1926, after which he handed the reins to Yicun, a junior disciple of his own master. Even though this temple's clergy subsequently traced their lineage through Yimin, and Yongding did not figure into the matter, the temple still counted as part of the Chaofeng Temple system. In 1913, Yimin took over another temple in Chiayi, the Miyuan Temple, and served as its abbot for three years, after which he turned it over to another disciple within his lineage named Miaoyuan. In 1922, Yimin founded yet another temple in Changhua called the Biyun Chan Temple. In 1940, another of Yimin's disciples from Yongding's generation, Yongli, founded the Baiyun Temple in Kaohsiung. In this way, Yimin proved much more inclined to outreach than Yongding, and took the initiative in propagating the Chaofeng Temple system geographically (Jiang Canteng 1993–1994, 38/5:31–32).

Other temples within the system came into being through Yongding's own tonsure disciples. For example, in 1918, Kaiji founded the Lianfeng Temple, also on Dagang Mountain, apparently so that visitors could have a temple with more convenient access and accommodations while repairs were underway farther up the mountain at the Chaofeng Temple (Jiang Canteng 1993–1994, 38/5:32–33). In all, the *1992 Gazetteer* lists forty-two temples within this system, all of them located south of Chiayi and most of them in Kaohsiung city or Kaohsiung county (*1992 Gazetteer*:143–145).

However, with no tradition of ordination or education, the system began to unravel even before the end of the Japanese colonial period. Yongding's vision for the Chaofeng Temple succeeded for a time, and during the two years before his death it drew some sixty thousand pilgrims annually (Jiang Canteng 1993–1994, 38/6:31). When Yongding died, Kaihui took over as abbess of the Longhu Convent, and Kaizhao took control of the Chaofeng Temple itself. However, their tenures were cut short by the intensification of the Pacific War. As Allied bombers began targeting Taiwan, the Japanese government felt that a brightly colored temple sitting on the top of a solitary mountain in the middle of a broad plain made too inviting a target, and so they gave all the temples on the mountain some financial compensation and ordered them to vacate. They then set to work demolishing them, and the Great Hall of Guanyin that Yongding spent over twenty-five years planning and building came down in 1942.

During this time, the residents of the three temples within the Chaofeng system—the Chaofeng Temple itself, the Longhu Convent, and the Lianfeng Temple—regrouped on the plain below and, under Yimin's leadership, quickly pooled their compensation funds and built the New Chaofeng Temple. Yimin served as the first abbot of this new temple, and Kaiji succeeded him. After the end of the war in 1945, many of the clergy from the Chaofeng Temple, led by Yongding's disciple Kaizhao, returned to the mountain and began the work of rebuilding, which was still in progress when I visited the site in 1993. Today, it is referred to as the Old Chaofeng Temple, while the New Chaofeng Temple continues its existence on the plains below.

Besides the lack of emphasis on precepts and the disruptions of the war, there are probably a number of other reasons that the Chaofeng Temple system failed to congeal into a viable lineage. It was the only one of the Four Great Ancestral *Daochang* not to associate with Japanese Buddhism for protection. Whereas the Fayun Chan Temple and Lingquan Chan Temple both associated with the Sōtōshū Myōshinji-ha, and the Lingyun Chan Temple affiliated with Rinzai, the Chaofeng Temple remained independent; and to the end of the war the Japanese government classified it as an "old customary temple" *(kyūkan jibyō)*, never reclassifying it as a "Buddhist temple" *(butsuji),* as had been the case when the other three temples gained affiliation (Jiang Canteng 1993–1994, 38/4:30). Also, we might speculate that, since the majority of residents in these temples never sought full ordination, they failed to gain recognition as legitimate Buddhist clergy when the refugee monks arrived from the mainland and took over the political infrastructure of Taiwan Buddhism in 1949; it is far more likely that these mainlanders simply looked upon them with the same distress and scorn with which they viewed the whole phenomenon of *zhaijiao.*

Whatever the reason, one of the anecdotes related by Jiang Canteng in his examination of the temple and its lineage illustrates the lack of cohesion that caused the association to dissolve after the war. In 1967, several members of temples within this system held a meeting to organize the "Dagang Mountain Dharma-Lineage Fellowship" *(Dagang Shan Benshan Famai Lianyihui).* Although the members succeeded in drafting a charter, the organization never materialized because the retired abbot Kaizhao, Yongding's successor, would not permit the leaders to set up an office within the Chaofeng Temple itself (Jiang Canteng 1993–1994, 38/4:31).

CONCLUSIONS

We have spent a great deal of time telling the stories of the Four Great Ancestral *Daochang* because they had significance, not only for the Buddhism of the period, but also for the events that followed Retrocession. First, the *Daochang* provided a formal network for temples that better enabled them to resist the encroachments of Japanese Buddhist customs and practices that offended Chinese religious sensibilities. Temples within these systems generally hewed to traditional Chinese Buddhist customs in not permitting clerical marriage or the consumption of meat and wine. Second, they provided the means for a more widespread dissemination of the ordination lineages of the Yongquan Temple on Drum Mountain (Gushan) in Fuzhou. It is perhaps ironic that this increased dissemination of Chinese ordination lineages came about at a time when Taiwan was not formally part of China. Third, it is my own speculation that the increased attention paid to Buddhist education for nuns, especially in the Fayun Chan Temple system under Jueli, helped set the stage for the very active role that nuns were to play in post–Retrocession Buddhism. Not only do nuns predominate over monks numerically, they are also held in equal or greater respect for their religious accomplishments in modern Taiwan; and I believe the roots of this phenomenon extend into the Japanese period.

This treatment has therefore shown how Chinese Buddhism continued to thrive under the Japanese colonial administration, but only at the local level. When we shift our perspective to the level of national Buddhist organizations, we see a much greater degree of interaction and cooperation between the Chinese Buddhist camp and the Japanese authorities and schools of Buddhism. Although the original motivation for this increased cooperation came from a combination of fear and realpolitik, it eventuated in some genuine rapprochement, at least between the nationally prominent monks and the *zhaijiao* adherents who joined the various associations that came into being in the 1910s and 1920s. It is to these national organizations that we turn our attention in the next chapter.

CHAPTER 3

—◦◦◦—

BUDDHIST ASSOCIATIONS AND POLITICAL FORTUNES DURING THE LATE JAPANESE PERIOD

THE NEED TO ASSOCIATE

Overview

The foregoing discussion of the major lineages and eminent monks of the Japanese period should help the reader understand the formation of the Buddhist organizations and associations that began to appear about twenty years after Japan took possession of the island. First, the reader is now familiar with the most important figures in the Buddhist world at the time, and is aware of why the Japanese authorities trusted and were willing to work with them. Second, the experience of the Chaofeng Temple in the years of Lin Shaomao's rebellion shows how easy it was for temples and other religious organizations to suffer guilt by association with the anti-Japanese movements and groups that prevailed during the early colonial period. This danger of implication in rebel movements affected both Buddhist temples and *zhaijiao* meeting halls.

With regard to this point, the *1971 Gazetteer* lists no fewer than fourteen major anti-Japanese insurrections and minor revolts that took place between 1895 and 1915, of which Lin Shaomao's was only one. Because rebel activity was so widespread, many religious people in Taiwan felt the need to cultivate good relations with Japanese missionaries and government officials from an early date. Thus, in 1912 we find the *zhaitang* of all three *zhaijiao* sects in Tainan city joining together to form the Vegetarian Mind Society *(Zhaixin She)*. However, as the preface to their contract of alliance makes clear, this step merely formalized what they had already been doing since 1895:

> We of the Longhua Sect, ever since the Japanese began ruling Taiwan, recognized ourselves as followers of the Sōtō School. Whenever we had a period of observing the vegetarian diet and making offerings to the buddhas, we would invite a Sōtō missionary over to chant sutras and preach *(1971 Gazetteer:*58a).

In 1915, with the so-called Xilai Hermitage Incident *(Xilai An Shijian),* the need to associate arose with special urgency. The "incident" was a widespread anti-Japanese conspiracy led by three men: Yu Qingfang, Jiang Ding, and Luo Jun. They plotted to overthrow the Japanese colonial government and set up Taiwan as an independent nation, and they used the Xilai An Temple in Tainan as their secret meeting-place. Unfortunately for the conspirators, Yu was too open in expressing his feelings about the Japanese and attracted the attention of the authorities, who subsequently uncovered the group's plans before the members had a chance to launch their rebellion. Eight hundred sixty-six conspirators were condemned by the Sōtokufu, of whom 95 suffered summary execution; 535 of them had their sentences commuted when the Crown Prince visited in 1923, and the remainder served long prison sentences at hard labor (Cai 1994:50–51).

What is most significant here is that Yu and his fellow rebels used a *zhaijiao* meeting hall as their base of operations, couched their revolutionary ideas in the language of *zhaijiao* rhetoric, and spread their ideas primarily among *zhaijiao* adherents. Here is an example of Yu's speech:

> The Three Teachings assist the dharma; sages and gods, immortals and buddhas all come down to ordinary mortals to propagate the Way, and their followers are myriads and thousands, their transformations are without end (*1971 Gazetteer*:59b).

After the plot was discovered, all *zhaijiao* devotees and their meeting-halls became suspect; and the majority of devotees, who were merely trying to live quietly and make the best of the circumstances, needed a way to show the authorities that they were loyal citizens of the empire. Their two most widely used methods for doing so were either to put their *zhaijiao* organizations and halls directly under the control of a Japanese Buddhist lineage, as exemplified by the actions of the Tainan *zhaitang,* or to form associations dedicated to both religious and patriotic purposes.

The Patriotic Buddhist Association

As a direct result of the Xilai Hermitage Incident, the Tainan Vegetarian Mind Society attempted to evolve into an islandwide religious organization, known as the Patriotic Buddhist Association *(Aiguo Fojiao Hui),* whose intention was to unite all the Buddhist temples and *zhaijiao* meeting-halls in Taiwan under the leadership of the Sōtō School of Japanese Buddhism, and to give the Japanese government a way to distinguish law-abiding Buddhists from rebels and bandits. This is clear from the preamble to its charter:

> Religion was established to enlighten all the people of the world, and to aid rulers in carrying out all good government. Sadly, the people of today are not like those of old. The enlightened are few, the superstitious are many, to the extent that even when they enter into a good religion [lit. dharma-gate], they practice it more and more confusedly from sunup to sundown. From this issue heresies and strange beliefs, to the extent that they practice *fuzhoushui,*[1] talk foolishly about fortune and misfortune, stir up the people with reckless speech, mislead them with heresies; these have infiltrated the ranks of *zhaijiao*. These people are criminals in [the realm of] religion, vermin in the gates of excellence! It may be that our meeting-halls *(zhaitang)* have failed to distinguish the sincere from the hypocritical, and have not known [the extent to which] bad elements have gotten mixed in. We sincerely fear that they have employed methods that go against the government's peaceful rule, that many innocent people have been impli-

cated, and that every religious retreat *(an)* has been handed the blame. Now, in this civilized age, can we really accommodate that set of fellows,[2] like fish-eyes among pearls? We have, in view of this, united together the congregations of each meeting-hall, extending to the entire ecclesiastical establishment, in order to resist incursions by outside trouble[makers] and maintain religious order. It is our hope that each [meeting-hall] will adopt and respect this arrangement (*1971 Gazetteer*:59a–b).

The desires to maintain the *zhaijiao* meeting-halls free from government suspicion and distance them from rebel activity are palpable in this preamble. As for the concrete measures taken to "resist incursions by outside troublemakers and maintain religious order," these are set forth in the charter itself. The following are the relevant clauses:

#3. The intent of this charter is first and foremost to respect the laws of the nation and imperial institutions, to pay all farm and excise taxes, to carry out our civic duties to the best of our abilities, and to act in accordance with the regulations governing religious activities.

#4. In order to become men perfected by religion, we will maintain ourselves pure and uncorrupted, love our brothers, be faithful to our friends, train our wives and educate our sons, be forebearing with others but uncompromising with ourselves, maintain clear boundaries between adjoining properties, each be diligent in our business, and earn our living in accordance with the law.

#6. Having entered into the way of religion, [members] may not go forming other associations; idle about in neglect of their proper occupations; form parties or cliques; engage in sedition, fornication, gambling, or theft; trick people out of their property by using the names of gods or buddhas; or practice *fuzhoushui*. All this goes against the true path of religion, and will be promptly reported to the authorities to be punished according to law.

#7. If there are [any members who] hold the government in contempt, slander those in power, flaunt their differences or brag about novelty, spread falsehoods, mislead the world or bring false accusations against people, or divide families and cause trouble; and if they will not correct themselves after admonition, then they will be expelled.

#9. Any member who wishes to introduce a new member should choose someone of upright moral character and sincere religious belief. These will be permitted to join. However, if there is anything wanton or reckless in their behavior but they repent and promise to reform, then

[their entrance] should be temporarily delayed and their behavior carefully monitored. If there is improvement, and if their introducer is willing to act as their guarantor, then they may join. But any follower who
is violent or deceitful will be refused.

#10. The meeting-halls of each [*zhaijiao*] sect must keep membership
records, one for the men and one for the women. These must include
everyone's name, address, and age, and information on members who die,
are expelled, or resign. These records must be carefully registered and ver-
ified (*1971 Gazetteer*:58b–59a).

In the provisions of this charter, we can see concerns that will be
common to all of the religious associations that formed under the
Japanese colonial government. The primary concern was to establish an
organization with enough credibility vis-à-vis the government that
membership in the organization would in itself be proof of good citizenship. The associations established this credibility by setting good citizenship as an explicit value to be inculcated in members in matters
such as paying taxes, obeying the law, not joining rebel factions, and so
on. In all these terms, the reader may see that the name of the organization was well chosen; they were indeed as patriotic as they were
Buddhist.

The Patriotic Buddhist Association (PBA) was not the only organization trying to provide asylum for the religiously inclined citizens
of the empire. In northern Taiwan, Huang Yujie, the leader of the
Xiantian Sect during that period, proposed another organization and
laid out a tentative charter including many of the same goals. The
organization he envisioned was to include not only Buddhist temples
and *zhaijiao* halls, but Daoist priests and temples as well. His draft
charter included ideas on how to organize the central governing body
and local chapters, as well as how to deal with infractions of the law;
and in his scheme, two copies of each member's dossier would be sent
to the government as a matter of course. However, his proposed association never materialized.

The Buddhist Youth Association

In April of 1916, the Japanese government completed their new headquarters building in Taipei. They marked the occasion by hosting the

first Taiwan Industrial Fair *(Taiwan Kangyō Kyōshinkai)* in an adjoining lot. At that time, the Religion *kochō* of Taipei *chō,* Shibata Kiyoshi, thought it would be a good idea if Buddhist leaders in Taiwan were to hold a series of lectures there; and so he consulted with two *zhaijiao* leaders, Chen Taikong and Lin Puyi, about organizing the event. They agreed; and the meetings began on April 1 and lasted forty consecutive nights, each featuring worship services and lectures on the sutras and teachings. The *1971 Gazetteer* records that these meetings proved very popular with the fairgoers, attracting over one thousand each night.[3]

It was during this time, when most of the major figures of *zhaijiao* were gathered in Taipei for the fair and the lecture-meetings, that all of the *zhaijiao* organizations in Taiwan formally submitted themselves to the Sōtō school, thus becoming administratively subject to the Sōtōshū Taiwan Betsuin and its chief officer, Ōishi Kendō. During the course of these negotiations, Lin Puyi conceived the idea of organizing a Taiwan Buddhist Youth Association *(Taiwan Fojiao Qingnian Hui)* in order to reverse what he saw as a severe decline in the quality of Taiwan Buddhism. (As we shall see, he was not the only one who perceived this decline.) Ōishi agreed, and asked Lin to draft a charter.[4]

The preamble to Lin's draft charter is a fascinating document, outlining a complete rationale for understanding the Japanese takeover of Taiwan in religious terms, for revering the Japanese emperor, and for understanding the religious needs of the modern age. For these reasons, I present here a full translation:

> Now, we hear that since the beginning of world civilization, the significance of the term "religion" means nothing more than its original intent of educating people. It has been thirty centuries since our honored ancestral [teacher] Śākyamuni appeared in the world. He preached sutras numbering as many as 5,700 scrolls, there are 84,000 dharma-gates that attest to the wonder of his profundity, his merits extend to the myriads of universes, and even the grains of sand in the Ganges could not rival their number. The key points of religion in the several myriads of worlds resolve down to three: In terms of religion, it enables people to escape suffering and attain happiness, pacify their bodies, and fulfil their destinies. In terms of ethics, it pushes people to forsake evil and do what is right. In terms of philosophy, it leads people to turn from superstition and attain enlightenment, and to contemplate Principle dispassionately. In the final

analysis, all of [religion's] endless variations come down to one thing, and none of them fall outside the limits of humaneness and compassion. Therefore, the most excellent things of religion are civilization that daily grows more prosperous, and customs that daily grow more deep.

Buddhism spread eastward and was propagated to China during Han times, and gradually entered into our country. It has been over one thousand years since then. It was vibrant during the period of China's middle antiquity. Afterwards it sank into decadence and one need not ask whether this [decline] has extended to the present day. But our country [i.e., Japan] has reversed this, and, ever since his majesty the emperor ascended the throne, his people have experienced constant renewal and improvement. At first it was like waves coming in layers and lapping over one another, and later came reports of success in the augmentation and consolidation of the nation's prestige. Respectfully quoting from the Meiji Emperor's Rescript on Education, whether a nation is order-ly or disorderly, prospering or in decline, depends upon the suitability or otherwise of its religion and education. Looking at the great successes reported in Japan's two great military campaigns in Russia and Germany on both land and sea, how could [his military] have such a spirit of loy-alty to their prince and love of their country if their religion and educa-tion were not suitable?[5]

Lately religion has undergone transformation. Western scholarship has become prevalent, twisted morals seem clever and tactful to those anx-ious for self-benefit, and the manners and morals of the times are wholly different from those of old. If the Buddha spoke of an age of world-destruction, he surely meant this [present] one! Recall that in ancient times the Yellow Emperor subdued the whole world by force of arms, but at the beginning used only bows and arrows, shields and spears. The western lands respected the old order in ancient times, but then they changed, first to machines and crossbows, then to firearms, and finally to bombs, machine guns, submarines, missiles, and things difficult for me to number, even if I go back and ponder them endlessly. These westward-looking, Europeanized demons mow people down like grass and feud endlessly. They are the exact opposite of those who still hold the chief Buddhist virtues of humaneness and compassion.

Now, everyone knows that in these long twenty years that the Japanese have ruled Taiwan, they have been diligent in encouraging and rewarding agriculture, industry, and commerce. It is only with respect to religious reform that we have not yet heard the first word. There are tem-ples both large and small everywhere that you look, and the pity is that their devotees['s religious practices] are all form and no spirit, and that the resident clergy are only out for their own benefit. Furthermore, the halls where people enshrine images of their ancestors are in the hands of gamblers and carousers. In a word, it's all just "superstitious Buddhism," not only of no benefit to its followers, but actually harmful to them. No wonder that in the years of Qing dynasty rule, from the Kangxi to the Guangxu reigns [i.e., from 1662 to 1907] there were no less than seventeen rebellions. Unexpectedly, in coming back to our own territory [i.e., Taiwan], one still has Zhan Arui in Taichung, Liu Gan in Nantou, and, more recently, the Xilai Hermitage [Incident] in Tainan. Had it not been for the errors of superstition, could these situations have developed?

The government has supervisors over this, and they do have plans to carry out investigations into religion, a complex undertaking, as we know. However, the issue is not that people's superstitions cannot be broken, it is just that the methods have not been good. Since this government has been ruling in Taiwan, the religious regulations have been good, and the achievements have been excellent. The problem is that the religious teachers do not speak Taiwanese, and so it has been hard for them to place believers in all parts of Taiwan. The delegates sent from the headquarters of the Sōtō School have been best at disseminating [their message], and that is why they have temples from the Lingquan Temple in Keelung, to the Longyun Temple in Daojiang, to the Jiantan Temple in Tachih, to the Fayun Temple in Miaoli, all the way to the Daxian Grotto in Chiayi. The resident clergy [in these temples] come from that school's lineages, and they draw not a few believers from among the Taiwanese. This all goes back to the Sōtō School's help and guidance. However, there are more people in Taiwan of correct belief and thought, and who are covered by the ruler's impartial, all-pervasive benevolence. Their only problem is that they are stumbling in the dark with no light to guide them.

Now I have a word to offer to my three million compatriots in Taiwan. If you wish to feel the ruler's impartial, all-pervasive benevolence covering you, you have only to respect the imperial Rescript on Education: the government's success or failure hinges on nothing more than the suitability of the people's religion and education. Like a skilled physician prescribing medicines according to the illness, the Buddha preached the dharma so that [people could] attain enlightenment in accordance with their capabilities. The religious outlook of the people of Taiwan is not all that different from that of the homeland [i.e., Japan], and so we should make good use of this opportunity to seek for an appropriate method to capitalize on it and expand its benefits to all.

We, being recognized as men of some intelligence, have accordingly come together in one mind to form the Buddhist Youth Association. Our purpose is to band together as members for the mutual cultivation of wisdom and virtue, and to respectfully emphasize education by stressing the Buddha's teachings. In upholding the spirit of the Rescript on

Education, we will eradicate existing superstitions, seek to serve the nation instead of self and family, and so come to enjoy the blessing of peace for all the people. I have been too verbose in making clear the aims of this Association, and I sincerely hope that men of humaneness and men of true virtue [lit.: Confucian gentlemen, *junzi*] will not reject [this plan], but will quickly approve of it and join up to bring great good fortune (*1971 Gazetteer*:60b–61b).

Several themes are apparent in this preamble. First, it presents the outlook of religious individuals who saw that, through association with seditious movements that co-opted their ideas and language, their own practices were endangered: there is explicit reference to the Xilai Hermitage Incident and two other revolts against the Japanese. Lin, a prominent *zhaijiao* leader, sought to put some distance between his own organization and these rebel movements by making the distinction between "religion," which he represents, and "superstition" or "superstitious Buddhism," represented by the rebels. Religion, he says, makes people ethical, benevolent, and enlightened; and, if the Meiji Emperor's Rescript on Education is correct, leads to the peace and prosperity of the nation. We have already seen this idea, that religion (and specifically the religion of the "men of antiquity") leads to peace and superstition leads to unrest, in the preamble to the PBA's charter.

This segues into an interesting implication: Since good religion conduces to the nation's health, then the successful expansion of Japan, even though brought about by military adventurism, still indicates the superiority of the Japanese religious and educational systems. This may smack of toadying to the reader, but there are two things to bear in mind when looking at this passage. First, it is a commonplace among scholars that Chinese religion is very pragmatic; if a person or a nation is successful in achieving its aims, it is a sign that they are worshipping the right deities in the right way. Second, the organizers of these associations had no way to foresee that Taiwan would one day be returned to China. From the perspective of 1916, the cession of Taiwan to Japan was a fait accompli, and Taiwan was and would continue to be an integral part of Japan. Resistance had been shown to be useless; the only reasonable course was to adapt.

Furthermore, there is in this preamble another explicit statement that Buddhism could be used as a bridge linking Chinese and Japanese culture—but with a new twist. Lin Puyi clearly saw the encroachments of Western culture as a threat and proposed that, if the Chinese in Taiwan could unite with the Japanese on the basis of their common religious heritage, they could put up a stronger resistance to the spiritual contamination emanating from these aggressive "demons." The language barrier, however, had proven a serious impediment to effecting this union, except in the case of the Sōtō School. This is no coincidence, considering the fact that this school included a significant number of Hokkien-speaking monks such as Shanhui and Jueli.

The charter itself is much more taken up with the technical details of the organization's structure and procedures than that of the PBA, but it still sets forth the basic principles and purposes that defined the organizers' goals. Article three codifies Lin's much-repeated intention to base the organization's goals on those outlined in the Meiji Emperor's Rescript on Education. Article four sets forth general principles governing members' conduct, and article seventeen sets expulsion as the punishment for violating them. However, in this respect the Buddhist Youth Association (BYA) was much more relaxed and confident than was the PBA. Whereas the PBA's charter gives a detailed list of infractions such as slandering the government, causing family disturbances, fornication, and so forth, the BYA charter simply exhorts members to act in accordance with "humaneness and compassion." It seems as if the BYA, at its inception having better government connections, did not need to advertise so precisely what sins its members would be free from. However, the BYA shared with the PBA a common method of quality control: Its charter also stipulated that prospective members needed an introduction by an existing member in order to join (article eighteen).

More than the PBA, the BYA seemed to see itself as an agent of education and uplift in Taiwan Buddhist circles; at least its charter is more specific about the means it would employ to pursue these goals. There was to be an annual newsletter (article thirteen); the association was to actively investigate the religious situation in Taiwan and find ways to proselytize efficiently among the Chinese population (article

fourteen); it was also to establish schools and lecture halls, and organize further ad hoc dharma-meetings for educational purposes (article fifteen).

Taiwan Friends of the Buddhist Way

The Taiwan Friends of the Buddhist Way *(Taiwan Fojiao Daoyou Hui)*
appears to have been a fairly minor organization, significant primarily
because it represents the entrance of the Rinzai School into the realm
of religious associations. As we have seen, the BYA was the brainchild
of the head of the Sōtō mission in Taiwan, Ōishi Kendō, who subsequently became the group's president. In 1918, the Myōshin Sect of
Rinzai sent one of its more eminent monks, Nagatani Jien, to work on
its behalf in Taiwan. He too lamented the sad condition of Buddhism in
Taiwan and immediately began to lay plans for its improvement. We have
already seen how Nagatani recruited Benyuan of the Lingyun Chan
Temple to help him set up the Chinnan Academy. At the same time, he
also urged the establishment of the Taiwan Friends of the Buddhist Way
Association, and he asked Lin Puyi to help draft its charter. As it was Lin
Puyi who composed the charter of the BYA, it is not surprising that the
two charters are virtually identical in content. Nagatani did seem to be
aware that he would be competing with the BYA for members, however; the last article of the charter stresses that membership is open to
all, both ordained and lay, male and female, orthodox Buddhist and *zhaijiao* devotee, and, perhaps as a jab at the Buddhist Youth Association, to
both young and old (*1971 Gazetteer*:63a–64a).

The leadership of the organization was very heavily weighted in
favor of Japanese members, which may explain why the group was so
ineffectual and short-lived. It issued its first monthly newsletter on
December 10, 1918, half in Chinese and half in Japanese, and published
thirty-one issues before suspending operations in 1922, the very year
of the founding of the most successful and influential of the island-wide
Buddhist groups, the South Seas Buddhist Association (SSBA). This
latter group was founded under the direction of Marui Keijirō, who was
also on the board of directors of the Friends of the Buddhist Way. It is
possible that when he helped to organize this new association, he simply
took the leadership of the Friends of the Buddhist Way with him.

The South Seas Buddhist Association

As stated above, the South Seas Buddhist Association (Ch: *Nanying Fojiao Hui;* Jpn: *Nan'e Bukkyōkai*) was the most successful and influential of all the islandwide Buddhist organizations founded during the Japanese period. Nevertheless, its success was still very limited, and its influence never spread beyond the Japanese population and the Chinese citizens whose positions and livelihood required contact with them.

To begin at the beginning: After the Xilai Hermitage Incident in 1915, the Japanese government decided to undertake an extensive investigation of all the temples and religious groups in Taiwan, and in 1917 set up the Office of Shrines and Temples *(shajika)* under the Bureau of Internal Affairs *(naimukyoku)* to oversee this work. The government appointed Marui Keijirō to head this office and oversee the survey (Cai 1994:54–55). During the course of the investigation, Marui became increasingly dismayed over the state of Buddhism in Taiwan, and saw the need for an islandwide umbrella organization to reverse the situation (Chen Lingrong 1992:129). The reader may remember that Marui was already on the board of directors of the Friends of the Buddhist Way during this time. He may have felt that this organization, tied as it was to the Rinzai School and having been founded in competition with the Sōtō School, would not be effective in unifying all Buddhists under one roof.

Marui expressed his concerns in an article published in the first issue of the SSBA's newspaper. In it, he wrote that the clergy, laity, and *zhaijiao* devotees in Taiwan were very ignorant about their own religion and unwilling to take leadership roles in addressing social concerns. He had come to see a pressing need to "engender an understanding of the spirit of Buddhism, encourage faith, broaden [believers'] perspectives, and strictly regulate their resolve" (*1971 Gazetteer*:64a). If Buddhists wished to improve their social standing, then it was necessary for them to set up a self-governing organization that would use the missionaries' training and techniques to influence all the people on the island.

Marui called his first conference on February 26, 1921 to present his proposals to the eminent monks of the time, including Shanhui and Benyuan, as well as representatives of all three sects of *zhaijiao*. They met in the Longshan Temple in Taipei; and in his keynote address, Marui urged the leaders to be of service to both the *saṅgha* and the members of *zhaijiao* by setting up an organization to promote Buddhism into the future. He further proposed that this organization have branch associations in every district of Taiwan. His proposal was accepted by acclamation, and the conference selected four people to serve on the steering committee, with responsibility for fundraising, recruiting potential members, and organizing similar steering committees in Hsinchu, Taichung, and Tainan.

Conferences in these localities followed in rapid succession, and the members of all the committees showed up in Taipei on the morning of April 4, 1922 for the official founding meeting of the SSBA. The meeting convened at three o'clock in the afternoon in the Longshan Temple for the first session; and the first order of business was to pass the charter that the steering committee had prepared during the preceding year, which was adopted with some minor amendments. Because this represents the fullest development of Japanese efforts to organize Buddhism in Taiwan, I present here a full translation of the charter as passed:

Charter of the South Seas Buddhist Association

1. The name of this organization is The South Seas Buddhist Association. It shall be provisionally headquartered in the Office of Shrines and Temples, Bureau of Internal Affairs, Taiwan Viceregal Government. It shall, in a timely manner, establish chapters in every locality, each of which shall write their own bylaws.

2. This Association is organized for the sake of all willing Buddhist clergy and friends of *zhaijiao* on this island, as well as for patrons of high social standing and good reputation.

3. The purposes of this Association are to raise members' knowledge and morals, maintain contact with Buddhism in the motherland [i.e., Japan], attempt to promote and develop Buddhism, and to broaden the minds of all the people on the island.

4. In order to fulfill these goals, the Association shall:

    A. organize short courses, study groups, and lecture series;

    B. carry on investigations into the key points of religion and publish a magazine.

5. The Association shall establish the following offices:

   A. one President (ed. note: to be nominated by the Board of Directors);

   B. one Consultant *(guwen)* (ed. note: to be nominated by the Board of Directors);

   C. one Vice-President (ed. note: to be nominated by the Board of Directors);

   D. a Board of Directors *(lishi)* with several members (ed. note: to be elected by the general membership);

   E. an Executive Council *(ganshi)* of several members (ed. note: to be elected by the general membership);

6. The President will be in charge of the Association's general affairs, and will represent the Association. The Consultant and the Vice-President will assist the President, and act as his proxy when he is unavailable. The Board of Directors will manage the Association's affairs under the President's direction. The Executive Council, acting on their supervision, will take care of general accounting.

7. The President will select from the general membership people of learning, virtue, and prestige, and appoint them as teachers to proselytize and spread the teachings.

8. Membership will be divided into four categories:

   A. Ordinary Members *(Putong huiyuan)*, who pay dues of two yen per year, one each in May and September;

   B. Regular Members *(Zheng huiyuan)*, who pay dues of five yen per year, due at the same time as those of Ordinary Members;

   C. Special Members *(Tebie huiyuan)*, who pay more than five yen in dues at any one time;

   D. Honorary Members *(Mingyu huiyuan)*, to be awarded upon recommendation of those of broad education and high morals or of outstanding contributions to the Association.

   Ordinary and Regular Members shall be able to pay their dues in one lump sum for a period of no more than ten years. If they do, then the Ordinary Members can pay sixteen yen, and the Regular Members can pay forty yen.

9. The Association will issue an identification card and badge to each member. However, members will have to pay for replacement badges.

10. Dues are not refundable in the event of withdrawal or expulsion.

11. Those desiring to join the Association must furnish proof of their name, address, and occupation, and must be introduced by an Association member in order to apply.

12. Any member who damages the Association's reputation or who fails to live up to the responsibilities of membership will be expelled.

13. The Association will hold its general convention in April of every year in order to discuss the preceding year's activities and accounts, and to deliberate on any new business.

14. Any amendments to this charter must pass by a two-thirds majority of the Board of Directors (Reproduced in *1971 Gazetteer*:65a–66a).

As is evident, this charter represents quite an evolution since the days of the founding of the PBA. It shows a level of sophistication and self-confidence completely lacking in the earlier document, and no trace of the former's pervasive apprehension. As an organization founded at the initiative of representatives of the Japanese government, its purpose was to upbuild Buddhism in Taiwan through educational and publishing activities. It was not, as was the PBA before it, an organ whose sole function was to provide members with credentials with which to represent themselves before the government as loyal Japanese citizens, and by which to distinguish themselves from seditious elements in society. While the SSBA charter certainly contains provisions that would have this effect, its goals were much more broadly and comprehensively defined.

In the discussion that followed the proposal of the charter, it was decided not to limit the site of the annual convention to Taipei, but to allow any local chapter with fifty or more members to host it. Marui Keijirō assumed the post of acting President, and thirteen representatives received positions on the Executive Council. These included Shanhui, Benyuan, Lin Delin, and Yongding among those from the Buddhist clerical establishment, and Xu Lin (the *taikong* of the Longhua Sect) and others from the ranks of *zhaijiao*. All were directly appointed by Marui, and it is notable that all were Chinese.

Marui called an ad hoc general meeting on December 17, 1922 for the purpose of electing permanent officers. Predictably, he was elected president, while the vice presidency went to the head of the government Education Office, Ikoma Takahisa. Marui might have continued indefinitely as head of the SSBA, but for the fact that in 1925 the government abolished the unit that he headed and transferred its responsibilities to the Social Affairs Office under the Bureau of Education. Marui returned to Japan. For the remainder of the SSBA's existence, the Board of Directors always nominated the head of the Bureau of Education as president, and the head of the Social Affairs Office as vice president (*1971 Gazetteer*:66b).

The SSBA did not wait until the ad hoc organizing conference to begin carrying out its mission as an agency for education and uplift. Its first short course opened on July 3, 1922 and lasted twenty days, at first in Taipei's Chengyuan School, then in the Eastgate Buddhist Junior School. Twenty-three students and six auditors came to hear lectures by Shanhui, Benyuan, Xu Lin, five Japanese monks of various schools, and Marui himself. The next short course took place in November of the same year at the Kaiyuan Temple in Tainan. This time, twenty-two students took part. Thereafter, the SSBA organized a two-week course of study every June and November, rotating the location. The participants in these events were mostly men; in 1925 the SSBA began organizing separate short courses aimed at women. The first, which began on June 18, 1925, attracted twenty-five women and took place under the direction of Jueli at the Yishan Temple in Hsinchu county without direct SSBA involvement. However, the SSBA quickly took notice of Jueli's educational offering for nuns; and, the following year, took over this event. From then on, women's courses became regular features of the SSBA's educational program (Shi Chanhui 1981:148).

In accordance with its charter, the SSBA also published a magazine, *South Seas Buddhism (Nam'e Bukkyō)*, which featured a mix of news, Buddhist thought, research reports, and poetry. The first issue appeared in July 1923. There were only two issues that year, but as the organization gained in membership, the magazine began to come out more regularly until, by 1930, it became a monthly journal. Most telling is the language of choice for writing. The first several issues were published solely in Chinese, probably in keeping with the wishes of the all-Chinese board of directors. However, the magazine began bilingual publication with volume four, number four. As time went by, Japanese began to occupy more and more space, until in the end the writing was exclusively in Japanese. Most likely, this linguistic shift was the result of the "Japanization" movement of the late 1930s, one component of which was the outlawing of the Chinese language in public discourse.

Be that as it may, some scholars and writers in Taiwan have seen this as emblematic of the general failure of this best and brightest of all Buddhist organizations to make an impact on the Chinese population of Taiwan. As is obvious from its history, the SSBA was never anything more than an agency of the colonial government for the regulation of Buddhist activities. As Chen Lingrong (1992) observes, the Japanese both in Taiwan and on the mainland saw Buddhism as a way to bridge the gap between them and the people they sought to rule. The "education" offered in lecture meetings and short courses probably included more than just Buddhist history and philosophy; there was probably a good sprinkling of official Japanese government ideology mixed in as well. Chen believes that Japanese Buddhism, despite these efforts, never extended its influence beyond the upper strata of Chinese society, who needed the contacts, or those who deliberately allowed themselves to be subsumed by a sect of Japanese Buddhism for protection, particularly when the government implemented its "temple restructuring" policy (Chen Lingrong 1992:130–131).

I am not so certain. There remains to this day a subcurrent of resentment against the Japanese colonial government, particularly with regard to their forceful attempts to suppress Chinese culture and language during their invasion of the mainland.[6] My own feeling is that Chinese scholars, given an opportunity, tend to interpret data so as to indicate the failure of the Japanese in these efforts. I wish to remind the reader that there really was not enough time for Japanese policies to work; Taiwan returned to the Chinese fold a mere twenty-three years after the founding of the SSBA. There is evidence that, in the later period, many ethnic Chinese people did in fact think of Japanese as their mother tongue and did assimilate Japanese values from the educational system. Thus, instead of failure, the SSBA magazine's shift from Chinese to Japanese may reflect success in reaching out to the general population. In any case, it was inevitable given the illegal status of Chinese. Had the Japanese continued to hold Taiwan after 1945, the

SSBA might have grown into a thriving and vital organization in the Taiwan Buddhist world.

THE "JAPANIZATION MOVEMENT" AND "TEMPLE RESTRUCTURING"

The term "Japanization Movement" has already appeared in several places; now it is time to look at this phenomenon directly and systematically. The Japanese expression *kōminka undō* literally means "the movement to turn [the people] into imperial citizens," and refers to an official government policy instituted in 1937 that attempted, as far as it was possible, to turn the Chinese population of Taiwan into ethnic Japanese citizens. They knew that the resulting hybrids would not be real Japanese, at least not at first; rather, they would be *kikeiteki nihonjin,* "deformed Japanese" (Chen Xiaochong 1991:499).

This is not to say that the Japanese viceregal government had not had this goal in mind before 1937; beginning in 1936, nongovernmental bodies had recommended a movement to inculcate Japanese values among the Chinese, improve the vulgar atmosphere that (they thought) prevailed at most temples, and curb wastefulness. Some local governments acted upon these recommendations and enforced some modest reform measures (Cai 1994:230–233). But this movement gained impetus and urgency on July 7, 1937, with the Marco Polo Bridge Incident which marked the outbreak of China's War of Resistance against further Japanese incursions into its territory. Japan needed soldiers to fight on the Chinese mainland, and could not afford to exempt the able-bodied men of Taiwan from military service. At the same time, it was feared that, once deployed on the mainland, Taiwanese soldiers would defect and fight against their Japanese commanders—in spite of the fact that this generation of young men had grown up in a Taiwan that was part of Japan, and had come through the Japanese educational system.

As a result of these considerations, the Japanization Movement that began in 1937 was more thoroughgoing in its goals and methods than previous movements. Among the measures enacted in quick succession were the following:

1. Use of the southern Fujian dialect (or any form of spoken Chinese) was outlawed, as was Chinese in all publications and periodicals. Japanese also became the medium of instruction in all public schools. At the same time, the law provided for the establishment of a great number of Japanese-language schools throughout Taiwan. Government statistics bear out the effectiveness of this policy, showing that in 1936, 32.9 percent of the population of Taiwan could speak Japanese; by 1944, this figure had risen to 71 percent (Chen Xiaochong 1991:500).

2. In addition to enforcing usage of the Japanese language, schools became vehicles for inculcating Japanese political ideology and thought. The language curriculum included songs extolling Japanese state militarism, and there were extracurricular clubs and activities organized for the express purpose of arousing Japanese nationalist sentiments (Chen Xiaochong 1991:503).

3. All citizens were required to adopt Japanese names. This was presented to the people as an option that they could choose as a convenience, but those who declined the offer sometimes found themselves sent away for national service in Malaysia or elsewhere (Chen Xiaochong 1991:502. However, given the virulently anti-Japanese tone of this source, I would be cautious in accepting the author's contention that all those who did not comply were shipped off. Such a policy would likely be impracticable on an islandwide scale.).

4. The government even intruded into private lifestyles, requiring women to wear Japanese-style clothes in public; and anyone renovating their house or apartment had to do so in Japanese style; for example, bathtubs had to be Japanese-style (i.e., not wide, but deep), bedrooms had to have *tatami*s for sleeping.

5. All Chinese cultural activities were proscribed. It became illegal to perform Taiwanese opera; instead, the government commissioned plays and dramas extolling Japanese cultural values (Chen Xiaochong 1991:504).

These measures demonstrate how seriously the Japanese government took their task. In the realm of religion, the government was no less thorough, at least on paper. They required all households to destroy the ancestral altars in their homes, and issued specific instructions on the erection of Japanese-style *butsudan* and *kamidana,* complete with diagrams. Citizens were to install paper amulets *(taima)* from the Ise Shrines (main imperial shrines to divine imperial ancestors) on these home altars and worship them regularly according to the rites of State Shintō (Chen Lingrong 1992:237–245; Miyamoto 1988:15; Cai 1994:172–201).

However, some local officials and others within the central government became convinced that traditional Chinese religious beliefs centered around temple practices, and unless the temples were brought into line with Japanese beliefs and values, all other efforts to eradicate Chinese culture would be useless. They therefore proposed the measure of "temple restructuring" *(jibyō seiri)*. This was, of course, a euphemism. In practice, it meant that the government proposed to raze temples, shrines, and *zhaijiao* meeting-halls, and burn their images (a process the Japanese called "sending the gods back to Heaven" [*shoshin shōten*]) (Cai 1994:236–240). Those buildings that were spared were to be "restructured" into Japanese state shrines *(jinja),* or Japanese-style Buddhist temples and missionary stations. For its part, the governor-general's office left local governments alone to do what they wished, and vacillated in its own view of the matter (Cai 1994:238).

As a result of the viceregal government's unwillingness to get involved, temple restructuring measures were unevenly promulgated and enforced. Since they were aimed specifically at "Daoist temples," the measures did not touch "pure" Buddhist temples at all (Miyamoto 1988:3). The official policy in Taiwan at this time was to encourage Buddhism (*1971 Gazetteer*:68b); and, at any rate, most Buddhist temples in Taiwan were already directly subordinate to the officially recognized schools of Japanese Buddhism, and their head monks had already shown themselves to be loyal citizens. The reader may remember that Shanhui had already built his Lingquan Chan Temple in a hybrid Chinese-Japanese style, and that the government used it as a place to receive Buddhist dignitaries from Japan; thus, it was not a candidate for "restructuring." The main brunt of this measure fell upon folk temples and shrines, Daoist temples, and *zhaijiao* meeting-halls.

The official explanation for this was that the religious practices at these temples were meretricious and antisocial. For instance, Chen

Lingrong cites a report issued in 1938 by Miyazaki Naokatsu, the governor of Chungli *gun,* that lists five specific complaints: (1) native temple beliefs are an obstacle to upward cultural progress; (2) they are unpatriotic; (3) they obstruct the development of healthy social thought because traditional beliefs and practices are self-serving and not conducive to putting the welfare of state and society above one's own good; (4) the way in which temples are currently run frequently leads to disputes and even bloodshed; and (5) the temples are only loosely administered, and private individuals sometimes embezzle temple funds originally designated for charitable purposes (Chen Lingrong 1992:247; see also Cai 1994:263–264 for the same material in Japanese).

The first restructurings took place in November 1938 in Hsinchu, and it was in the Hsinchu-Chungli area that the local authorities pursued this policy most vigorously. As it went into effect, temples and shrines scrambled to find ways to escape, and many appealed to the Japanese Buddhist establishment for protection, promising to subordinate themselves and their property in return. For instance, the *1971 Gazetteer* records an instance of an attempt of this kind, reported by Miyazaki Naokatsu:

> Among these was the Fengtian Gong on Yangmei Street. It had long before placed itself in contact with the Rinzai School, and so a few dozen of the temple's devotees sent a petition to the main Rinzai temple in Taiwan *(Rinzai-shū Taiwan Betsuin),* saying that they would take all of the temple's property (ed. note: their land was appraised at 10,000 *yen)* and transfer it over to Japanese Buddhism. In addition, they would hang a sign over the temple's door declaring it a missionary station of the Rinzai Temple for Protecting the Nation *(Gokokuji).* The supervisor of the Rinzai mission in Taiwan, Takabayashi Gentaka, went in person to the Yangmei neighborhood government office, showed them the certificate appointing him the deputy of the temple's devotees, and said, "I have been given the management of this temple in trust, and I do not approve of you 'renovating' the Fengtian Gong. Plus, I am personally not willing to participate in the enshrinement ceremony for the Yangmei neighborhood (i.e., the opening of the official Shintō *jinja* in this neighborhood). If the local authorities make any move to renovate the Fengtian Gong or its images, the Rinzai School will never give its consent, you may be sure of that!" He also said, "Japanese Buddhism will never permit the local authorities to violate the right to freedom of religion guaranteed to citizens by our constitution. If the authorities step over this line, we will not

only contact the viceregal authorities to rectify the matter, we will also call our representatives in the National Diet and get them to put the matter on their agenda so as to investigate [who is] responsible for ruling in Taiwan" (*1971 Gazetteer*:68b).

However, even Takabayashi's influence proved insufficient, and the temple came down. The government in Taiwan was committed to carrying out restructuring, convinced of its necessity to insure that the Taiwanese would ultimately come to see themselves as Japanese citizens and thus be willing to fight other Chinese on the mainland. In the records of a government meeting held on February 2, 1939, a delegate named Nagano, in responding to criticism that the temple restructuring policy was being overzealously enforced, defended it thusly:

> In order to enforce the abolition of the Chinese language, culture, and tradition, we must exert ourselves in the destruction and re-structuring of the temples that are their centers, the burning of ancestral tablets, and the ban on wearing Chinese dress, and thus bring about the Japanization of the people of the island. No matter what objections there may be to this movement, I believe that whatever degree of success we may have in abolishing Chinese and depriving our Taiwanese compatriots of their literature, instilling the true spirit of our rule over them, and especially in destroying their culture in such things as the temples around which their religion centers and the ancestral tablets that are the objects of their veneration, the most important thing is to influence their hearts (Taiwan Sōtokufu Bunkyōkyoku 1943, no pagination).

Not all parts of Taiwan went through the same experience as Chungli *gun;* it depended upon how much importance the local authorities gave this task vis-à-vis the other tasks of government. Chungli *gun* chief Miyazaki seems to have pursued the implementation of this policy more vigorously than any other local official, with the result that in this area, twenty-nine temples, four *zhaijiao* halls, seventy-eight devotional societies *(shenming hui),* and eight ancestral worship societies were either razed or disbanded; and their property was confiscated and put into the hands of a holding company charged to administer the funds for educational purposes. This property totalled 197 *jia* (or about 82 acres) of paddy land and 78 *jia* (about 32.5 acres) of dry fields, worth a total of 500,000 yen and producing annual rental income of about 42,000 yen (Chen Lingrong 1992:262). In fact, both Chen Lingrong and Cai assert that the prospect of acquiring substantial money and property through confiscation constituted one of the major motivations for the movement (Cai 1994:235).

How much of an impact did this policy have across the island? When one looks at the numbers, it appears that it was not that great. Government surveys taken in 1936 and 1942 provide the following statistics:

	TEMPLES (BUDDHIST, DAOIST, AND FOLK)	ZHAIJIAO MEETING HALLS	DEVOTIONAL SOCIETIES
1936	3,403	246	5,345
1942	2,327	224	4,017

Source: Statistics from Chen Lingrong 1992:255

Further statistics show that during this period, 361 temples and 9 zhaijiao halls were destroyed, while 819 temples and 27 halls were transferred to other uses. In addition, the government burned 13,726 religious images from temples and 153 from zhaijiao halls, while 4,069 and 202 respectively were shipped off to museums and other new homes. Finally, scholars working in Taiwan have frequently lamented the fact that the authorities destroyed many temple and meeting-hall records and historical documents during this time, making a reconstruction of pre-Japanese religious history extremely difficult.

The Japanization Movement was not only pursued by the government; the Japanese Buddhist establishment itself saw this as a tremendous opportunity to expand membership. A policy statement issued by the Kogi Shingonshū (a subsect of the Shingon school) in the early 1940s included among its eight goals the following four items: (1) embodiment of the spirit of nation-building; (2) the Japanization Movement; (3) the eradication of individualism and libertarianism; and (4) the completion of the essence of Imperial Buddhism (kōdō Bukkyō) (Kogi Shingon-shū [1940?]:2). (The other four goals have to do with the propagation of specifically Shingon rituals and doctrines.) The statement goes on to list eighteen specific actions, the first of which stipulates that the Shingon

School would carry out its own temple restructurings with the advice and consent of the local authorities. Number two states that the School would work to regulate and improve traditional life-cycle rituals, altering Chinese rituals into a Japanese form. Number three says that, henceforth, only Japanese priests from the main Japanese islands would be permitted to carry out rituals, and these were to be compatible with the imperial house. Number four proposes sending native Taiwanese clergy to Japan for indoctrination. Number ten pledges to use only Japanese as a medium of instruction in all Shingon functions; and the rest bear on issues of accountability, propaganda work, and management (Kogi Shingon-shū [1940?]:3–4).

The policy statement then reports on the progress in implementing these measures. In 1940, the secretary of the Kogi Shingonshū had come from Kōyasan to Taiwan to make two inspection tours and certify that things were proceeding smoothly. Furthermore, the School did pay for thirteen native Taiwanese clergy to travel to Kōyasan, where they listened to lectures on Shingon lore (such as the life of Kūkai, chanting, the Three Dhāraṇī, and so forth), and then toured Japan, stopping at Nagoya, Nara, Ise, Tokyo, and Kyoto, among other places. These measures must have had some effect; one of the clergy reported that he had learned the importance of always speaking in Japanese (Kogi Shingon-shū [1940?]:5–10).

The colonial government's temple restructuring project clearly was the most far-reaching and disastrous in its effect on religion in Taiwan. However, it is equally clear from the figures given above that the government fell far short of its stated goal of the complete abolition of all Chinese temples before, in the face of severe criticism in 1939, it pulled back, leaving some token temples in operation (Chen Lingrong 1992:264). In several localities, the policy was not enforced at all. For example, in Taichung *shū*, the authorities could not decide how to implement the policy and so did nothing, while in Taipei, most of the temples had good government connections and were able to escape restructuring (See Chen Lingrong 1992:252–253 for a summary of local enforcement). As stated above, while several *zhaijiao* halls did fall beneath the wrecking ball, Buddhist temples were generally not affected because they had long since proved their loyalty to the colonial government.

The movement finally halted with the arrival of a new governor-general in November, 1940. By the time he arrived, protests against the unconstitutionality of the measures, both in Taiwan and in Japan proper, had reached such a pitch that he decided to "suspend" all enforcement of them and appoint a commission of academics to study the situation. When the commission finally submitted its report, the war was almost at an end, and the government had many other concerns; and so the new governor-general's suspension of the movement in fact became its demise (Cai 1994:273–281).

Consequently, the ultimate importance of the Japanization Movement and its concomitant temple restructuring policy does not lie in the concrete results, but in the atmosphere it created. As the policy was promulgated in the various political districts around Taiwan, temples and *zhaijiao* halls sought ways to survive. Most, if they had not done so already, accomplished this by submitting to the authority of Japanese Buddhist establishments. Many that did not take this step on their own were soon forced to in order to comply with the policy. The result was that by the time Japan returned Taiwan to China in 1945, the Taiwanese viewed Buddhist and *zhaijiao* temples and organizations as simply appendages of the Japanese Buddhist establishment and the government to which it had given its full cooperation. When the Japanese government pulled out, the organizations collapsed, victims of the very measures that they thought would save them.

THE FATE OF *ZHAIJIAO*

The events outlined above, beginning in 1912, had steadily eroded *zhaijiao*'s foundations; and the temple restructuring policies of 1938 left it badly wounded. This point becomes very clear when we remember the characteristics that defined *zhaijiao* and differentiated it from "orthodox" Buddhism during the Qing period: First, it defined itself as lay Buddhism, and existed in complete independence of the monastic community. Second, it was a derivative of the Luo religion of mainland China, and relied either on Luo Qing's *Five Books in Six Volumes* or other texts composed in-house as its basic scriptures, holding them equal or even superior in stature to traditional Buddhist sutras. Third, even though it leaned toward Buddhism when it needed to identify itself, it was still officially committed to combining Daoism, Confucianism, and Buddhism into a single system, and incidentally adopted many of the concepts and practices of folk religion as well. Fourth, it saw its commitment to vegetarianism as its defining quality; it was, after all, the "vegetarian teaching" *(zhaijiao)*.

All of these qualities and ideological commitments unraveled during the long years of the Japanese occupation. Beginning with the formation of the PBA in 1912, and running through the organization of the SSBA in 1922 and the temple restructuring calamity of 1937–1940, *zhaijiao* followers became increasingly subject to Japanese Buddhism, especially the Sōtō School. In so doing, they gained their survival, but they completely lost their independence from monastic oversight.[7]

Two other results followed from their submission. First, they lost their scriptures and liturgies. The Japanese monastic establishment had no more use for Luo Qing's *Five Books in Six Volumes* or any other *zhaijiao*-composed scripture than had the orthodox Chinese monastic establishment during the Ming and Qing dynasties. Neither did the establishment have any use for liturgies directed toward non-Buddhist divinities such as the Unborn Venerable Mother *(Wusheng Laomu)* or the eschatological mythology connected with her. Second, as stated above, the followers of *zhaijiao* came to be seen as collaborators with the Japanese by the incoming Nationalist forces who were to determine the political future. While the Buddhist monks who streamed into Taiwan from the mainland after the war at least felt that the native orthodox Buddhist temples and organizations were salvageable, there was no such sympathy for *zhaijiao*, which consequently was left to its own fate.

It even came about that, in some quarters, *zhaijiao* followers began eating meat, thus letting go of their most essential defining characteristic and the one practice that gained them respect in the eyes of their more orthodox compatriots. The man responsible for this development was Su Zeyang, and the vehicle was the "New Covenant Longhua Sect" *(Xinyue Longhua Jiao)* that he established.

Su Zeyang (1873–1934) lived a quiet life as a Western-style pharmacist until 1900, when, while out on a business trip, he was held up at gunpoint. This event depressed him greatly, and impressed upon him the uncertainty and transitoriness of life. He sought solutions to these conditions in religion, but did not seem to find anything satisfactory for quite a while, for he joined one religious group after another in quick succession: *zhaijiao* in 1901, Sōtō Zen in 1903, another *zhaijiao* sect in 1904. He wrote books and displayed quite a talent for doctrine and administration. Consequently, in 1906 a *zhaijiao* group asked him to open a new meeting-hall in Mengjia (the present Wanhua district of Taipei); but other *zhaijiao* groups protested, and so he changed his plan. On the basis of his credentials as a Sōtō devotee, in 1907 he opened the "Mengjia Baoan Buddhist Hall and Dharma Preaching Station" *(Mengjia Baoan Fotang Shuojiaochang)*, for which he took on the responsibilities of chief missionary and executive manager.[8]

Six years later, in 1913, Su formally established the "Taiwan New Covenant Longhua Buddhist Shengguo Mountain Baoan Hall" *(Taiwan Xinyue Longhua Fojiao Shengguoshan Baoan Tang)*. His "New Covenant Longhua Sect" also called itself Laoguan Zhaijiao, thus implicitly claiming to descend from the earliest *zhaijiao* groups on the mainland. This claim gained added respectability in 1929 when the head of the Yishi Sect of Longhua *zhaijiao*, Zhou Pujing, came for a visit from Fujian and conferred the title of *taikong* upon Su's wife, Chen Ying, and gave her the dharma name of Pulie. Su and his wife spent the remaining five years of his life administering their small sect, which at its height had only seven halls in northern Taiwan. After his death, his New Covenant Longhua Sect went into a decline, although at least one hall in the Tienmou area of Taipei has remained active.

Despite the putative connection with the Yishi branch of the Longhua Sect of *zhaijiao*, Su's New Covenant group was vastly different in several respects. For one thing, Su did away with Luo Qing's *Five Books in Six Volumes* and substituted scriptures of his own composition. He simplified the nine-level hierarchy of Longhua down to six. Most importantly, he did away with the vow to observe a vegetarian diet at all times.

Most sects of *zhaijiao*, with the exception of Xiantian, gave adherents the option of choosing the *huazhai* initiation, which only involved observing vegetarianism at selected times, or *changzhai*, "permanent vegetarianism." Su, feeling that the second option was too great a strain for even the most committed devotee to maintain, decreed that all members should pick four days each month to observe vegetarianism. In so doing, he succeeded in instituting a paradoxical branch of the "vegetarian teaching" that did not observe vegetarianism, at least not in daily life (Zheng 1990:77–78).

The innovations of one small sect do not indicate a complete decline in *zhaijiao,* but their development, along with some other factors, show how weak and diluted *zhaijiao* had become by the late 1920s and mid-1930s. The other factors include the fact that by 1945, several halls had been demolished and almost all their religious images were gone. The remaining halls were being administered by Japanese (or Japanized) monks; followers had lost the use of their own scriptures and liturgies in their daily religious life; they had lost control of their properties and funds; and some had even given up on vegetarianism. The little bit of authentic *zhaijiao* that remained bore the taint of collaborationism after Retrocession.

This is not to say that these groups died out completely. Zheng reports that, as of 1990, there were still fifty "fellowship centers" *(lianyi zhongxin)* connected with the Longhua Fellowship Association *(Longhua Lianyi Hui)* (Zheng 1990:77). However, most of the halls have gone in one of two directions since Retrocession: either they have been taken over by more orthodox Buddhist monks or nuns and become Buddhist temples, or they have become Daoist and folk temples (Zheng 1990:85). Other groups cast about for ways of revitalizing their corporate life to meet the challenges of existence under the Chinese Nationalist government.

We may look at the Xiantian Sect as an example of the difficulties *zhaijiao* faced in this new situation. When Huang Yujie passed away in 1918, his brother Huang Jian succeeded him as head of Xiantian in Taiwan. Huang Jian was active, both in his capacity as provincial leader and as a founding member of the SSBA board of directors; and in 1935 he traveled to the mainland and there received from a Xiantian leader both a confirmation of his commission and appointment as head of the entire Fujian–Zhejiang region. He survived into the new regime, and passed away in 1958. The next leader was Zeng Yuhui, who, more than Huang, saw that the sect needed new ideas in order to adapt to the new political and social climate. That year, he drafted a set of proposals to reorganize and reform the sect, and sent them to all the halls in

Taiwan. The response was generally favorable, so Zeng called a conference in Changhua which convened in March, 1960. At this meeting, participants clarified the sect's lineages and doctrines, ratified a new charter, and set up new headquarters there.

Zeng Yuhui passed away in 1961 and was succeeded by Xu Wentong, another active leader who worked hard to propagate the sect. Xu died in 1967, and Zheng Rongsheng took over. Zheng had some new visions for the Xiantian Sect, and arranged for its involvement in social welfare work. He also helped organize a Poetry Convention in Changhua, which attracted the participation of 740 poets from all over Taiwan. Additionally, he oversaw the construction of a new, four-story meeting hall called the Xinde Hall, whose completion was marked by a forty-nine day religious observance (*jiao*) attended by many government officials (Lin Wanchuan 1984:I–234–236).

In addition to the Xiantian Sect, the Longhua Sect continues to thrive to some extent around Taiwan. From this evidence, it appears that *zhaijiao* remains a vital minority religious tradition in Taiwan, and that the expulsion of the Japanese government and the arrival of mainland refugee monks in 1949 returned it to its normal, adversarial relationship with more "orthodox" Buddhist institutions. As some scholars in Taiwan have noted, this return has put *zhaijiao* into the interstices between academic fields: It is not quite a topic for the researcher in Buddhist studies, nor do anthropologists think of it as folk religion; thus, it remains largely unstudied to this day, providing a fertile research field for interested scholars. However, since our study is concerned primarily with Buddhist history, we will part company with *zhaijiao* at this point.

CONCLUSION: HOW GREAT AN IMPACT?

Most Chinese scholars working in Taiwan do not believe that the Japanese occupation influenced religion on the island to any great extent. The Japanese were not in Taiwan long enough to have a lasting impact, and their policies never significantly touched the masses. I believe that is true as far as the uneducated and working classes go; their lives were probably touched much more in terms of having to join the Japanese army, provide corvée labor, and adopt a new language and mode of dress than in having to alter their religious beliefs and practices. However, we must note that the "temple restructuring movement" had the effect of driving their worship of folk and Daoist divinities underground for a time, and even engendered some widespread agnosticism as the curses and calamities that they feared would accompany the razing of a temple failed to occur (Cai 1994:290–299).

It also appears that the withdrawal of the Japanese from Taiwan was less traumatic for Buddhism there than it was for Buddhism in other colonies when the Japanese were forced out. For example, Robert Buswell reports that in Korea, the exit of Japanese Buddhism left Korean Buddhist monks deeply factionalized between those who had adapted to Japanese customs by taking wives and rejecting vegetarianism, and those who wished to return to the more stringent customs of earlier eras. This factionalization resulted in open hostility when the two groups competed for control of monastic property, and it was years before the issues of ownership and leadership were sorted out (Buswell 1992:30–36). Taiwan was spared these effects for two reasons. First, the Japanese had permitted the influx from the Chinese mainland of Buddhist ordination lineages that actively worked to keep the traditional Chinese precepts. I have not uncovered any evidence that the Japanese pressured monks like Jueli or Benyuan to refrain from transmitting the full monastic precepts, or coerced them to accept clerical marriage and other infractions. Second, unlike Korea, Taiwan had been part of a larger nation, and as soon as it returned to China, monks of national eminence began coming in with the authority to suppress whatever they took to be the lingering ill effects of the Japanese administration.

And yet I also believe that the Japanese viceregal administration had an enormous impact upon those whose occupations and aspirations brought them into close contact with the government. These were the people like Shanhui and Benyuan, Yongding and Jueli, Xu Lin and Huang Yujie, people who actually ran things within Taiwan Buddhist circles and had the highest visibility. Apart from the fact that these men had all passed from the scene by 1945, the institutions they created, the temples, schools, and associations that provided outlets for the energies of the Buddhist elite, vanished along with the Japanese colonial government.

One may discern in the history of the activities and institutions of these leaders a curious double movement. On the one hand, in creating associations such as the South Seas Buddhist Association, along with various schools and temples, these men deliberately fostered ever-closer ties with the Japanese colonial administration and Buddhist establishment. This was natural and inevitable since, as indicated before, they had no reason to believe that Taiwan would ever be part of China again. On the other hand, despite this resignation, there was a pull towards traditional Chinese Buddhist customs and practices. One sees this aspect in the stories of the four primary ordination centers that brought strictly Chinese ordination platforms to the island for the first time in its history, as well as in various efforts at Buddhist education aimed at the ethnic Chinese clergy. This double movement points to a pattern of cooperation with the Japanese without assimilation on the part of Chinese Buddhism in Taiwan. Given the fact that, despite one hundred years of domination by other linguistic groups, Hokkien remains the mother tongue of an overwhelming majority of the islanders to this day, one may speculate that this sort of accomodation without assimilation would have remained the case for a very long time had Taiwan not been returned to the Chinese nation.

Such was the pattern of religious life molded by the leaders of Chinese Buddhism in Taiwan during the Japanese colonial period. If Retrocession had been the end of the story, it is possible that the people who succeeded these leaders could have built up new religious institutions within the framework of the Taiwan Branch of the BAROC along the same lines as their predecessors. However, as we shall soon see, Generalissimo Chiang Kai-shek's retreat to Taiwan in 1949 brought a wave of mainland monks from the eastern seaboard, men who had been leaders of national stature and sought to do for Chinese Buddhism what the Nationalist government was trying to do for Chinese politics: make credible claims to positions of national leadership while in exile on Taiwan. The aftermath of this influx, among other things, will be addressed in the next chapter.

PART III

FROM RETROCESSION TO THE MODERN PERIOD

(1945–1990)

CHAPTER 4

—✺—

RETROCESSION AND THE ARRIVAL OF THE MAINLAND MONKS

The Japanese colonial era in Taiwan ended in 1945, when, as part of its terms of surrender, Japan returned the island to Chinese rule. The people and government refer to this event as *guangfu,* "the return of the light." The Taiwanese, remembering their second-class status under Japanese rule and the excesses of the Japanization Movement, rejoiced at the prospect of returning to the Chinese fold. However, Retrocession came upon the public quickly, and most people did not have time to consider what this sudden change of fortunes might portend. In any case, no one at that time could have predicted the far more active role that the central structures of the Nationalist (Kuo Min Tang [*guomindang*], or KMT) government would soon play in Taiwan's political affairs, or that, under the new regime, Taiwanese (meaning southern Fujianese) language and culture would once again be banned from public discourse. Most importantly, no one would have predicted that the entire central government of China would be retreating en masse to Taiwan a short four years later.

INTERLUDE: 1945–1949

The Expulsion of the Japanese and the Reorganization of Taiwan Buddhism

The period between Retrocession and the arrival of the retreating Nationalist government in 1949 marks the only four years out of the past century in which Taiwan has been a province of greater China in any real sense. The major task for Buddhism, as for all other sectors of public and private life in Taiwan, was to find its appropriate role under the new regime. The main question was: to what extent would Taiwan Buddhism be able to set its own course, and to what extent would it have to accept governance and supervision from the mainland?

The transition was slow, of course. After fifty years, the greater part of a generation of ethnic Chinese living in Taiwan had known nothing but life under Japanese rule; and almost half of the 488,000 ethnic Japanese living in Taiwan had grown up there and knew nothing of life in Japan proper. For all of these people, what followed was a time of intense upheaval. The new Nationalist authorities reorganized all of the old Japanese political administrative units along Chinese lines, and changed all street names (which must have made giving directions a daunting task for a time); and all of the Chinese people who had been forced to adopt Japanese names ten years earlier resumed using their original Chinese names. Japanese government officials and military men, long used to privileged positions in society, now found themselves selling vegetables or noodles by the roadside, or pulling rickshaws (Huang Zhaotang 1994:254–255).

However, the biggest disruptions were yet to come. On December 25, 1945, the Nationalist government began to repatriate all Japanese citizens in earnest. One can imagine the chaos that ensued as 459,928 people were shipped out in the space of four months. These people lost everything that they had built up over the past fifty years, only being allowed to take with them 1000 Japanese yen in cash and one backpack of daily necessities, and to ship two thirty-kilogram suitcases separately. Everything else—houses, shops, businesses, bank accounts, government buildings, Shintō shrines and (most significantly for our purposes) Buddhist temples—went to the new Taiwan Provincial government (Huang Zhaotang 1994:256–257; Kerr 1976:97–113). The last viceregal governor of Taiwan, Andō Rikichi, was put in charge of the repatriation liaison unit, a duty he found so shameful that he never even went to the dingy office given him, instead letting his subordinates handle the actual work. He and several other Japanese viceregal officials were arrested on charges of war crimes the day after the repatriation efforts were officially closed. They were sent to Shanghai for trial, but Andō committed suicide rather than face this final humiliation.

Those who moved in Buddhist circles, no less than those in the political realm, found themselves suddenly operating in a power vacuum. Two of the "Three Great Monks" of the Taiwan Buddhist world during the Japanese era, Shanhui and Benyuan, were still on the scene. Accustomed to enjoying islandwide prominence as heads of various Buddhist associations, they reacted to the sudden evaporation of the South Seas Buddhist Association and the deportation of their Japanese colleagues by proposing the establishment of a new organization, to be called the Taiwan Provincial Buddhist Association *(Taiwan Sheng Fojiao Hui)*. However, Shanhui died unexpectedly a mere twenty days before the organizational meeting on December 31, 1945 *(1992 Gazetteer:*209). Nevertheless, a nine-man steering committee proceeded to lay plans for the new organization; and the founding meeting took place on February 25, 1946, when delegates elected Benyuan as the first president *(1992 Gazetteer:*148).

The Taiwan Provincial Buddhist Association's autonomy did not last very long. The BAROC[1] reconstituted itself in Nanjing on May 28, 1947 in its first post-war meeting; and the Taiwan Provincial Buddhist Association sent delegates to attend. After the ratification of the organization's new charter, the Taiwan group submitted itself to the BAROC's authority and renamed itself the Taiwan Provincial Buddhist Branch Association *(Taiwan Sheng Fojiao Fenhui),* in compliance with the BAROC's organization into provincial branches *(fenhui)* and local chapters *(zhihui).* After returning to Taiwan, the group began to reorganize Taiwan's Buddhist establishment yet again into city and county chapters *(1992 Gazetteer:*149). Benyuan died in the midst of all this activity on July 7, 1947, the last of the major Buddhist leaders of the Japanese colonial era (*1992 Gazetteer*:205).

The *[1992] Revised Gazetteer of Taiwan Province* reports all of these developments with a blandness that makes them appear unremarkable, as if it were right and fitting that the Taiwan Buddhists should immediately subordinate themselves to the newly reconvened BAROC. However, one cannot help but notice that this subordination came just three months after the "2/28 Incident" *(er er ba shijian* or *er er ba shibian)*. While we remain mindful that positing a connection between the two events may constitute a *post hoc ergo propter hoc* argument, we will present the facts and let the reader judge.

The 2/28 Incident

On February 28, 1947, six agents of the Nationalist Government's Monopoly Bureau found a woman named Lin Jiangmai on the streets of Taipei selling contraband cigarettes. They stopped her and confiscated all her merchandise and cash. She went down on her knees and begged them to return her goods and money; in response, one agent pistol-whipped her until she fell, unconscious and bloody, to the pavement before a crowd of horrified onlookers. A melee ensued as the enraged mob set out in pursuit of the agents. One of the agents, cornered near a movie theater, fired into the crowd and killed a man. The six then took refuge in the Yongle neighborhood police station, were transferred to the central police station, and finally went into the custody of the military police.

The incident crystallized the resentment and frustration that had been steadily building over the Nationalist provincial government's abuses and corruption. What followed was a confrontation lasting all night and into the next day, as people crowded outside whatever police station the six were in, demanding that they be turned out to face public wrath. When the agents were not forthcoming, the crowd grew angry and overturned one of the Monopoly Bureau's trucks, setting it alight. Word of the incident quickly spread, especially when it appeared on the front page of the *New Life News (Xinsheng Bao)* the next morning (along with photos of the six agents). Crowds gathered in several parts of Taipei, and civil disturbances spread rapidly. A mob attempted to storm the government headquarters in Taipei but were met by the army, who opened fire, killed or injured several people, and set the rest fleeing in panic. Others broke into the China Broadcasting Corporation building and took over the facilities long enough to broadcast an account of the incident and call for a mass uprising against Nationalist rule. A dispute over contraband cigarettes had now turned into a rebellion aimed at liberating Taiwan from Chiang Kai-shek's government.

The Nationalists responded with a ruthless crackdown; and over the next several months, untold numbers of people suspected of involvement with Taiwan independence movements were rounded up and were executed, or disappeared. The victims came from all levels of society, from workers to scholars and county magistrates. The numbers are unclear because the government has kept the records sealed until just recently, and the actual totals may never be known. However, the people of Taiwan learned the lesson that the government on the mainland was in firm control and had the means and will to remain so. During the aftermath, which the Taiwanese refer to as the "White Terror," partisans of Taiwan independence, or of Taiwan's language and culture, learned to keep their views to themselves. Those who would not keep quiet went into exile to the mainland after the Communist Victory, or to the West (Dai and Ye, 1992:189–231. An English account and analysis of this event can be found in Kerr 1976, Chaps. 11 through 15, and Mendel 1970:31–41).

It is impossible that the founders of the Taiwan Provincial Buddhist Association would have been unaware of these events, or of the dangers of appearing to assert too large a role for Taiwanese autonomy in any sphere, religious or otherwise. The reorganizational meeting of the BAROC in Nanjing that the Taiwan delegates attended took place three months after the 2/28 Incident, during the height of the ensuing repression. Seen against this backdrop, the swiftness with which the Taiwan group became part of the BAROC and set about reorganizing Taiwan Buddhism according to the BAROC charter is understandable. The reader should remember that this was the same group of people who formed the South Seas Buddhist Association for similar reasons: to cooperate with the government and distance themselves from revolutionary groups.

However, the language barrier remained a practical problem. During the period between Retrocession and the retreat of the Nationalists in 1949, affairs were very chaotic in Taiwan; and there was no time to put in place a universal system of public education in Mandarin (which has since been implemented). Whatever clerical education the Buddhists in Taiwan wanted to implement had to be done in the southern Fujian dialect in order to be effective; and so when Buddhist leaders looked for teachers from the mainland, they invited those from Fujian. The best example of this is the Ven. Cihang (1895–1954), one of the best-loved figures in post-Retrocession Taiwan Buddhism, and whose career in Taiwan bridges the period before and after 1949. Welch regards Cihang *(Tz'u-hang)* only as an example of a trend toward the gilding and worshipping of "flesh bodies" *(roushen),* and indeed, Cihang's body is still on the altar of the Cihang Hall in the Taipei suburb of Hsi-chih, gilded and seated in the lotus position (Welch 1967:343–344). However, as far as understanding Buddhism in Taiwan is concerned, his life story is far more illuminating than the disposition of his corpse. (All of the information concerning Cihang, except where otherwise noted, comes from Jiang 1992:37–75.)

Cihang and his Times

Cihang was born in 1895 in Jianning, a small town about 250 kilometers inland from the coastal city of Fuzhou in Fujian Province, and entered the *sangha* at seventeen. After receiving the full precepts, he wandered from temple to temple, studying both Chan and Pure Land under various masters. In 1927 he entered the Southern Fujian Buddhist Seminary *(Minnan Foxue Yuan),* one of the seminaries founded by Taixu (FG 5803b). However, he was already over thirty years old at the time, older than the other students. His age, lack of education, and rustic background elicited the open ridicule of one of the teachers (Daxing, whom he would encounter again in Taiwan), and so he left after only three months and never again attempted formal Buddhist education.

After that, Cihang went on to a distinguished career, becoming the abbot of the Yangjiang Temple in Anqing. Despite this success, he felt ashamed to occupy such a responsible and respected position while still ignorant of Buddhism and unable to understand the scriptures; so he tried another avenue of getting an education. In 1929 he saw an advertisement for correspondence courses offered by another of Taixu's seminaries, the Wuchang Buddhist Seminary. He wrote for the materials and received in the mail a textbook on Consciousness-Only *(Weishi)* philosophy, which he found completely incomprehensible. He dropped off the rolls of formal correspondence students, but kept the book; and for the next ten years he carried it with him at all times, coming bit by bit to understand its contents. From then on, whenever he was invited to give a lecture, his favorite subject was Consciousness-Only thought.

Through his exposure to two of Taixu's seminaries, he became enthusiastic about Taixu's plans to reform the Buddhist *saṅgha* and the BAROC. He followed Taixu during the latter's tour of Southeast Asia in 1940, but did not return with him to China. Instead, he stayed around Malaysia and Singapore, working tirelessly for Buddhist education and founding seminaries and study groups (FG 5803b,c). Finally, in 1948, Miaoguo invited him to come to Taiwan and help establish the Taiwan Buddhist Studies Academy *(Taiwan Foxue Yuan)* in the Yuanguang Temple in Chungli. Cihang came amid great hopes that he would do wonders for Buddhist education in Taiwan, and he spent the last six years of his life on the island.

These were not six happy years. The Taiwan to which he came was highly unsettled and its economy was in chaos. During his first year there, the Nationalist government retreated to Taiwan, bringing in its wake a flood of refugees that included many young monks. The United States–Taiwan Mutual Defense Treaty was not signed until 1954 and did not go into effect until 1955, which meant that the atmosphere was nervous to the point of paranoia during Cihang's entire time in Taiwan. As an outsider to the Taiwan system who did not come in with the Nationalists, he had an especially hard time of it.

Cihang came on the understanding that he was to help the Taiwan Buddhist Studies Academy set up a three-year curriculum, spend the first six months teaching a basic training course, and then move on to teach more advanced research courses. After his arrival, he found that the Yuanguang Temple had almost no money for its proposed academy, and in fact provided little more than the buildings. Cihang's first task was to tour the island, giving lectures and trying to attract students. He raised money for textbooks from his contacts among the overseas Chinese living in Southeast Asia, and he himself never received a single paycheck during his entire tenure in Chungli. He began the basic training class in the late fall of 1948 with forty-odd students, but when the course concluded six months later and the advanced research class did not materialize, he came to feel he had been taken in.

Nonetheless, he did not let bitterness interfere with his educational efforts; and what he lacked in formal education, he made up for with energy and enthusiasm. He worked around the clock lecturing, meeting privately with students, administering the school, and trying to raise money. He was enormously popular with the students, many of whom took his enthusiasm for education into distinguished careers of their own. His primary problem was his relationship with the Yuanguang Temple. He stayed there at the pleasure of the abbot, and was in no position to enforce any decisions he might make about the academy's curriculum and administration. This problem became especially acute in the spring of 1949.

The event that triggered Cihang's break with the Yuanguang Temple and its Taiwan Buddhist Studies Academy was the arrival of the Nationalists in 1949· and the refugee monks who followed them. This event takes us from Taiwan's four-year interlude as a part of Greater China into the next phase of its history.

This interlude had been a time of upheaval and transition. The mass deportation of the Japanese population and the dismantling of the Japanese political system left a vacuum for Buddhists as much as for everyone else. With the deaths of Shanhui and Benyuan, the stage was set for a new generation of leaders to emerge; and some, like Miaoguo, took the lead in trying to establish Buddhist education on a firmer footing. They were stymied by a lack of qualified teachers and of financial resources, as well as by the general instability of the period. Still, they expected that future developments in the Buddhism of the island would take place within the context of Taiwanese language and culture (though the 2/28 Incident taught them to be careful about asserting any degree of Taiwanese autonomy). Thus, the first teacher invited to help in the revival of Buddhist education was Cihang, who was qualified as much by his ability to speak the Southern Fujian dialect as by his educational accomplishments.

More turmoil lay ahead, however. The arrival of 1.5 million mainlanders in the first months of 1949 altered the balance of power in Buddhist circles, and brought in some of the most eminent mainland Chinese Buddhist monks of the day. As we look at the events of this period, we will finish the story of Cihang's life and work, and then turn our attention to the establishment of BAROC's new headquarters in Taipei and the events that followed.

THE MAINLAND MONKS ARRIVE IN TAIWAN

Cihang had only been teaching at the Taiwan Buddhist Studies Academy for two months when the Nationalist government fled to Taiwan, bringing with it 1.5 million refugees from China's eastern seaboard. This included monks and nuns, some who came as refugees and some as soldiers. The monks about whom we will have the most to say later were highly respected, eminent monks from Zhejiang and Jiangsu provinces, who had been active at the regional or national level, and so were well connected and able to find accommodations in Taiwan soon after their arrival. First, however, we will look at the situation of the younger and less-distinguished monks, who made up the vast majority of those who fled to Taiwan, and had much more difficulty finding food and lodging.

Many came as soldiers in the Nationalist army. In its need for military manpower during the War of Resistance against the Japanese and later against the Communists, the Nationalist government drafted monks along with other able-bodied Chinese males. The recruitment of monks had begun in earnest in 1936, during which time Taixu, working closely with Nationalist Party Chairman Lin Sen, convinced the National Assembly to exempt monastic recruits from doing any work that would force them to break their precepts, and let them train as battlefield medics, do sanitary work, aid in the disposal of bodies, and perform other compassionate jobs (Dongchu 1974:2/468–469; Welch 1968:45). However, by the 1940s the government was hard-pressed and apparently no longer willing to grant such concessions; all army personnel had to be prepared to do any kind of work. Accounts by Shengyan and Chen-hua *(Zhenhua)*, men who were junior monks at the time and have since risen to prominence in Taiwan Buddhist circles, show them scrambling to find work that would not involve breaking their vows and trying to maintain a vegetarian diet while in the army (Chen-hua 1992:199–212, and Zhang Shengyan 1968:151–215). Their stories are vastly different and show how varied a soldier-monk's experience could be. Chen-hua *(Zhenhua)* was drafted at gunpoint along with many other young monks at Putuo Island, and left the army as soon as he could. However, in spite of maintaining a vegetarian diet out of compassion, he surprised his captain one day by declaring that if the need should arise to fire his rifle and kill an enemy soldier, he would do so without hesitation (Chen-hua 1992:210).

Shengyan, on the other hand, volunteered for military service, but avoided having to kill others by testing into the Signal Corps (radio and communications specialists). He went on to enjoy a fairly distinguished ten-year military career before retiring in 1955 to rejoin the *sangha.* Both these men shared a common struggle to maintain something of their monastic identities and lifestyles in a military setting, but did so with very different attitudes and means. These monks came to Taiwan with their units for training and were already on the island when the Nationalists retreated in 1949.

Other monks and nuns came with the rest of the refugees and did not have the benefit of barracks and mess halls to maintain their livelihood. Their only solution was to do what clergy have always done: go to a temple and apply for lodging in the visitors' quarters. However, the times were chaotic, and Taiwan abbots were suspicious of strangers and vagrants, even those with monastic garb and shaved heads. We have another firsthand account of these times by a junior monk of that time who has since also risen to eminence, Ven. Hsing-yun *(Xingyun)* of Fo Kuang Shan *(Foguangshan),* here quoted at length:

> I first arrived in Taiwan in 1949. At the time, the war in Mainland China had caused widespread panic and many monastics were fleeing the country ... Within the Buddhist circle, the confidence of young monks and nuns was shaken—temples would not accept monastics from other places, ... and it was impossible to rely on the Buddhist community for survival.

That same year, I traveled from Taichung to Taipei. Within a short interval of two days, the following happened to me. At a temple on Nan Ch'ang Road, a master demanded of me, "What qualifications do you possess to stay in Taiwan?" He must have not liked my answer for I was not allowed to stay there that night. I went on to a temple on Chung Cheng Road and was again rejected. The night was cold and wet, and the only place to rest was under a large bell where I slept in my soaked clothing.

Another time, I arrived at a temple in Keelung at 1:00 P.M., in the hope of getting lunch which I had missed the day before, only to find that the temple had been ordered not to give food to traveling monks.

Yet another time, I hoped to stay at Ch'eng Tzu Liao on Mount Kuan Yin. However, on my way there, I discovered that the road was blocked because of a heavy flood. Stuck at a bus stop, peering into the gusty wind and pouring rain, I, hungry and cold, wondered to myself if there was any place I could go (Xingyun 1994:180–181).

This passage could have been written by any of the young monks and nuns who fled to Taiwan in 1949.

At that time, the Taiwan Buddhist Studies Academy was the only institution of its kind in Taiwan; and many of the refugee monks applied there for an education, hoping to find lodging and meaningful work. Cihang, seeing their plight, took pity on them and admitted them all, and found himself with about twenty extra students. But there was a problem: Cihang himself was only a guest at the Yuanguang Temple, and not in a position to offer food and lodging to extra boarders. His indiscriminate acceptance of all comers strained the temple's already shaky financial foundations and ultimately led to a confrontation with Miaoguo, who adamantly refused to allow him to accept any more students. This vexed Cihang considerably, but he seemed to accept the ultimatum. However, when ten more refugee monks arrived a short while later, Cihang pleaded for their lodging and was again turned down. This refusal, along with the lack of financial support for his educational endeavors, the overwork, the failure of the school to hire even half of the teachers it had promised, the failure of the advanced research class to materialize, and the tenuousness of his position at the Yuanguang Temple, finally led Cihang to walk out along with twenty of his refugee monks.

The temple, for its part, decided that the financial burden of running the academy was too crushing. Cihang and Miaoguo met one more time, in June 1949, to host the graduation exercises and to discuss the academy's future. At that meeting, Miaoguo informed Cihang that the Yuanguang Temple could no longer afford to run the school, and that it would be shut down directly after the graduation ceremony. The Taiwan students were disappointed, but at least had the option of returning to their home temples. The mainland refugee monks, however, had nowhere to go; and at this point, Cihang himself was left homeless. Still, he negotiated fiercely with Miaoguo, who in the end reluctantly agreed to let ten of the mainlanders stay on. Cihang's next problem was to find shelter for himself and the other ten.

Fortunately, Cihang had made a lot of friends during the happier time of his triumphant entry into Taiwan and his subsequent lecture tour. One, Wushang of the Lingyin Temple in Hsinchu, was also trying to start a Buddhist seminary; and he invited Cihang to come and give lectures. Cihang and his group set forth; however, they were intercepted before reaching their destination. The times were very unsettled, and the government did not tolerate large groups of people of unknown background roaming freely; aside from his original group of refugee students, Cihang had picked up another ten mainland monks, so his group was large enough to attract attention. It also did not help that Cihang, influenced by the time he spent in Southeast Asia, wore not the traditional Chinese grey or black monastic robes, but instead the eye-catching bright yellow of the Theravādan countries. Thus, he and his group were picked up by government agents on suspicion of vagrancy and banditry, and spent some time in prison.

Cihang was not alone in having these sorts of difficulties. Dongchu (1908–1977) writes in his memoirs that he also had to be wary of attracting attention as he traveled around the countryside. His solution was to travel alone, and to eschew staying in large urban temples in favor of more isolated, smaller temples on the outskirts of towns (Jiang 1992:62). Another contemporary account, by Shengman of the Linji Temple in Taipei, describes how wary the police were of temples and their residents: Police would come by the temple and check all of the clergy's ID cards and entry permits (Jiang 1992:63).

Cihang got off fairly lightly; he spent only one night in jail, and then the authorities transferred him to the Dongda Temple in Taipei for detention. The Dongda Temple at that time housed many monks that the government wanted to confine but not to feed and clothe, and so Cihang and his fellow detainees depended on the charity of devotees for their livelihood. In the meantime, their friends worked for two weeks on all their government connections to get the detainees released, both those in the Dongda Temple and those left behind in the Hsinchu jail.

Once freed, Cihang still had to find a place to stay. At this point, two of his pupils from the Taiwan Buddhist Studies Academy, the nuns Ciguan and Guangwen, got permission for him to lodge at the Jingxiu Hall *(Jingxiu Yuan)* in the Taipei suburb of Hsi-chih *(Xizhi);* but Cihang had great difficulty in getting around without attracting official notice. He still wore his bright yellow robes, and he had no citizen's ID card. At this point he determined that he had no future in Taiwan and decided to return to Southeast Asia, but the nuns prevented this by hiding his passport. After taking care to conceal his movements, his former students finally succeeded in getting him settled into the Jingxiu Hall.

From that time, Cihang's life calmed down a bit. He raised some money from among his friends and established a new school, the Maitreya Inner Hall *(Mile Neiyuan)*. Since it was his own school, he could accept any students he wanted without opposition, and so he was finally able to house the remainder of the refugee monks who had looked to him for shelter as well as education. He remained just as overworked as ever and, in 1952, decided to undergo a three-year period of sealed confinement.

He never came out. The strain of his life had taken its toll, and he suffered a stroke and died on May 6, 1954. In his will he stipulated that his body should be placed, seated in the lotus position, in a large urn, which was to be reopened after three years. If the body had not decayed, he said, "then it should be plated with gold and placed in a pagoda." His will ends with the following verse, which he wanted recited at his funeral:

> Coming with empty hands, empty-handed going;
> Of comings and goings, there is no respite.

Holmes Welch tells the rest of the story. The urn was opened five years later, and the body was adjudged intact—although photographs that I have seen, taken just after the opening, show that time had not been kind to the "flesh-body." Still, it was gilded as per his instructions and placed on the altar of the Cihang Hall (which had been built for this purpose next to the Maitreya Inner Hall), where it sits to this day (Welch 1967:344).

This account of Cihang's life shows the plight of the ordinary refugee monk and the suspicion of the native Buddhist establishment during the turbulent period following the fall of the mainland. Jiang, in his recounting of Cihang's life story, sees another facet to this drama: the continuation of the struggle between Taixu's reformist faction and the traditionalists who controlled the BAROC on the mainland until its reconstitution in 1947. Cihang found himself caught in the middle of this struggle, especially as it played itself out in the educational arena.

The reader will remember that Cihang first attempted formal education in Taixu's Southern Fujian Buddhist Seminary and (by correspondence) Taixu's Wuchang Buddhist Seminary, and felt himself greatly moved by Taixu's reformist spirit. He had also accompanied Taixu on his tour of Sri Lanka, India, and Southeast Asia. However, others of Taixu's reform group, such as the influential layman and national legislator Li Zikuan, and Daxing (the teacher under whose derision Cihang left the Southern Fujian Buddhist Seminary), felt that Cihang had betrayed Taixu's spirit on at least two counts. First, he had questioned Taixu's proposals to redesign monastic garb. Second, and more importantly, while in Penang, Malaysia, he had accepted the dharma-transmission in 1947 from Ven. Yuanying, a fellow Fujianese and Taixu's main nemesis within the BAROC.

The struggle carried over into Taiwan. When the BAROC set up its new offices in Taipei, the reform group and the traditionalists, represented mainly by Baisheng, competed for control. The reformers won, and Baisheng retreated to the Shipu Temple, a former Japanese temple in Taipei.[2] The victorious reform faction took the opportunity to bring in other famous educators who seemed more solidly within the Taixu reformist axis, such as Yinshun and Yanpei. These were men of such broad learning and scholarly ability that Cihang paled in comparison, and many of his own students left him to study with them. The rancor between the two factions at this time was so great that Daxing openly gloated when Cihang was arrested, and tried to discourage others from bailing him out.

In the end, Cihang must be seen as a transitional figure. He was never a great scholar, due to his lack of early formal education and rustic background. He came to Taiwan at a time when no one suspected that there would be such a massive influx of mainland monks in one year's time, and when everyone thought that Southern Fujianese would remain the language of education well into the future. Though not a refugee himself, he found himself caught in the tide of refugees, and in power struggles that he may not have fully understood between rival factions of the BAROC. He is remembered today mostly for his energy, affability, compassion, and devotion to the task of inspiring others to seek an education; and many of today's prominent Buddhist leaders are his former pupils. The altar where his gilded "flesh-body" sits remains a popular spot for visitors, and as the memories of the bitterness of those early days fade, people think of him with ever-increasing fondness.

THE BAROC'S ASSESSMENT OF BUDDHISM IN TAIWAN AND OF ITS OWN TASK

We turn now to the group of monks who re-formed the BAROC on Taiwan and came to dominate Taiwan Buddhism until the 1970s, when economic growth and a more relaxed political environment ushered in a more pluralistic atmosphere. One of the most significant facts about these monks is that almost all of them came to Taiwan after distinguished careers in the areas of Jiangsu and Zhejiang provinces and the city of Shanghai. These are the very areas in which Buddhism was the most active and vibrant, where the monasteries were kept in the best repair and had the largest monastic populations, where the clergy kept the precepts most scrupulously and were most serious about spiritual discipline, and where they enjoyed the greatest degree of respect and patronage from the laity (Welch 1967:246–252). Some examples of eminent mainland monks from the early post-Retrocession period include Yinshun, who was from Zhejiang; Daxing, Taicang, Dongchu, Xingyun, Shengyan, and Nanting, who were all from Jiangsu; and Zhenhua, who was originally from Henan and received tonsure in the north but took full ordination and studied in the seminaries of Zhejiang and Jiangsu. (There are exceptions, of course: Daoan spent his childhood and early monastic life around Hunan, the Zhangjia Living Buddha was Mongolian, and Baisheng was from Hubei.) When these monks arrived in Taiwan, they reacted with disgust and disdain to the Buddhism that they found there.

A report by Dongchu best examplifies their attitude: In 1950, the BAROC asked him to tour Taiwan and report on the state of Buddhism as he saw it (Dongchu 1979:105–113). In the course of his travels, he says, he saw "new and old, flourishing and declining, the Buddhistic, the theistic, and the superstitious, immaturity of religious consciousness, and a basic lack of education." But the biggest problem, he said, was the lack of any kind of Buddhist order. During the Japanese period, *zhaijiao* had been allowed into the various Buddhist associations; and some *zhaijiao* halls even used the term "Buddhist" in their names. Although I doubt that the heads of these *zhaijiao* halls would have considered themselves members of a clerical order, Dongchu took their existence within Taiwan Buddhist circles as representing a group of clergy who ate meat, drank wine, married, and did not shave their heads. Thus, he concluded, "… The order of life among Buddhists [in Taiwan] does not strictly adhere to the principles of Buddhist order. There is no clear boundary between clergy and laity" (Dongchu 1979:106).

Another problem that Dongchu found was the halfhearted way in which the Taiwan Provincial Buddhist Branch Association had implemented BAROC rules and regulations, especially at the local level. In many areas, he found chapters headed by laypeople or (worse yet) members of *zhaijiao* halls. In some places he found that the local BAROC chapter had no clerical members at all, and that the clergy and laypeople were not even on speaking terms. Since the BAROC charter stipulated that local chapters be headed by clergy, he called for immediate steps to remedy this situation.

A problem that appeared to pose a threat to Buddhism's continued existence in Taiwan stemmed from the fact that, during the Japanese period, Taiwan Buddhists had been largely cut off from their religious tradition on the mainland and had had to rely on the Japanese model for their training and inspiration. Most of the leaders in Taiwan Buddhism had been trained under the Japanese system. Of these, many were now quite old and could not be counted upon to carry the torch into the future. Of those leading figures who remained, many had refused to join BAROC, while others had signed up as nominal members without becoming active. Dongchu quotes a Japanese-educated Buddhist layman as saying that if BAROC did not become more active in contacting the people directly, then the Christian missionaries would overwhelm them, and Taiwan would become a Christian district in thirty years' time.

A large section of Dongchu's assessment is given over to reporting on the "childishness" *(youzhi)* he saw in the Taiwan people's basic consciousness *(genben yishi)*. As he describes his findings in the field, it becomes clear that he is referring to their failure to understand, and subsequently to follow, the rituals and procedures of Chinese Buddhism. In most temples he went to, the residents' monastic garb was idiosyncratic; the residents were just as likely to recite a Daoist scripture such as the *True Scripture of the Jade Emperor (Yuhuang Zhenjing)* or the *Blood-Basin Scripture (Xuepen Jing)* as a Buddhist sutra; most temples had images to Daoist and folk divinities alongside, and sometimes in positions superior to, images of Śākyamuni Buddha, Amitābha Buddha, or Guanyin. Perhaps worst of all, temples in which monks and nuns lived together appeared to be the rule rather than the exception.

The cause of these problems, and the key to their solution, could be summed up in one word: education. Illiteracy and lack of education both directly contributed to syncretistic tendencies and caused Buddhism to lose the respect of the intelligentsia. On this point, Dongchu revealed a profound pessimism with regard to what the BAROC could realistically hope to accomplish in this area. Buddhist education must ultimately rest on the foundation of a sound general education; you cannot teach a person to read and understand Buddhist books if he or she cannot read at all. Dongchu estimated that only about ten percent of the Buddhists and *zhaijiao* adherents in Taiwan were literate enough to receive a true Buddhist education.

Lack of facilities constituted another stumbling block. There were still at this point no islandwide Buddhist seminaries, and scant resources for founding them. In the past, Taiwan could depend upon the resources of Japanese Buddhism to hold lecture series, summer institutes, and training schools. Now that Taiwan was cut off from both Japan and the mainland, it had to depend entirely upon its own resources to bring any educational schemes to fruition. But the effort must be made; Dongchu estimated that, of the clerical population in Taiwan, only about 30 percent could be considered young, a much lower figure than on the mainland. Without more young monks and nuns, Buddhism in Taiwan faced an uncertain future.

As Dongchu saw it, one important aspect of educational reform lay in an amendment of the ordination system. Fifty years of Japanese rule had taken its toll on the transmission of the pure precepts; Dongchu guessed that only about 10 percent of monks and less than 1 percent of nuns aged forty and over could receive the pure precepts.[3] Thus, most of the "clergy" in Taiwan could not even be considered clergy at all; their ordinations were invalid according to the standards of the *vinaya*. This was due to three factors: First, there was a general lack of concern for *vinaya* study and training. Second, Taiwan had no "public monasteries" *(shifang conglin)* such as existed on the mainland and served as ordination centers.[4] Third, laypeople controlled the financing and administration of most temples in Taiwan, and so the clergy who cared about reforming the ordination system lacked the authority to implement measures. If the BAROC wished to reform Buddhist education, then it needed to begin with reforming the ordination system; taking control of temples out of lay hands, reemphasizing training in and adherence to the pure precepts, and establishing public monasteries as centers for these reforms.

Dongchu's report sounds several themes that we will see again and again as we move through the modern history of Buddhism in Taiwan. Some of the problems he raises continue to tax the resources of Taiwan's Buddhist world to this day: Education remains a top priority, and even relatively minor vexations such as the standardization of monastic garb occasionally come to the surface for loud debate.[5] Other issues that troubled Dongchu and his compatriots at the BAROC have since faded and been accepted as the status quo, most notably the cohabitation of monks and nuns. Finally, the BAROC did find solutions for some problems, such as breaking the connection between *zhaijiao* and orthodox Buddhism, thus bringing to an end this anomalous alliance. Other issues were resolved in creative and unexpected ways. For example, the problem of establishing public monasteries has been solved, but not by actually establishing public monasteries. We will return to this later.

EARLY DOCTRINAL CONTROVERSY: PURE LAND BUDDHISM

The Continuing Influence of Yinguang's Pure Land Revival

In terms of practice, Pure Land Buddhism dominates in Taiwan today. All over the island, one may see devotees wearing small rosaries *(nianzhu)* as a visible symbol that they have formally taken refuge in Buddhism at a temple under a master. One may also observe that they use the name of Amitābha Buddha as a substitute for "hello," "good-bye," "excuse me," and most other social expressions. Even temples that profess to emphasize Chan meditation practice find that the largest numbers of participants are drawn by Buddha-recitation events. Laurence Thompson noted that, between 1941 and 1960, the people of Taiwan constructed more temples enshrining Amitābha Buddha than any other buddha, bodhisattva, or deity (Thompson 1964:326). Much of this modern Pure Land thought and practice stems from the revival of Pure Land teachings that took place in the Lingyan Temple in Suzhou under the leadership of Ven. Yinguang, and which his direct disciple Li Bingnan subsequently transmitted into Taiwan.

Yinguang (1861–1940) and his Pure Land Revival. Yinguang is one of the most important modern Buddhist reformers. National Taiwan University philosophy professor Yang Huinan once commented that Yinguang and Taixu were the two "bookends" of Republican-era Buddhism (Jianzheng 1989:2); and Shengyan lists him alongside Taixu, the modern Chan master Xuyun, and the *vinaya* reformer Hongyi as one of the four greatest monks of the modern period (Jianzheng 1989:1). Western scholars have noted Yinguang's contributions as well, although they generally emphasize his personal appeal and charisma, and offer no information on his actual teachings concerning the Pure Land (for example, see Chan 1953, 65–68; Welch 1967, 91, 100; and Welch 1968:195).

Yinguang was born in December 1861, the third son to a farming family in Shanxi province. He spent his early monastic career in the north in order to avoid his family's efforts to take him back. During this time, he was in charge of the libraries of two temples, and had the job of sunning the scriptures, a task that gave him the time and opportunity to read broadly in the Buddhist classics.[6] He was most attracted to the Northern Song dynasty text *Longshu Jingtu Wen* (T.1970), a Pure Land miscellany composed by the layman Wang Rixiu around 1160 and comprising outlines of Pure Land teachings, exhortations to practice Buddha-recitation, and biographies (Jianzheng 1989:20). This work had a decisive impact on the development of Yinguang's thought and practice.

After full ordination, he spent some years at the Zifu Temple on Hongluo Mountain, and both this site and the events of his life there have significance for the emergence of his Pure Land devotionalism. This temple had been the home of the twelfth patriarch of the Pure Land School, Chewu (1741–1810), a monk who gained fame for his advocacy of Pure Land practice despite his status as a widely acknowledged Chan master of the Linji School (FG 5947c–5948a). Yinguang's education afforded him the opportunity to serve again as custodian of the temple library; and during this time he read Chewu's works. He was impressed with Chewu's active discouragement of Chan meditative practice in favor of Buddha-recitation, and later in his life Yinguang was also to advise his disciples to make a clear distinction between the teachings of the two schools (Jianzheng 1989:21).

For example, chapter seven of the *Felicitous Sayings of Yinguang (Yinguang Fashi Jiayan Lu)* is devoted to the subject of separating Chan and Pure Land. Here Yinguang states that Chan is an unreliable path to enlightenment as it requires unswerving effort over many lifetimes, and every moment brings the possibility of distraction onto other paths. As for sudden enlightenment, this is as unlikely as feeling full and satisfied after taking the first bite of rice. Intensive Pure Land practice, on the other hand, allows one to attain the Pure Land even if one still carries the burden of bad karma, and once one attains rebirth in the Pure Land, one is assured of never again returning to the cycle of samsara (Yinguang 1991, 4:1579).

In 1893, Yinguang accepted an invitation from Ven. Huawen to work in the library of the Fayun Temple on Putuo Island. While there, he received many requests to lecture on scriptures and teachings; but he was reluctant to stand in the spotlight, so he asked for two consecutive three-year periods of sealed confinement in order to deepen his own Pure Land practice. Even when not strictly in sealed confinement, until 1911 he used a false name in order to practice incognito. His later fame and recognition as the thirteenth patriarch of the Pure Land school came about despite his efforts at anonymity.

Even during his periods of sealed confinement and anonymous practice, Yinguang gathered dozens of lay disciples who were attracted to his erudition, wit, and simple piety. Since his confinement made personal access difficult, many contacted him through letters; and he proved a faithful correspondent. Beginning in 1917, his lay followers began collecting his letters, some small pamphlets he had written, and notes from his dharma-talks, and published them in order to give them wider circulation. This marked the beginning of his fame as a modern Pure Land master (Jianzheng 1989:22).

In 1930, at the age of seventy, he moved to the Baoguo Temple in Suzhou for another period of sealed confinement. This temple was not far from the temple most often connected with his name, the Lingyan Shan Temple. During this time, even before he went to live in the latter temple, he helped it to revise its rules and practices, and turned it in the direction of Pure Land cultivation. In 1937, Beijing and Shanghai fell to the advancing Japanese army, and Yinguang moved into the Lingyan Shan Temple, where he continued to live in seclusion away from all worldly affairs. He continued his routine of Buddha-recitation, study, corresponding with followers, and receiving visitors at the small window of his room until his death in 1940 (Jianzheng 1989:25). His fame was such that all over China people heard of his death and mourned his passing.

We have already delved into his thought with the above consideration of his separation of Chan and Pure Land. A few more important observations about his conception of Pure Land practice must be elucidated. First, he conceptualized the Pure Land as a concrete goal, and not as a purified state of mind. In a letter to a follower, he said,

> [Some worldlings and followers of outer paths] say, "the inconceivable grandeur and solemnity of the Pure Land is a fable or a metaphor for the mind, it is not a real place." If one holds this kind of heretical concept or ridiculous view, then one loses the benefit of rebirth in the Pure Land. You must know the harm there is in this (Yinguang 1991, 4:1939).

To put this in context, for several centuries in China there had been two competing ways of thinking about Pure Land practice. The first was "Mind-Only Pure Land" *(Weixin jingtu),* which held that the Pure Land appears when the mind is purified; or, to put it another way, that the transformation of the mind that comes with the attainment of Buddhahood also purifies one's surroundings. This style of thought has its roots in the *Vimalakīrti-nirdeśa-sūtra,* and was further developed by the Tiantai school in its exposition of Pure Land practice. The opposing stream was "Western Pure Land" practice *(Xifang jingtu),* which held that the Western Paradise of Amitābha Buddha was a real, concrete destination, and that the goal of Pure Land practice was to attain rebirth there after death. Yinguang clearly belonged to this latter camp (Jianzheng 1989:48).

Also, unlike the thought of some Japanese Pure Land reformers of the Kamakura period such as Hōnen and Shinran, Chinese Pure Land thought never lost faith in the importance of morality and keeping the pure precepts. For Yinguang, this morality was based squarely in Confucian values and Buddhist precepts. Buddhism, he argued, had to work for people in the world; and so it could not be opposed to the proper fulfillment of one's societal role as defined by Confucian ethics. A person who was unfilial and who failed to fulfil the duties implicit in his or her social role would have a much harder time perfecting his or her practice and attaining rebirth in the Pure Land. Filiality constituted the root of all morality, and the unfilial son or daughter could not enter the path (Jianzheng 1989:58–59).[7]

Another area in which Yinguang differed from some of the later Japanese elaborations of Pure Land theology was in his insistence that *nianfo,* inward contemplation of the Buddha or outward invocation of his name, was a strenuous, lifelong practice. In this he stands firm with the rest of Chinese Pure Land thought, which has never heard of the "one-calling" versus "many-calling" debates that took place in Japan.[8] For Yinguang, Buddha-recitation was a method of purifying the mind and harmonizing it with the Pure Land along with its reigning Buddha in such a way as to create affinities that would lead one there upon death. Thus, he advocated many practices of *nianfo* whose purposes clearly go beyond simply calling upon the Buddha for induction into the Western Paradise. For example, Yinguang invented the technique of reciting the Buddha's name ten times exactly, but without counting or using a rosary, a practice that puts the mind in a state of intense concentration by occupying it with counting at the unconscious level, as well as with oral invocation at the conscious level (Jianzheng 1989:84–85).[9]

As is evident from the above presentation, Yinguang provided his followers a fully articulated rationale for a very specific conception of Pure Land practice. However, his main contribution may well lie in the zeal with which he defended Pure Land thought from its detractors and resolved doubts as to its efficacy. For example, his severe critique of Chan came as a response to some vicious attacks upon Pure Land practice from Chan practitioners. By quoting Chan sources that themselves speak approvingly of Pure Land practice, and by asserting that Pure Land practice was both easy and reliable compared with the riskiness of Chan practice, he demonstrated superiority of the former over the latter. In this manner, his Pure Land "theology" was constructed over the years as he sought to encourage his followers to persevere in their practice in the face of very real obstacles, whether slander from without or doubts from within.

The life and thought of Yinguang is important to understand because it constitutes the framework of modern Pure Land belief in Taiwan, and yet has been little studied in the West. We will now turn to two of the direct channels through which Yinguang's influence entered Taiwan: the breviary, and Yinguang's disciple Li Bingnan. After that we will be in a position to understand the controversy surrounding Yinshun's book, *A New Treatise on the Pure Land*.

The Adoption of Lingyan Shan Temple Liturgies into the Taiwan Breviary. Although there is no agency to regulate the compilation and use of breviaries (books containing liturgical texts to be

recited at various monastic offices), and any temple or devotional society is free to adopt whichever texts they wish to use, one breviary in
particular has gained wide acceptance throughout Taiwan: the *Fomen
Bibei Kesongben* (Essential recitations for the Buddha-gate), revised and
published in Taipei in 1954. In order to understand how the adoption
of this breviary marks a shift toward Pure Land theology, it is necessary
to understand the kind of breviary that it succeeded.

Most early breviaries consisted of various texts compiled by individual temples for internal use during morning and evening devotions,
and these compilations could be quite diverse. Some of the earliest contained both Buddhist and non-Buddhist texts. In 1600, the Ming
dynasty monastic reformer Yunqi Zhuhong (1532–1612), at the request
of a lay patron, produced the first attempt to rationalize and standard-
ize the Buddhist breviary, the *Zhujing Risong* (Daily recitations from the
sutras) (Günzel 1994:13). This breviary, and its 1662 reprint, contained
both canonical and noncanonical materials (such as vows, admonitions,
and mantras).

Another group of breviaries emanated from the Haichuang Temple
in Guangzhou, which in 1792 produced the *Chanmen Risong* (Daily
recitations for the gate of chan). Other breviaries by this name came
into use in other temples; and although the extent to which the 1792
edition influenced them is not clear, a comparison of earlier and later
editions shows a steady accretion of texts adopted for liturgical use. One
of the later versions, produced at the Yongquan Temple in Fujian
Province, was imported to Taiwan during the Japanese period along
with the influx of monastic lineages from that temple; and it formed
the basis for the first breviary in Taiwan to go by the name of *Fomen
Bibei Kesongben,* which was produced in Taichung in 1940 (Günzel
1994:14–15).

A glance at the *Chanmen Risong* of the Tianning Temple in
Changzhou, produced in 1900, reveals the wide variety of ritual texts
selected for inclusion: After morning and evening devotions, one finds
liturgies for repentance; the Mengshan liturgy for making offerings to
hungry ghosts; a series of Pure Land texts *(jingtu wen);* "little prayers"
(xiao qidao); a ceremony for "lonely souls" *(guhun yi);* praises for various buddhas, bodhisattvas, sutras, and rituals (a very long section); the
"Huayan Ceremony" *(huayan yi);* the ceremony for "Reverencing the

Lotus Sutra" *(li Fahua Jing yi);* and so forth. The texts are followed by many short mantras, extracts from various sutras such as the *Sutra in Forty-two Sections* and the *Platform Sutra of the Sixth Patriarch,* liturgies for various monastic ceremonies such as tonsuring a disciple, and finally a section on the essential teachings of the Chan School *(chanzong fayao)* and lists of various Chan lineages (*Chanmen Risong* 1988). While the Pure Land school is represented along with the Chan, it is by no means emphasized or given any prominence.

After Yinguang took over the abbacy of the Lingyan Shan Temple in Suzhou, he called for the compilation of a new breviary that would exhibit a definite doctrinal slant towards the Pure Land. This was the first conscious attempt to produce a breviary for a particular form of Buddhist thought and practice, and it resulted in a drastic reduction in content. Yinguang omitted much of the material contained in the *Chanmen Risong,* in particular the instructions and materials concerning the traditions of the various schools, which had made up almost one-third of the previous breviary (Günzel 1994:15–16). This breviary, the *Lingyanshan si niansong yigui,* came out in 1938, and was a direct antecedent for the one currently in use.

The *Fomen Bibei Kesongben* currently popular in Taiwan is much smaller and more streamlined than the older Chan breviaries. Morning and evening devotions occupy over one-third of its space, and the rest is clearly biased toward Pure Land practice. After a short section on mealtime devotions, and a somewhat longer liturgy of praise to several buddhas and bodhisattvas for use in the ceremony known as the "Ritual for the Universal Buddhas" *(Pufo Yigui),* there is a lengthy set of rituals for a "Seven-Day Buddha-Recitation Retreat" *(foqi),* daily recitations for the Buddha-Recitation Hall, and a "Ceremony for Invigorating a Buddha-Recitation Retreat" *(jingjin foqi yigui),* all taken directly from the Lingyan Shan Temple's breviary. The remainder of the breviary, comprising about the last third and listed as an "appendix" *(fulu),* contains a variety of short praises and liturgical verses for different occasions, such as bathing the Buddha on his birthday or for dedicating the merit of one's spiritual practices (*Fomen Bibei Kesongben* 1954). Missing are the Chan lineages, the outlines of Chan teaching, and liturgies for any specifically Chan practice such as a "Seven-Day Chan Meditation Retreat" *(chanqi).* Thus, the direct influences of

Yinguang's Pure Land revival and the Lingyan Shan Temple breviary are apparent. The fact that the calligraphy that graces the cover of the breviary is by Yinguang's most influential disciple on the island, Li Bingnan, may also signify the strength of the master's vision in contemporary Taiwan.

Li Bingnan. Li Bingnan (1890–1986), one of the most influential laypeople in post-Retrocession Taiwan, was Yinguang's direct disciple and worked ceaselessly for over forty years to spread Yinguang's message within Taiwan Buddhist circles.

Li Bingnan was born in Shandong province not far from the ancient states of Qi and Lu, the homes of Confucius and Mencius. He came from an educated family, and during his youth received a broad education in the Confucian classics. However, his education took place against the backdrop of the events leading up to the Wuchang Rebellion and the fall of the Manchu dynasty, and he imbibed the revolutionary atmosphere of the times. Thus, besides Confucianism, he also read widely in law and politics, and chose a career in governmental service in the hopes of putting his studies to practical use. He held a series of minor posts, and by 1926 was the warden of the Ju County prison in Shandong.

During his tenure at the prison, he obtained a copy of one of Yinguang's works, which he read intensively, with the feeling that he had found the crucial missing ingredient in his education and training. He began corresponding with the master, and within a year he journeyed to Shanghai to take the Three Refuges under him.[10] From this point on, he completely reformed his life in accordance with Buddhist precepts: Whereas before he had been a revolutionary famous for his seemingly endless capacity for alcohol and meat, he now undertook a strict vegetarian diet, began rising early and retiring late in order to do the morning and evening devotion services, and practiced *nianfo* constantly. He maintained this rigorous practice for the remaining sixty years of his life, and devoted as much energy to the study of Buddhism as he did to his work.

His reputation spread, and in 1931 he received an invitation to go to Nanjing to assume the directorship of the "Agency for Making

Offerings to the Past Masters Who Achieved Sagehood of the Republic of China" *(Zhonghua Minguo Dacheng Zhi Sheng Xianshi Fengji Guanfu),* a minor governmental organization with about ten employees. The move to Nanjing put him in closer touch with Yinguang, but this situation was short-lived; in 1937, when the Japanese took the Shanghai area, Li was forced to move with the government to Chongqing (Chungking) in central China. In the winter of 1948, about six months before the Nationalist government retreated to Taiwan, Li's agency was transferred to the island, and they set up their main office in the central town of Taichung. Li would remain here in this post for the rest of his life.

Because he had a license to practice Chinese medicine, he quickly became known to the citizens of Taichung. In addition, he began writing a regular question-and-answer column for the magazine *Bodhi Tree (Puti shu),* which gained him wider recognition around Taiwan. Building on this base, he founded the Taichung Buddhist Lotus Society *(Taizhong Fojiao Lianshe)* as a lecture hall and an agency for mutual support in the practice of *nianfo.* He founded several other Buddhist enterprises as well, including the Ciguang Library, the Ciguang Kindergarten, the Bodhi Clinic, the Lingshan Temple, and the Wufeng Missionary Station *(Wufeng Bujiaosuo).* He enjoyed great fame as an effective and moving speaker and a practitioner of great integrity, and his lectures regularly drew above-capacity crowds. Later, he trained a mostly female corps of speakers to spread the teachings; another step forward for Chinese Buddhist women.

He lived a spartan existence in a small apartment, never marrying, but never taking the monastic vows, either; in this he exemplified Yinguang's ideal of the layperson leading a pure life and sincerely practicing Buddha-recitation. He continued to study all his life, and gained such a reputation for erudition, not only in Buddhism but also in the Confucian Classics, Chinese medicine, and poetry, that he won teaching appointments at Chung Hsing and Tung Hai Universities in Taichung. In these capacities he inspired many college students who later went on to become Taiwan's leading Buddhist intellectuals. He retained his health well into old age, taking only a year off from his rigorous work and teaching schedule from 1984 to 1985 because of stomach problems. Finally, on April 13, 1986, he died at the age of ninety-seven surrounded by friends reciting the Buddha's name on his behalf (Chen Huijian 1994:329–341).

I believe it would be difficult to overestimate Li Bingnan's importance in spreading Yinguang's Pure Land revival into Taiwan. He was enormously popular with the Buddhist laity, his lectures reached thousands of people over the thirty-eight year period between his move to Taiwan and his death in 1986, his college posts gave him a position from which to influence at least two generations of Taiwan's rising intelligentsia, and his writings have assured his continuing influence even after his death. Like Yinguang, he propounded a fusion of Confucian ethical standards with intensive study of Buddhist doctrines, the strict observance of precepts, and simple Pure Land piety; and this has remained the model for most of Taiwan's Pure Land practitioners to this day.

With this background in mind, we are prepared to understand the depth of Li Bingnan and his followers' outrage when the contents of Yinshun's *A New Treatise on the Pure Land* became known. What follows is a classic story of piety versus academic inquiry.

The Controversy over Yinshun's New Treatise on the Pure Land

Yinshun. Yinshun (1906–) represents the other side of Chinese Buddhism's modern revitalization. Although he is careful to distinguish his own thought from that of his mentor Taixu (as we shall see at the end of this section), he still acknowledged his heavy debt to Taixu's vision of a modernized Buddhism.

Yinshun was born in 1906 in the town of Haining in Zhejiang province, and his lay name was Zhang Luqin. Although his family was not well-to-do, he was able to go to school until financial difficulties forced him to abandon his studies at the age of fourteen. Even though his own education was thus incomplete, he went back to his old school two years later, this time as a teacher; and during the next eight years he taught other students and devoted his free time to reading books on all of the religions of China (Chen Huijian 1994:2). According to his brief autobiography, his introduction to Buddhism came from a book on the Daoist sage Zhuangzi, whom the author extolled as a precursor of Buddhism. Yinshun, curiosity piqued, went to some local Buddhist temples to pick up some further literature, and obtained additional reading through mail order. His limited education left him ill-prepared to absorb very much of what he read; but he persevered, ordering more books, consulting dictionaries whenever they were available, and generally, as he puts it, "groping in the dark" (Yinshun 1985:4).

During these early years, while reading and visiting temples, he encountered the problem that would focus his studies for the remainder of his life. The books that he read presented a philosophical vision of both reality and the path to liberation that was highly abstract, pristine, and profound, that excited and intrigued him; yet the monks whom he met (he says there were no nuns in his district at that time) seemed almost completely ignorant of this intellectual heritage, and spent their days idling about or performing funerals for paying clients. For their part, the local Buddhist laity seemed interested only in the pursuit of this-worldly benefits and mostly belonged to the Xiantian and Wuwei Sects, both derivatives of Luojiao. Despite their ignorance of basic Buddhist doctrine, the laity practiced their religion in temples and considered themselves pure Buddhists. Yinshun came to the conviction that Buddhism had become corrupted at some point in its transmission from India to China; and he set about to recover and disseminate the primitive dharma, which his narrow range of reading led him to believe consisted of Chinese Mādhyamaka *(Sanlun)* and Consciousness-Only teachings (Yinshun 1985:4–5).

In order to pursue his questions further, he left his job at the school and went to the Fuquan Temple *(Fuquan An)* on Putuo Mountain to seek ordination in the fall of 1930. From 1934 to 1936 he lived in the Huiji Temple on Putuo Mountain, reading through all seven thousand fascicles of the Qing Canon (Chen Huijian 1994:2). Yinshun records that he did not absorb much of what he read, since he was racing through seven or eight fascicles each day. But he did gain an appreciation for the breadth and variety of Buddhist teaching, which he now saw extended far beyond the boundaries of Mādhyamaka and Consciousness-Only thought. He became impressed with the persistent encouragement in the Mahayana scriptures to practice for the sake of all sentient beings, while at the same time he found a dose of realism in the sutras of the Dīrghāgama and the stories in the *vinaya* that counteracted the often fantastic imagery of the Mahayana texts (Yinshun 1985:8–9).

During the period of Communist insurgency, Yinshun relocated to Sichuan province, where he made the acquaintance of two of his most important pupils, Yanpei and Miaoqin. He remained in Sichuan for eight years, but in 1946 was forced to flee again because of the Communist revolution. By 1947 he finally made it back to the east coast, where he received word of Taixu's death. He spent a year working with his disciple Xuming editing Taixu's *Collected Works,* and then resumed travelling south, where he reached Xiamen [*Amoy*] in 1949. When the mainland fell, he fled across the border into Hong Kong. In 1952, responding to an invitation issued by his old teacher Daxing, he relocated to Taiwan (Yinshun 1985:10). Although the fourteen years from his arrival in Sichuan to his move into Taiwan were marked by severe health problems, political unrest, and war, he still considered them an especially fruitful time for his study and teaching. Many of his shorter works come from this period of his life and as a result of his students collating their notes and publishing them as books. One of the books from this time, transcribed by his disciples Xuming and Yanpei, was his *New Treatise on the Pure Land (Jingtu Xinlun).*

The New Treatise on the Pure Land. It is difficult to read Yinshun's *New Treatise on the Pure Land* without perceiving his distaste for the kind of Pure Land piety advocated by Yinguang and popular throughout China. This simple and exclusive devotion to the practice of reciting Amitābha Buddha's name in the hopes of gaining rebirth in the Western Paradise must have appeared to him to be at the heart of the crass, popular Buddhism that he had vowed to reform in his youth. In his *New Treatise,* he draws on his broad reading of the Chinese Buddhist canon to show that there are many more Pure Lands than the Western Paradise, many more ways to reach them than by reciting a buddha's name, and many more motivations for seeking rebirth in a Pure Land than a lack of confidence in one's ability to carry out Buddhist spiritual practices in this world.

Yinshun begins his discussion by pointing out that "purity" is a basic concept for all the historical varieties of Buddhism, but that this purity has two aspects: purity of one's own personal consciousness, and purity of one's environment. Chinese Buddhism classifies karmic recompense into two types, "proper recompense" *(zhengbao),* and "dependent recompense" *(yibao).* According to Yinshun, Hinayana Buddhism only recognizes the first kind of recompense, whereas Mahayana recognizes both. Thus, in all branches of Mahayana, the purification of one's own consciousness necessarily leads to the creation of a "pure land," i.e., a purified environment (pp. 2–4; in this discussion, all in-text page references are to Yinshun 1992, 1–75.). Thus, Mahayana Buddhism, with its innumerable buddhas, necessarily acknowledges innumerable Pure Lands, although the most widely known are Amitābha Buddha's Pure Land in the West; Akṣobhya's Pure Land in the East; and the Tuṣita Heaven, where Maitreya, the Buddha of the future, awaits his final rebirth (pp. 6–7).

Among devotees, Pure Lands are psychological constructions of idealized worlds. In China, these Pure Lands have four characteristics: (1) They are level, with no mountains, valleys, rivers, oceans, or sharp stones. Yinshun believes that this represents the terrain of the Gangetic plains where the earliest Pure Land scriptures were composed; (2) They are symmetrical and well-ordered: the trees are evenly spaced and in rows, and the landscape is balanced. Yinshun here comments that this aspect is not so important within Chinese culture, as a glance at a typical Chinese landscape painting will reveal; (3) They are very clean, and are free of any impurity whatsoever; (4) They are very rich, adorned with golden sands and jewel-laden trees. This last item Yinshun takes to be a peculiarly Mahayana conceit, and reveals the popular origins of the Mahayana schools: Whereas Hinayana taught contentment with what one possessed, Mahayana scriptures are full of images of wealth and grandeur (pp. 9–10). More importantly, the presentation of the Pure Land as found in the Indian sutras reveals how scriptures reflect the social and geographical contexts of their authors; for example, the notion of many bathing pools and shady trees in the Pure Land would have naturally occurred to authors living in the hot, dry climate of central India (p. 11). In a direct jab at the Pure Land school, Yinshun points out that it really resembles a Marxist utopia (p. 12); one can imagine how the citizens of the ROC after 1949 would have reacted to this comparison!

In one of the more controversial chapters of his *New Treatise,* Yinshun discusses the possible origin of the figure of Amitābha Buddha within the context of Hindu solar worship. Several factors led him to believe that Amitābha derived directly from the Hindu solar deity Mitra, and perhaps also from Persian antecedents.[11] First, the name "Amitābha" itself means "limitless light." Second, the first visualization prescribed in the *Meditation Sutra* (*Guan Wuliangshou Fo Jing,* T.365) is that of the setting sun, a vision that would be consonant with the western localization of Amitābha's Pure Land (pp. 22–23). Although this is all Yinshun had to say on this topic, and the discussion only occupies one page of his *New Treatise,* it must have proven very offensive to the average Pure Land devotee who conceived Amitābha as an existent Buddha and not a constructed deity whose derivation could be elucidated historically. At the very least, this is one aspect of his Pure Land theories that several commentators on the ensuing controversy have all fixated upon.[12]

Yinshun goes on from this discussion of Amitābha's origins to his pairing with two other Buddhist figures generally represented as residing in the East: Akṣobhya and Bhaiṣajya-rāja. In the first instance, he points out how in the *Vimalakīrti-nirdeśa Sūtra,* Akṣobhya, whose name means "unmoving," represents wisdom. Thus, in following the motion of the sun from the east to the west as a metaphor for the believer's progress in the Buddhist path, this juxtaposition of Akṣobhya and Amitābha reflects the movement of the devotee from initial wisdom and enlightenment to full buddhahood (pp. 26–28). Those who rely on reciting Amitābha's name to attain rebirth in the Western Paradise while ignoring the symbolism of Akṣobhya are seeking buddhahood without first aspiring to the cultivation of wisdom or enlightenment (p. 29).

The juxtaposition of Amitābha and Bhaiṣajya-rāja Buddha represents another sort of symbiosis that, unlike the relationship between Amitābha and Akṣobhya, has actually received attention within Chinese Buddhist culture. Bhaiṣajya-rāja, or Medicine King Buddha, brings healing for illness, and protection from accidents, financial ruin, natural disasters, and the like. When paired with Amitābha, he represents happiness and longevity in this life, while the latter represents salvation after death. Again, this is consonant with their directionality: Bhaiṣajya-rāja dwells in the east, where the sun rises; Amitābha in the west, where it sets. However, after the establishment of this symbolism in India, Pure Land devotionalism in China came to neglect Bhaiṣajya-rāja and concentrate on Amitābha alone, which effectively turned Buddhism into a cult of the dead (pp. 31–32).[13]

Yinshun finds much to criticize in the aspiration to seek rebirth in Amitābha's Western Paradise *(wangsheng jingtu)*. He points out that there is another way to achieve rebirth in a Pure Land, and that is to "adorn" a Pure Land oneself *(zhuangyan jingtu)*. In this connection, Yinshun reminds the reader that Amitābha himself did not attain his present life in the Western Paradise by merely reciting a buddha's name; rather, he first generated *bodhicitta,* the vow to achieve perfect enlightenment out of compassion for all sentient beings, and then worked to reach this goal over several aeons. The Pure Land that came into being as the "dependent recompense" of his exalted state represented the fulfillment of this vow. In Yinshun's view Buddhists ought to take this as their model of practice, since it reflects the Mahayana ideal of personal striving for the perfection of one's own wisdom and compassion, and does not seek rebirth in a Pure Land in utter dependence upon a buddha's saving power. This latter path makes the Pure Land into just another heaven and the buddha who creates it just another savior-deity (pp. 38–41).

Yinshun argues that the elevation of calling the buddha's name into a single, all-sufficient practice may be traced to a misunderstanding that confuses *nianfo* with *chengming* (calling upon the name [of the Buddha]). *Buddhānusmṛti,* a rich and varied meditation upon the excellent qualities of the Buddha, is one of the earliest forms of Buddhist practice, and in Yinshun's view constitutes the true form of *nianfo,* the Chinese term used to translate the Sanskrit. However, since the word *nian* means both "to contemplate" and "to recite aloud," the Chinese came to believe that the term *nianfo* referred to oral invocation. Calling upon the Buddha's name, on the other hand, is not a form of religious cultivation at all according to Yinshun, but an expedient means reserved for situations where the believer is in danger, or as a last resort for someone on his or her deathbed with no time for proper repentance and confession. Yinshun then analyzes various scriptures, related to methods for attaining rebirth in various pure lands, that had been translated more than once into Chinese, and shows that the vocabulary of these sutras gradually shifted over time from "reflecting on" or "contemplating" the Buddha to "reciting the Buddha's name" (pp. 56–61).

In a move certain to infuriate his critics, Yinshun illustrates the above point further by referring to a story from a Jin dynasty historical work called the *Record of Foreign Lands (Waiguo Ji),* in which the people of Parthia, who are very stupid and understand nothing of Buddhism, come upon a golden parrot who recites the Buddha's name. Convinced that the parrot was an incarnation of Amitābha, they all began joining in the recitation and thus attained rebirth in the Western Paradise. After relating this story, Yinshun points out that the Pure Land scriptures were among the first to be translated into Chinese, and indicates that this was not a compliment to the Chinese people. On the contrary, he takes this as evidence that the earliest Buddhist missionaries to China thought the Chinese people to be as stupid as the Parthians of old, and gave them this lowest form of practice because they did not think the Chinese capable of anything more. Otherwise, they would have translated works on Buddhist doctrine and cultivation (pp. 62–63). So the Chinese go on mindlessly repeating the Buddha's name, spurred on by ignorant teachers such as Yinguang, whom he singles out by name for criticism at the end of this discussion (p. 64).

Finally, Yinshun attacks a commonly used apologia for Pure Land practice: Relying on comments made by Nāgārjuna in his *Daśabhūmika-vibhāṣā-śāstra* (*Shizhu Piposha Lun,* T.1521), devotees assert that reciting the Buddha's name constitutes an "easy path" for those unable to take the "difficult path" of attaining the six perfections over several aeons of practice. Yinshun points out that Nāgārjuna prefaces his remarks on the "easy path" with some rather sarcastic comments to the effect that it constitutes a path of last resort for those lacking in the bodhisattva's resolve and compassion. Even after introducing the path of buddha-recitation, Nāgārjuna denies that it is a sufficient means for attaining perfect enlightenment. In fact, Yinshun asserts that "easy path" and "difficult path" are misnomers, with his dictum "It is hard to become a buddha by taking the easy path, but it is easy to become a buddha by taking the difficult path." To illustrate, he relates that Maitreya chose to take the easy path, while Śākyamuni Buddha chose the difficult path. Even though Maitreya took his vows forty aeons before the Buddha, he is still in the Tuṣita Heaven awaiting the ripening of his practice, while Śākyamuni has already achieved his goal (pp. 64–70).

It is not within the scope of this discussion to evaluate the merits of Yinshun's case; such an undertaking would constitute a book in itself. Our purpose here is simply to see that Yinshun consistently attacked the very form of practice that Yinguang spent his life advocating, relegating it to the very lowest form of cultivation, to be used only as a last resort by the dim-witted and those in dire straits. For Yinshun, to take buddha-recitation and make it the sole form of practice for all people, even those with the intelligence and leisure to undertake true bodhisattva practice, represented a degradation of Buddhism; and his contempt for this way of thinking comes through clearly on every page of his *New Treatise.*

The Controversy and its Aftermath. The *New Treatise* came about as a result of a series of lectures Yinshun delivered in the winter of 1951 at the Jingye Monastery *(Jingye Conglin)* in Hong Kong. His students Yanpei and Miaoqin revised their notes and published them that same year, perhaps conscious of the stir the treatise was likely to cause. The following year, Yinshun received the invitation from his old teacher Daxing to come to Taiwan, and he was installed as the Guiding Master *(daoshi)* of the BAROC's flagship institution, the Shandao Temple in Taipei. Because of his sudden prominence, his works began circulating among Buddhists, among them the *New Treatise on the Pure Land.*

In his autobiography, Yinshun makes little of the trouble that followed, saying only, "It appears to have elicited some disgust from those people who only want to practice calling the name of Amitābha" (Yinshun 1985:20). This is an understatement. According to Yang Huinan, Yinshun's critics mounted a whisper campaign against him; and in Taichung, Pure Land devotees burned his books publicly (Yang 1991:23). Jiang asserts that Yinshun's disciple Li Bingnan himself directly incited the burnings (Jiang 1988:58); but Yang disagrees, saying instead that it was a group of local clergy, recently ordained after having retired from military service (Yang 1991:23, n. 60). I was also told by friends in Taiwan who have spoken to Yinshun that he does not believe Li Bingnan was involved. Yinshun's attackers sent flyers to all the branches and chapters of the BAROC asking that he be ostracized and his works boycotted, and some within the BAROC even used their influence with the government to have certain Nationalist Party officials issue a statement that Yinshun's writings were infected with the poison of Communism (perhaps because of his comparison of the Pure Land to an ideal Marxist state?), and requesting that increased attention be given to extirpating his influence (Yang 1991:28).

Yinshun finally gave in to the combined pressure of the BAROC and its Nationalist friends. He stepped aside from his position at the Shandao Temple and issued a statement asking pardon for his offense, saying that his treatise was written when he was in flight across China and had no access to the Tripiṭaka; perhaps his memory of certain canonical passages was faulty. He concluded by humbly asking the government to help him correct his views (Yang 1991:29). Although he has remained active in some facets of Buddhist life in Taiwan, notably as an ordaining master in several BAROC-sponsored ordination sessions, he has mostly retired from public life, preferring to pass his days in quiet study in his Fuyan Vihara in the town of Chiayi.

Yang interprets the ferocity of the reaction against Yinshun as yet another manifestation of the power struggle between the traditionalist and reform factions, spearheaded on the mainland by Yuanying and Taixu respectively, and which continued after the disciples of these two great monks retreated to Taiwan (Yang 1991:21). There is some plausibility to this claim; other eminent monks and lay scholars in Taiwan have criticized the Pure Land tradition of Yinguang and its advocacy of the single practice of buddha-recitation, with no worse consequences than brief flurries of editorials (Jiang 1988:48–49). Also, as related in the biography of Cihang given above, Yinshun came to Taiwan at the invitation of Ven. Daxing, who had opposed Cihang's educational efforts partly on the grounds of his suspicion that Cihang had betrayed the spirit of Taixu's reforms. At this time, the reformers had won control of the Shandao Temple; and the traditionalists, represented by Yuanying's disciple Baisheng, retreated to the Shipu Temple. The appearance of Yinshun's controversial book just at the time that Yinshun assumed a high post at the Shandao Temple may have provided the traditionalist faction the opportunity to reassert control over this temple and over

BAROC affairs. The fact that the controversy involved Pure Land practice had symbolic significance to Yuanying's traditionalist followers as well. When Yinguang passed away and popular sentiment began to identify him as the thirteenth patriarch of the Pure Land school, some opposition ensued on the ground that two other candidates for this honor, Xuyun and Yuanying, were still alive. These dissenting voices argued that the mantle of thirteenth patriarch should be withheld until all three had passed on, so that a choice could be made from among them all (Jianzheng 1989:105). The inclusion of Taixu's archrival Yuanying among the candidates shows that the traditionalist faction identified itself strongly with the conservative view of Pure Land practice that Yinshun had attacked.

As we shall see, Baisheng eventually did lead the traditionalists to regain control of the BAROC. In 1960, not long after this controversy, he was elected as president of the organization, and either he or other members of his close circle have held this position ever since. My own speculation is that the public vilification of Yinshun was one of the first stages of their comeback. To this day, Yinshun maintains an ambiguous position within Taiwan Buddhist circles. As a young monk at a Pure Land temple once said to me with a cluck of the tongue and a shake of the head, "Yinshun is a great scholar, but he just doesn't understand the spirit of the Pure Land."

Yinshun's "Buddhism for the Human Realm." Despite his retreat, Yinshun has not been completely without influence on Taiwan Buddhist thought. After the controversy died down and tempers cooled, Yinshun, along with other members of the reform faction, was able to gain acceptance for some of Taixu's ideas about a modern reformulation of Buddhist ideals. One of the most successful of these is actually a modification of one of Taixu's guiding ideas, that of "Buddhism of Human Life" *(rensheng fojiao),* which Yinshun reworked as "Buddhism in the Human Realm" *(renjian fojiao).* The primary difference between these two theories consists in their diagnosis of what constitutes Chinese Buddhism's main impediment to meeting modern social needs.

When Taixu surveyed the Buddhism of his day, he thought that its major problem was its excessive focus on conducting funerals and placating spirits. Thus, he coined the term *rensheng fojiao* in order to emphasize his vision of a Buddhism more directly engaged in the affairs of the living than the dead. He based his program on two assumptions: First, that progress in the Buddhist path occurs most rapidly during a human life and not after death; and, second, that the religious life must consequently emphasize the affairs and morals of the living. Taixu expressed this ideal in his concrete programs for the reform of the Buddhist *saṅgha* in order to rationalize its organizational structure and to purge it of superstitious practices, and in his efforts to involve Buddhists more in social welfare activities (Yang 1991:92).

In changing *rensheng* (human life) to *renjian* (the human realm), Yinshun expressed the primary difference between his and Taixu's diagnosis of the source of Buddhism's degradation. Whereas Taixu thought that Buddhism concentrated too much on spirits and the dead, Yinshun thought the problem had roots in the history of early Indian Buddhism. During that time, Buddhism became progressively more theistic *(tianhua* or *shenhua)* (Yinshun 1985:18). Taixu decried Buddhism's preoccupation with the spirits of the dead but not the trend toward worship of deities; and so Yinshun believed that Taixu remained caught in traditional, outmoded Chinese conceptions of Buddhism. For example, Yinshun believed that Taixu failed to critique the Chinese interpretation of the *dharmakāya,* or "dharma-body" of the Buddha, in very theistic terms. The reader may recall from the discussion above that Yinshun criticized contemporary Chinese Pure Land practice for making Amitābha Buddha into a kind of god and his Pure Land into a kind of heaven. As stated in the essay, "The Buddha is in the Human Realm" *(Fo Zai Ren Jian):*

> The Buddha was not a god, nor a demon, nor did he claim to be the son of a god or the prophet of a god. He frankly stated: "All buddhas and world-honored ones arise from the human realm and not from the gods" *(Ekottarikāgama).* This is not only true of Śākyamuni Buddha; all who become buddhas arise from the human realm, not from a heaven. ... When a buddha is in the human realm, he wears clothing, eats, comes in and goes out (Yang 1991:115).

Thus, in changing *rensheng fojiao* to *renjian fojiao,* Yinshun sought to go further than Taixu in secularizing Buddhism.

This emphasis has taken hold in many segments of Taiwan Buddhism. The socially progressive Buddhist magazine *Buddhist Culture (Fojiao Wenhua)* took as its guiding editorial policy the "founding of the Pure Land among humanity" *(renjian jingtu)*. Many temples that I visited in Taiwan, especially in urban areas, posted signs that expressed the purpose of the temple's programs in terms of creating this earthly Pure Land; such temples frequently offered social welfare programs and tried to implement environmentally conscious practices, such as eschewing disposable dishes and chopsticks in favor of reusable ware.[14]

This concept of *renjian fojiao* appears also to be peculiar to Taiwan. Jiang reports that this term, familiar to most Buddhists in Taiwan, is unknown elsewhere. He says that when Lan Jifu, a prominent historian of Buddhism in Taiwan, went to Japan to participate in the third Sino-Japanese Buddhist Scholarly Symposium, no one that he spoke to had ever heard of the term (Jiang 1992:171). Thus, despite his early humiliation, Yinshun has exerted some influence over Buddhist thought in Taiwan, and many Buddhists, particularly scholars and intellectuals, have continued to pay attention to his life and work.

CONCLUSION

This chapter has outlined several trends that emerged during the early years after Taiwan returned to the Chinese fold in 1945. In terms of the politics of organizing China's Buddhists, Taiwan Buddhists quickly came under the direct supervision of the nationwide establishment, particularly the BAROC. Before the latter organization relocated to Taiwan with the Nationalist government in 1949, it had been subject to years of internecine power struggles between a traditionalist faction led by Yuanying, and a reformist faction led by Taixu. After 1949, the disciples of these two figures carried on this struggle, which seemed to go to the reformers at first but ultimately resolved in favor of the traditionalists. The result has been that Taiwan Buddhism has tended to incline towards conservatism, especially in the retention of very traditional Pure Land practices. However, it must also be noted that after the conflicts of the early 1950s, the two sides seem to have reached a rapprochement as the economic development of Taiwan has forced even the most conservative believer to face issues of modernization and progress.

The BAROC continued to be the chief political player in Taiwan Buddhism for many years, although its power base has been steadily eroded by an increasing atmosphere of pluralization. The BAROC will be the subject of the next chapter, and the forces of pluralization will be examined in chapter six.

CHAPTER 5

—⁓⁓—

THE BUDDHIST ASSOCIATION OF THE REPUBLIC OF CHINA

In the last chapter, we saw how Buddhism was organized in Taiwan in the period immediately following Retrocession, when Taiwan resumed its place as a province of China. Buddhist organizations on Taiwan at that time operated at the provincial, not the national, level. We also looked at the human side of the retreat to Taiwan, concentrating on the concrete problems of individual monastic refugees and on their perception of Buddhism in Taiwan as they found it. In this chapter, we will shift our focus to the Buddhist Association of the Republic of China (BAROC) as it accompanied the Nationalist government in its retreat to Taiwan; and we will see how it managed to establish its own "government in exile" on the island, reorganized and adapted itself to fit its new circumstances, and perceived its role during the period of its dominance.

THE EARLY PERIOD, 1949–1960

The Flight to Taiwan

Like the Nationalist government itself, the BAROC landed on Taiwan in a shambles and had to act quickly to find lodging for its officers and its operations. However, it worked under some disadvantages not shared by the government. First and foremost, its officers did not come to Taiwan as an organized group. Like other private citizens who wished to flee the mainland, they had to find their own passage, and not all chose Taiwan as their first refuge. Some, like Daoan and Yinshun, fled first to Hong Kong and came to Taiwan only later (on Daoan, see Jiang 1990:175; on Yinshun, see Chen Huijian 1994:3). The senior monk Wuming, later to be the president of the BAROC, came to Taiwan in May, 1949 dressed in a soldier's uniform, and went to live in a funeral home that was being used as temporary housing for refugee monks (Chen Huijian 1994:132). A few officers came to Taiwan before the Nationalist retreat, such as Baisheng, who had accepted an invitation to assume the abbacy of the Shipu Temple in Taipei and so was able to make a relatively smooth transition to Taiwan (Chen Huijian 1994:90). Some eminent clergy from the BAROC never came to Taiwan at all. Yuanying himself, a past president of the BAROC and the leader of the conservative faction on the mainland that opposed Taixu's reforms, remained on the mainland after 1949 and was even elected to lead the Chinese Buddhist Association *(Zhongguo Fojiao Xiehui)* under the Communist government.[1] Dongchu estimated that in all, fewer than one hundred monks came to Taiwan from the mainland, and of those, only a handful had any leadership capabilities or the status to participate in BAROC decisions (Jiang and Gong 1994:145).

However, enough leaders finally gathered in Taipei to begin rebuilding the organization. Of the three-man standing committee that convened on the mainland beginning in 1945, two came to Taiwan early. One of these, the national legislator and lay disciple of Taixu, Li Zikuan, pooled his resources with another lay leader, Sunzhang Qingyang, to purchase the Shandao Temple in Taipei, which gave the BAROC a place to meet (Dongchu 1974:2/539). The other member, the Zhangjia Living Buddha, was the current president of the

BAROC. He arrived at the end of 1949 just ahead of the Nationalist government. The committee asked Baisheng, who was already in Taiwan, to serve on the standing committee in order to have a quorum, and the group began planning for a National Congress in order to rebuild the BAROC's legislative and executive infrastructure (Nanting 1954:308). They met in a provisional office provided by Baisheng in the Shipu Temple (*1992 Gazetteer*:149).

The problems the BAROC faced in deciding whom to seat in its congress paralleled those of the secular government. As an organization that was ostensibly nationwide in scope, it needed delegates from all the provinces and major cities in China to ensure that all branches *(fenhui)* and local chapters *(zhihui)* were represented. However, the reality was that Jiangsu province was overrepresented, many other provinces had only a few members, and others had none at all. In order to put together its assembly, the standing committee decided that each province would have exactly two representatives, a solution that left some of the refugee monks dissatisfied. For example, Dongchu, the monk deputed earlier to tour Taiwan and prepare for the BAROC's move, blasted this decision, saying:

> In selecting representatives for the Second National Congress, [the BAROC] proceeded by naming two delegates from each province as if they were dividing spoils, which was blatantly unfair. For instance, there were over 100 delegates from Jiangsu Province, but there were only two representatives. There were only a few delegates from Anhui Province but only two representatives. There were two delegates from Fujian Province, and they got two representatives. ... Some provinces had many delegates in Taiwan, and some had only a few, and there were some provinces that lacked even a single delegate. The contradictions arising from this provisional apportionment of two delegates per province have been endless: someone from province A pretending to represent province B, and someone from province B pretending to represent province C (Jiang and Gong 1994:146).

Another problem arising from the exigencies of the times was the elevation of large numbers of lay Buddhists to positions of leadership within the BAROC. Nanting, in his assessment of the BAROC's first six years on Taiwan, lamented the fact that laity filled about one-half of the official positions within the organization, while the BAROC charter specifically limited them to one-third of all official posts (Nanting 1954:308).

Nonetheless, with a roster of representatives and officers in place, the BAROC prepared to hold its first National Congress since its move to Taiwan. This meeting took place on August 30, 1952, in Li Zikuan's Shandao Temple in Taipei. At that meeting, the BAROC elected a full slate of officers, directors, and supervisors. The Zhangjia Living Buddha won a second term as president, and mainland clergy and laity dominated all other committees and boards. The Zhangjia was to remain in the office of BAROC president for the remainder of his life.

The Zhangjia Living Buddha (or Zhangjia Hutuktu) was a native of Inner Mongolia, and part of a line of Living Buddhas who served as liaisons between the Qing dynasty government and the Dalai Lama. As Welch points out, "Zhangjia" is a title, not a name, and can refer to any of the Living Buddhas of this line (Welch 1968:302, n. 28). According to his entry in the *Foguang Dacidian* (pp. 4837–4840) and the brief biographical sketch given by Dongchu, the figure under discussion here is the nineteenth and last of this line of Living Buddhas. He was born in 1891 (or 1889, according to Dongchu), and his name is variously given as Ye-śes rdo-rje and Saṅs-rgyas-skyabs. He trained in several temples during his youth and was honored by the Qing government at the age of eight. After the founding of the Republic in 1912, the Nationalist government continued to honor him, recognizing him as one of the "Four Great Lamas of the Republic."[2] While on the mainland, he had temples under his authority not only in Inner Mongolia and Qinghai province, but also in Beijing, Liaoning, Wutai Mountain, and other places, with lamas numbering between three and four thousand in the larger temples and three to four hundred in the smaller.

Besides having extensive religious authority and prestige, he also worked for the Nationalist government as a member of the Tibetan–Mongolian Affairs Commission. During the Republican period on the mainland, the Nationalist government placed some importance on its relationships with the Tibetan and Mongolian peoples, and so found his advice quite useful. This gave him a direct link to the secular government; and because he argued before the government in favor of fair treatment for Buddhists of every sect, he became a figure of major importance within the Buddhist world as well. He was active in organizing China's Buddhists as early as 1917, when he helped revive the Chinese Buddhist Association (CBA) (*Zhonghua Fojiao Hui,* Beijing, 1917), although that organization collapsed two years later. When Taixu died unexpectedly in March 1947, the Zhangjia Living Buddha was elected president (Welch 1968:39, 46, 174).

Welch contends that the Zhangjia won this election because of his influence within the Tibetan community and the importance this gave him in government eyes (Welch 1968:47). As we shall see, such government interference does in fact occur from time to time, and may well have had a decisive influence in allowing him to attain his position; however, this contention fails to explain why he was elected to a second term as president after the BAROC moved its operations to Taiwan and lost contact with Tibet and Mongolia. Might there have been internal factors at work in the BAROC?

Jiang suggests another reason related to the reformer-versus-traditionalist struggle that came across the Taiwan Straits with the mainland monks. Although the two main adversaries were no longer on the scene, Taixu having died and Yuanying having remained on the mainland, they each had disciples among the clergy and laity vying for control of the BAROC even as it tried to find its footing in Taiwan. Among Taixu's disciples one could count Daxing and Li Zikuan, upon whose influence within the government the clergy still relied. Both these men were intimately connected with Taixu. On the other side, Baisheng had met Yuanying on the mainland in 1935 and had accompanied him on his travels for two years, receiving the dharma-transmission from him in 1937. Daoyuan, another monk who would be very active in the BAROC on Taiwan, is the monk who invited Baisheng to meet Yuanying (Chen Huijian 1994:86). These monks, therefore, were very much identified with the traditionalist faction that opposed Taixu's efforts at reform.

As Jiang interprets the situation, the Zhangjia Living Buddha was an outsider to this struggle, and his reelection as president of the BAROC was a compromise between two unyielding factions (Jiang 1992:66–68). I will add my own speculation that this internecine struggle explains why, when the Zhangjia died in 1957, the BAROC switched to government by its standing committee and did not elect any president at all until 1960. However, although the two factions were deadlocked in seeking to gain control of the BAROC, the scales tipped in favor of the reformers in terms of the governance of the Shandao Temple itself. Baisheng tried to gain the abbacy of the temple, but Li Zikuan was determined to have a reformer in charge and succeeded in giving Daxing the call. Baisheng subsequently settled into the Shipu Temple that he had bought. Thus, for Jiang, these two temples not only represent the bastions of the two most economically powerful Buddhists in Taiwan, they also represented the strongholds of the reformist and traditionalist factions respectively (Jiang 1992:68).

The BAROC's Organization, Mission, and Activities under the Zhangjia's Presidency

Organization. Since the BAROC reconvened in Nanjing in 1947, its organizational structure has remained essentially the same, although some administrative committees have been renamed, and the number and function of its special committees change as the need arises. The base of the organization is the membership, which is divided into corporate and individual memberships. Corporate members—temples, lecture halls *(jiangtang),* clubs, and any other Buddhist organizations— have no vote within the BAROC National Congress. Individual members are divided into clerical and lay houses.

The highest authority within the BAROC is the National Congress, which convenes every year. This is composed of elected delegates from all the branches and local chapters under the BAROC's jurisdiction. The representatives elect a board of directors, whose duty is to implement all resolutions passed by the National Congress and report on such implementation at the following year's Congress. The board of directors elects a standing committee from amongst its own members, which in turn elects the president, who must be a monk. The board of supervisors is also elected at the Congress; about one-third the size of the board of directors, it serves to audit the BAROC's books and provide independent confirmation of the directors' prosecution of their duties. The board of supervisors also elects a standing committee from amongst its members to meet regularly.

Directly subordinate to the BAROC central administration are the branch associations, which properly indicates provincial- or metropolitan-level organizations, and local chapters, which could include any city or county with a significant population of Buddhists (Welch 1968:48). Daoan, in his 1957 report on the BAROC's first eight years in Taiwan, says that at the Second National Congress, there were representatives from forty-five branch associations covering all of China, from Liaoning to Guangdong and from Jiangsu to Xinjiang. At that time, all of Taiwan province fell within the jurisdiction of the Taiwan Provincial Branch Association, which oversaw twenty-two local chapters (Daoan 1979:117–118).

However, as the years passed and the Nationalist government remained unable to retake the mainland, the BAROC legislative structure suffered the same problem as the National Assembly. That is, delegates, who on paper represented provinces on the mainland, aged and passed away with no one to replace them, until it finally became impossible to maintain even the pretense of jurisdiction over any area outside of Taiwan Province. At that point, the BAROC, like the government, had to deal with the problem of redundant jurisdictions. In other words, it had a national organization whose jurisdiction extended over only one province. The national government solved the problem by elevating Taipei City to the status of "special municipality" in 1967, and Kaohsiung, Taiwan's second-largest city, to the same status in 1979, placing both outside of the jurisdiction of the Taiwan Provincial Government and subordinating both directly to the central government (Copper 1993:xviii, xxi). In the same way, by 1990 the local chapters of both Taipei and Kaohsiung had been elevated to the status of branch associations, removing them from the jurisdiction of the Taiwan Provincial Branch Association and putting them directly under the supervision of the BAROC central administration. Thus, by 1990 the BAROC had only three branches under it; and of these, only the Taiwan Provincial Branch had any local chapters reporting to it. There are currently twenty-one of these local chapters (*BAROC and Buddhism in the Taiwan Area* 1990:6).

Relations with the Government.   As was the case on the mainland prior to 1949, the BAROC maintains close relationships with both the central government and the ruling party. Article five of the BAROC charter as amended in 1936 put the Association directly under the oversight of the Ministry of the Interior; and it was this ministry, along with the Ministry of Social Affairs, that gave Taixu the mandate to reorganize the BAROC in 1945 (Welch 1968:46, 140–141). In the contemporary ROC, the government does not include a separate Ministry of Social Affairs, and so the BAROC deals most directly with two offices within the Ministry of the Interior. The Bureau of Social Affairs *(Shehui Si)* oversees the BAROC as an organization, and it is the bureau most concerned with reorganization, and with meetings and conferences. The Bureau of Civil Affairs *(Minzheng Si)* is responsible for religious affairs within society, and so the BAROC looks to it for guidance when holding large dharma-meetings and other religious functions. There are occasions, of course, when the BAROC has to deal with other branches of the government: with the Ministry of Foreign Affairs to invite foreign visitors to attend BAROC functions, with the local government to register property, and so on. Before 1989, the BAROC also acted as the direct intermediary with the Ministry of the Interior and the Ministry of Foreign Affairs in obtaining passports, and exit and reentry permits for monks and nuns going abroad. However, as of July 1989, the Ministry of the Interior decided to stop requiring BAROC certification of such applications, stating that Ministry employees lacked the means to judge the veracity of certification by religious bodies. From that point, monks and nuns were to apply individually for their own documents as ordinary citizens under their lay names, thus removing BAROC's ability to control clergy travel. (*Zhongfohui Kan* [*BAROC Newsletter*] 76 [July 20, 1989]:1).

This relationship with the government has been reciprocal. The government solicits the BAROC's advice on any proposed changes to ROC laws dealing with religious matters, as in 1983, when the Ministry of the Interior was considering new regulations on religious freedom (*Zhongfohui Kan* [*BAROC Newsletter*] 22 [August 25, 1983]:1), or changes to the laws governing religious organizations in 1990 (*Zhongfohui Kan* [*BAROC Newsletter*] 84 [April 30, 1990]:1). The BAROC can also look to the government for assistance in matters impinging on its activities or image, as when it prevailed upon the Government Information Office to ban a movie it felt poorly depicted clergy (*Zhongfohui Kan* [*BAROC Newsletter*] 15/16 [October 10,

1982]:1). The government relies on the BAROC to help maintain contact with temples and Buddhist organizations and disseminate information on government policies and suggestions for implementing them. (Examples of this type of meeting can be found in *Zhongfohui Kan* [*BAROC Newsletter*] 31 [February 15, 1984]:4; and 53 [June 30, 1987]:1.) In addition, representatives of the Ministry of the Interior and the Bureau of Social Affairs, and often the Interior Minister himself, usually attend all BAROC National Congresses to observe, give speeches on government policy, and give advice.

Mission and Activities. The BAROC charter lists the organization's mission under the following eleven items:

1. to propagate and engage in research into the dharma;

2. to maintain and administer the organization's bylaws;

3. to protect and supervise religious property;

4. to register temples, along with their property, resident population, and religious artifacts;

5. to supervise the preservation of temples and to arrange for the restoration of religious artifacts and sites of historical significance;

6. to engage in Buddhist cultural and educational work;

7. to work for social welfare and education;

8. to encourage clergy to engage in productive work;

9. to correct inappropriate customs and practices among believers;

10. to encourage social movements of all kinds; and

11. to engage in other activities for the revival of Buddhism (*1992 Gazetteer*:151).

In BAROC literature, this statement of purpose is frequently compressed into the slogan, "protect the religion and defend the nation." *(hujiao weiguo)* During the early years of the Zhangjia's presidency, the BAROC found itself much more vitally concerned with the former than with the latter. In 1954, Nanting, then the BAROC secretary-general, published an assessment of the BAROC's first six years in Taiwan in the December issue of Dongchu's *Rensheng* (Human life) magazine, in which he noted the following accomplishments:

When, in 1951, the BAROC received word that soldiers were being billeted in several temples, it interceded with the Ministry of the Interior and the Ministry of Defense, and received assurance that this practice would be prohibited in the future; or if this were impractical, then at least the military would first obtain the permission of the temple's governing agency. As of 1954, Nanting reports that there were still some temples being forced to house soldiers, but not as many as before.

Second, also in 1951, the BAROC convinced the Ministry of the Interior that temple lands were nonproductive and should not be subject to land taxes.

Third, the "land-to-the-tiller" provisions of the Land Reform laws exempted educational and charitable institutions from having to sell to the government for redistribution any land whose income they relied on. Because this law did not specifically exempt religious institutions, many Buddhist clergy and laity feared that the government would force them to sell their land for resale to its tenant farmers. The BAROC petitioned the Taiwan Provincial Government to amend the law to specifically exempt religious institutions as well. This, Nanting says, relieved the fear that temple lands would be requisitioned, as well as the fear that temples would have to begin cultivating their land in order to keep it. While Nanting's report does not state clearly that the provincial government accepted the BAROC's request, we shall see shortly that it may have had its intended effect.

The fourth item concerns laws passed by the Taiwan Provincial Government in 1952 in an effort to abolish *baibai,* a form of native folk religious worship in Taiwan. One clause of the law stated that "the erection of new temples or the molding of new Buddha-images is strictly forbidden." The BAROC, whose constituency was as much threatened by these prohibitions as were the adherents of folk religion, protested on the grounds of the ROC constitution's guarantee of freedom of religious belief. The provincial government tried again two years later to pass a similar law, and the BAROC again protested.

Nanting's third point raises the matter of land reform, and so a brief digression is necessary here in order to clarify the issues involved. The "land-to-the-tiller" *(gengzhe you qi tian)* program was the third and final part of the Nationalist government's land reform program (the first two were the imposition of rent ceilings and the sale of public farmland, mostly former Japanese properties, to local farmers). Passed on January 26, 1953, this measure stipulated that any land over a certain area that a landlord owned but did not personally cultivate must be sold to the government in exchange for government bonds and shares of government enterprises. The land would then be resold to farmers for their own cultivation.

Welch commented many years ago, "it [i.e., the "land-to-the-tiller" policy] made no distinction between a lay landlord whose rents brought luxury to a few, and a monastic landlord whose rents made it possible for hundreds of people to practice religious austerities" (Welch 1967:242). In this he was wrong. The law enacted by the KMT government on Taiwan made specific provision that temples would only be required to give up half as much land as private landlords. This meant that, despite confiscation by the Japanese Sōtokufu, and despite the Nationalists declaring large amounts of temple-owned land "ownerless" and taking them over, some temples could still derive significant income from agricultural land rentals. Chen Ruitang, in his legal study of temples in Taiwan, lists a few such temples: the Chaofeng Temple in Gangshan; the Quanhua Hall on Lion's Head Mountain near Hsinchu; the Yuanguang Temple in Chungli; the Fayun Chan Temple in Miaoli; and so on. However, he emphasizes that these temples comprised a small minority of all temples in Taiwan (his study embraces Buddhist, Daoist, and folk temples), and none of them had the kind of extensive landholdings held by their counterparts on the mainland. (Chen Ruitang 1974:188–191).

In addition, David K. Jordan, in his article on changes in popular religious practice in Taiwan after 1945, gives a bit of anecdotal evidence. During his stay at the Kaiyuan Temple in Tainan, he found that the various land reform measures adopted by the government had made it increasingly difficult for this temple to hold onto its land. Because of land consolidation and prohibitions on alienating arable land from agricultural use, the temple could only retain its land by erecting more buildings and augmenting its "footprint." To this end it built "a hospital, an old people's home, a kindergarten, and a building designated as an orphanage but intended for immediate use as a pilgrims' hostel" (Harrel and Huang 1994:147).

Despite Jordan's claim that land reform and related laws "reduced drastically" the landholdings of Buddhist temples, there remains a need for perspective on this issue. In chapter one we saw that, while Buddhist temples in Taiwan did indeed own land, the tracts recorded in the gazetteers are not large by any standard, and certainly do not approach the extent of holdings cited by Welch with regard to temples on the mainland before 1949. Welch reports personally knowing of more than twenty temples that owned over one thousand *mu* (about 151.5 acres) of farmland (Welch 1967:240). Also, as Chen observed, much temple land had already been confiscated by the Japanese between 1895 and 1945, which forced temples at that time to begin seeking other sources of income. After 1945, temples lost even more land to Nationalist rapacity. Taken together, this evidence suggests that farmland rental never constituted a major source of income for any Buddhist temple in Taiwan. Nonetheless, we should recognize that the potential loss of any property, however large or small, was a genuine concern for temples at this time.

We now return to Nanting's report. With regard to the other half of the BAROC slogan, "protect the nation," Nanting mentions a few other activities during this early period. First, in the spring of 1950, the BAROC sponsored the first of what would become an annual event, the Benevolent Kings Dharma Meeting for the Protection of the Nation and the Averting of Disaster *(Huguo Renwang Xizai Fahui)*. This is a large, three-day dharma-meeting *(fahui)*, the purpose of which is to gather both clergy and laity of all sects to pray together for the welfare and safety of the nation, and to generate merit by reciting the *Sutra of the Benevolent Kings*. As an ecumenical event meant to unite all of Chinese Buddhism, it employs several altars. During the first meeting in 1950, the Zhangjia Living Buddha, as a representative of the Tibetan Yellow-Hat Sect, tended the Esoteric Altar *(mitan)*, while Nanting himself tended the Exoteric *(xiantan)*.

In other patriotic activities, the BAROC circulated a letter for all members to sign in the autumn of 1951, pledging their support of efforts to fight the Communists and resist Soviet influence. At the 1952 meeting of the World Fellowship of Buddhists in Japan, the BAROC introduced a motion condemning totalitarianism and reporting on Communist abuses against Buddhism; it also became a corporate member of the Asian Anti-Communist League *(Yazhou Renmin Fangong Tongmeng)*. These activities all served to support its claim to represent all the Buddhists of "Free China" (Nanting 1954:308–309).

The BAROC's Efforts to Reform the Monastic Ordination System. When Dongchu toured Taiwan and made his report to the BAROC, he perceived three major groups of Buddhists on the island: Japanese (or Japanized), Chinese, and *zhaijiao*. The first attracted the intellectual and political elite, but it was too liberal, and by 1950 had largely disappeared from Taiwan because of the repatriation of Japanese citizens. The second was more conservative, and centered around the transmission of the monastic precepts through the Yongquan Temple in Fujian Province. The third was, he said, a "peasant cult." Of all three branches, he thought that only the second, consisting of the Gushan Yongquan Temple monastic ordination lineages, led an acceptably austere life and had received the precepts correctly (Dongchu 1979:109–110).

However, despite the BAROC's apparent approbation of the "conservative" faction, the Gushan lineage was to become inactive after 1949. Although the "four great temples" remained active, the climate had changed so that they could no longer offer ordinations independently as they had done during the Japanese period. The Lingyun Chan Temple on Guanyin Mountain did make an effort to hold an ordination session in the spring of 1949, but "conditions were not ripe." The Shandao Temple tried in 1951, but its plans also fell through; and it seemed that individual temples had no way to hold ordinations. There were probably three reasons for this.

First, the times were still very unsettled in Taiwan. Clergy found it difficult to travel freely around the island, and the government was suspicious of mass gatherings of any kind. Second, the clergy connected with the BAROC saw it as their clear duty to reform the ordination system to conform to that which had existed before in their home provinces. It will be recalled that Dongchu, during his inspection tour, was disturbed by the lack of "public monasteries," the institutions which had served as the primary centers of ordination on the mainland. The "four great temples" had, after all, been technically "hereditary temples," subject to all the abuses and cliquishness inherent in a system where disciples could receive the tonsure and the full precepts at the hands of a single master.

The third reason was the prestige that the mainland monks enjoyed on Taiwan. As noted before, many of them who came to Taiwan were the cream of the Chinese Buddhist order, monks of nationwide stature and impressive credentials. Xingyun adds an interesting note of support to this contention: He reports that during the 1954 ordination session at the Yuanguang Temple on Lion's Head Mountain near Hsinchu, every effort was made to call the "three ordaining elders and seven witnesses" *(sanshi qizheng)* from the ranks of native Taiwanese clergy. However, "there was still insufficient manpower"; and so in the end, all of them, "even the preceptor" yielded their duties to mainlanders (Xingyun 1954:313). Among all the native clergy in Taiwan in 1954, the BAROC monks could not find even one whom they considered eminent enough to ordain others.

For all these reasons, the first post-1949 ordination session was held under the BAROC's supervision in the winter of 1953 at the Daxian Temple in the centrally located town of Chiayi. Although largely satisfied with the outcome of this ordination, the BAROC still saw a need for further reforms. First, the Daxian Temple received many donations from people who came to observe the session, and made a significant profit over and above its expenses (Xingyun 1954:313). It is perhaps for this reason that the *1992 Gazetteer* reports that "temples in every place began helter-skelter arranging to transmit the precepts" (*1992 Gazetteer*:159). The BAROC felt that ordinations should be conducted in a more orderly manner and not as a for-profit business. Second, there was still the problem of Taiwan's lack of public monasteries. No matter where the ordination was held, it would be in a hereditary temple; and the resident clergy of that temple would be training and ordaining their own tonsure disciples along with novices from other temples, allowing for the possibility of favoritism.

Consequently, the BAROC ruled that henceforth there would be one ordination per year, and that temples desiring to hold ordinations would be required to register with the BAROC, who would put them on a rotation. Furthermore, the BAROC itself would provide all of the necessary personnel: the preceptor, the *karmācārya,* the catechist, the seven witnesses, and all of the lecturers and deans. The host temple would still enjoy the prestige and increased income from hosting the event, but its role would be limited to providing facilities and support services. In this way, the host temple would, in effect, become a public monastery for the duration of the ordination session. This has remained the procedure for BAROC-sponsored ordinations in Taiwan ever since.

This was a significant development in terms of the BAROC's authority over Buddhism in the ROC. It must be clearly understood that the BAROC has no real supervisory authority over Buddhists in Taiwan, as it is well aware. For example, in 1990 an editorial appeared in the BAROC newsletter to address reader queries as to why the organization did not intercede in a libel suit filed by a temple against a lay Buddhist. In this editorial, the writer reminds readers that the BAROC lacks any binding authority to arbitrate internecine disputes; it is a service organization, nothing more (*Zhongfohui Kan* [*BAROC Newsletter*] 85 [May 25, 1990]:1).

However, having the responsibility of running and staffing the annual ordination session gave the BAROC control over entry into the clerical ranks. In November 1993, I went to the Guangde Temple in Kaohsiung County at the end of the monks' ordination session, where I had the opportunity to interview the elder Jingxin, who at the time was both preceptor and abbot of the temple.[3] He indicated to me that about one hundred of the people who had come for ordination had been eliminated during the course of the session for failing to meet standards. This demonstrates the power that the BAROC held over entrance into the clergy during the period when it had a legal monopoly over ordinations.

It also explains why the ordination lineages emanating from the Yongquan Temple in Fujian Province, which had predominated during the Japanese period, became inactive. As we have seen, monks from the mainland dominated the BAROC infrastructure. Thus, even when, as in 1956, 1962, 1965, and 1973, the annual ordination took place at one of the "four great temples" of the Japanese period, the ordaining elders came from the outside. The dominance of the mainland monks and the institution of the new ordination system effectively put an end to the transmission of the Yongquan Temple lineages.

The Vitality of the Nuns' Order after 1952. When the BAROC reformed the ordination system, its efforts produced one consequence that it could not have foreseen. Since the first ordinations in 1952, nuns have increasingly come to predominate numerically over monks, a situation that only exists in Taiwan and Hong Kong (*Sakyadhītā: Daughters of the Buddha* 1988:121). Japan has very few nuns (*Sakyadhītā* 1988:124), and there are technically no nuns at all in the Theravāda countries.[4] What are the reasons for this situation, and what is its significance?

First, let us look at the actual numbers. Yao Lixiang provides a statistical table of all ordination sessions conducted on the island between 1953 and 1986. With only one exception (1961), the BAROC has consistently ordained more women than men; and frequently the ratio has been 3:1 or higher. In all, 2,030 men were ordained during this period, as compared to 6,006 women (Yao 1988:239). This trend has shown no signs of alteration since 1986; the ordination session I observed in 1993 had 126 male and 485 female ordinands.

To the best of my knowledge, no researcher has yet undertaken an investigation of this phenomenon, and so there are no scholarly or theoretically informed studies to help us understand this discrepancy. However, while in Taiwan, I have heard and read many explanations, some of them mutually contradictory. Here I will present a sampling of some of the more credible ones.

The first is the least precise and scientific, but it is the most universally voiced opinion on the subject in Taiwan: Women are simply more religiously inclined than men. Without delving into the issue of whether this proposition applies across cultures and historical periods, I can say from my own fieldwork that, at least for modern Taiwan Buddhists, it appears to be true. Most dharma-meetings (*fahui*), buddha-recitation sessions, and other religious functions that I observed were attended by many more women than men; interestingly, the discrepancy was generally consistent with the ratio of nuns to monks. The only exceptions were public lectures on Buddhist scriptures, and group Chan meditation sessions. At these events the participants' gender distribution was about equal.

Another theory seeks to explain the predominance of nuns in modern Chinese society by contrasting modern times with the conditions of the past. For instance, Kenneth Ch'en reproduces a monastic census taken during the Kangxi reign (1662–1721) that counted 110,292 monks, as opposed to only 8,615 nuns (Ch'en 1964:452). According to this theory, the relevant factors are the changing legal and social environments. The Qing government required women to be at least forty years old before they could consider ordination, although in some localities (such as Fujian province), this law often went unheeded (Chen Ruitang 1974:9). In addition to the age requirement, the imperial government in 747 CE began the practice of requiring prospective ordinands to obtain an ordination certificate from the government. Generally, this required the candidate to memorize a certain number of scripture passages, which prejudiced the system against women, who lacked access to education (Ch'en 1964:224, 246–247). Although one might also purchase a certificate and avoid the examination, the conditions that made ordination valuable (i.e., exemption from corvée labor and taxation) appear to apply more to men than to women; and so I would speculate that far fewer women purchased their certificates. Even though the government stopped issuing ordination certificates by the end of the Qing dynasty, the combination of legal restrictions with lack of an ordaining temple in Taiwan meant that, at the end of the Qing period, there were no nuns in Taiwan (Chen Ruitang 1974:11). Currently, there are no legal restrictions on ordination, nor does the government issue certificates or examine candidates for ordination. In addition, clerical status no longer brings any tax advantage or exemption from military conscription, so men are no longer motivated by the prospect of avoiding civic obligations to seek ordination. Thus, the legal environment is much more conducive for women who want to become nuns.

As to the social environment, it is widely observed that population pressures have severly reduced the average family size in contemporary Taiwan. Couples usually restrict themselves to one or two children, and so it is common for families to have only one son. This means that the obligations to produce heirs to carry on the cult of the family ancestors and to develop a successful career in order to provide for parents in their old age, which in the past might have been carried by several sons, now frequently devolve upon only one or two. This increased pressure serves to discourage men from seeking ordination. Another factor is Taiwan's current economic prosperity, which makes it easier for families to provide for their sons and thus has decreased the number of sons they give up to Buddhist temples (Shih Yung Kai 1988:121).

The above factors also affect daughters, though to a lesser degree. However, the relaxing of traditional Chinese family values, especially in urban areas, has made it easier for daughters to seek ordination despite parental objections. The overall increase in educational levels for all members of society has also given women more career options, and the resulting sense of freedom leads many more women to consider ordination than might have previously (interview with Prof. Shih Heng-ching, National Taiwan University, December 15, 1993). However, the opposite explanation appears to hold true for women from rural areas; many still appear to choose ordination as an escape from marriage and children, and as an opportunity to pursue an education and a meaningful career (Tsung 1978:189–206).[5] Whereas urban women seek ordination from a feeling of empowerment, the rural ones choose it from a position of disempowerment.

Another question that elicits contradictory responses concerns the social position of nuns in Taiwan society. All my informants in the areas of Taipei and Sanhsia considered nuns at least as respectable as monks, or even more so. Although most of my fieldwork concentrated on a temple renowned for the strictness of its discipline and the high educational levels of its resident clergy, which meant that my informants had a particularly illustrious group of nuns in mind when this topic came up, I still feel that this assertion has a certain plausibility. The temple had approximately six times as many nuns as monks, and many more women than men seeking ordination; and so it rejected many more women than men. I was told that a woman seeking ordination there would be scrutinized very closely and made to undergo a trial period of two or three years before she received the novice's tonsure. Since men were much scarcer, a man would be more readily accepted and could be tonsured after a matter of months. Thus, it seems credible that the nuns, having passed a longer and more intense period of vocational testing, during which they risked a greater likelihood of elimination, would be of higher average quality. In contrast, however, Shiu-kuen Tsung found in Taipei county that female clergy were viewed with some suspicion by society. She reports that while outsiders did not necessarily regard their vocation as unworthy of respect, they still tended to view the nuns as social misfits (Tsung 1978:182).

Within the *sangha,* nuns have also come to play a more active role in monastic affairs since Retrocession. Jiang points out that some of the early mainland monks, such as Cihang and Daoan, saw the talent and potential of Taiwan's nuns and deliberately drew them out of their kitchens and buddha-recitation halls. They encouraged the nuns to pursue further education and to take leadership roles in religious affairs and temple management. The result of this early encouragement has been increased prominence for the female clergy in social activism, education, temple management, and lay organizing (Jiang 1992:77–85). Today, one of the most powerful figures in the Buddhist world is the nun Zhengyan, founder of the Buddhist Compassion Relief Tzu-Chi Association, whose career will be examined in the next chapter.

While the quality and numbers of nuns have been increasing over the years, those of the monks have done the opposite. Yao's statistics show that, while the number of female ordinands has risen steadily since 1953, when there were 132 women, to 1986, when there were 417, the number of male ordinands has stagnated. In 1953 there were only 39 new monks, and only in 1983 did the number of new ordinands exceed 100. During this time, the population of Taiwan has climbed from 7.5 million to over 20 million, and so the numbers of male clergy as a percentage of the overall population have fallen dramatically.

At the same time, some observers have raised concern about the monks' commitment to their vocation, and their overall quality. In 1967, Shengyan observed that monks studying abroad in Japan were likely to leave the monastic order; the same was not true of nuns (Zhang Mantao 1979b:165). Almost twenty years later, Jingxin, then president of the Taiwan Branch Association of the BAROC, presented a report to the BAROC board of directors on the 1985 and 1986 ordination sessions. In his closing remarks, he commented that there seemed to be very few young men seeking ordination, and that those who did were very fickle. Many reverted to lay life, others retreated to the mountains to perform austerities, while others simply wandered aimlessly and never settled down to work in a temple (*Zhongfohui Kan* [*BAROC Newsletter*] 49 [February 28, 1987]:2). It is clear that Taiwan's Buddhists need to find ways to address these trends, or face an ever more serious decline in the order of monks.

The above discussion, while offering no tested explanations for the remarkable increase in the population of nuns, should at least give a sense of how the people of Taiwan understand the phenomenon. With that, we return to the main narrative concerning the BAROC.

After the Zhangjia. The BAROC held its Third National Congress on August 28, 1955 in Taipei, at which time the Zhangjia Living Buddha won reelection for a third term as president. However, he was soon diagnosed with cancer and on March 4, 1957, passed away in the National Taiwan University Hospital (Daoan 1979:116). His death left a vacuum at the BAROC, whose charter contains no provisions for succession in the event of an unexpired term. At the next National Congress, which took place the following June, the BAROC decided to do away with the office of president, and adopted the system of government by the Board of Directors' standing committee instead.[6]

Because the records do not indicate precisely why the National Congress decided to abolish the office of president, it is difficult to impute a motive for this action but, it seems reasonable to speculate that factionalism continued to influence the congress' deliberations, and that no other compromise figure like the Zhangjia Living Buddha was available for the office. Doing away with the office altogether may have been a new and more creative solution. However, this is only speculation; and there were other factors at work as well. Yang, quoting extracts from Daoan's diaries, notes that the Third National Congress of 1955 suffered from unspecified interference from the Nationalist Party and that, as a result, the conservative faction roundly defeated the reformers in the elections for most BAROC official posts (Yang 1991:35). Although this helps round out our picture of the climate in which the BAROC conducted its business at this time, it is difficult to see how this may or may not have contributed to the Zhangjia's reelection or the decision to abolish the presidency after his death.

The BAROC continued to be governed by standing committee for the next three years. The Fourth National Congress convened on August 28, 1960, at which time the congress voted to reinstate the office of the presidency and elected Baisheng to the post. From then until his death on April 3, 1989, Baisheng remained a controlling presence in BAROC affairs, despite the fact that he did not hold the presidency continuously during this period. At times the BAROC returned to governance by standing committee, and at others someone else held the office of president. However, it was Baisheng who provided the vision and, by some accounts, the energy necessary to keep the BAROC a vital organization.

THE MIDDLE PERIOD UNDER BAISHENG, 1960–1986

A Biography of Baisheng[7]

Born on August 13, 1904, Baisheng was a native of Yingcheng County in Hubei Province, and his lay name was Hu Bikang. By his own account, despite frequent illnesses, he was an extremely active and rebellious boy who regularly ran off to play rather than attend the private Confucian school in which his father had enrolled him. His father responded by putting him in a small Christian school that offered games; this way, he felt, the boy might actually stay in school. This situation did not last, however, and young Bikang returned to the Confucian school once again.

Of his conversion to Buddhism, Baisheng recalls that it happened at about the age of ten. One day, he fell while playing and permanently crippled his right hand; later, his mother told him that she had once had a vision of a paralyzed right hand. From that point, he says, he believed in the doctrine of cause and effect. As with so many other great monks, he also had the experience of loss and grief during his childhood. His mother suffered from poor health, and his elder sister took most of the responsibility of looking after him. This sister died when he was fifteen years old, and his mother passed away the following year. At the same time, he heard a dharma-talk given by Ven. Zhimiao of Nine-Flower Mountain *(Jiuhua Shan)*, which gave him the idea of seeking ordination.

His family disapproved strongly and gave him heavy responsibilities to carry out at home. In 1921, he took advantage of a flood to flee to Hankou, the site of Nine-Flower Mountain, and seek ordination from Zhimiao. After ordination, Zhimiao sent him to the Gaomin Temple in Yangzhou for further study. Baisheng wanted to reside there but received word that his brothers had come looking for him, which prompted him to take refuge in another temple. His brothers found him anyway and convinced him to return home by telling him their father was on his deathbed and wished to see him one last time. When Baisheng arrived home, he found that they had lied, but it was too late; he was trapped once again in family life. He soon found another opportunity to run away and returned to Nine-Flower Mountain to be with his tonsure master. Later, when Zhimiao was asked to take over as abbot of the Baoguo Temple in Suzhou, Baisheng accompanied him. He stayed there until 1926, when he left on a pilgrimage to Mount Wutai.

His first involvement in transmitting the monastic precepts came about in 1929, when he was invited to join the resident clergy of the Baotong Temple in Wuchang. The abbot there solicited ideas for activities to promote the dharma, and Baisheng suggested that they hold a series of sutra-lectures followed by a monastic ordination. He himself served as an ordination instructor. During the session, however, he came to feel that the ordination he had received at age eighteen on Nine-Flower Mountain did not conform to Buddhist standards, and so he decided to take ordination a second time.

During this period, he also made progress in Chan meditation, having already participated in several Seven-Day Chan Meditation Retreats *(chan qi)*, practiced "nourishing the breath" *(yangxi)* for an hour every day, and reduced his need for sleep. Shortly after his reordination, he entered a period of sealed confinement, during which he developed dysentery. His abbot advised him to come out, but Baisheng refused. He said that all beings are fated to die anyway, and if he died while in confinement, he wanted his body placed in an urn and left in the retreat chamber until the time of confinement had elapsed, at which point the temple should cremate him. (In his memoirs, he indicates that he had been joking when he said this; had he actually died, he hoped that they would have cremated him immediately.)

In any event, he did not die, and he came out of sealed confinement at the age of thirty-one. He records that this was another turning point in his life: Before this, he had devoted himself to cultivation and study; afterwards, he gave himself over to more outwardly directed work such as temple administration, social work, teaching, and evangelism. He accepted many invitations to lecture on the sutras and *vinaya;* during this time he met Yuanying and spent the next two years travelling with him. It was while traveling with Yuanying that he first became active in the BAROC, becoming one of its "managers" *(ganshi)*. In addition, he often took the lecture dais on Yuanying's behalf and helped him perform ordinations. Finally, in the summer of 1937, Yuanying transmitted two dharma-lineages to Baisheng: those of Qita and Gushan.[8]

In 1937, the War of Resistance erupted, and Baisheng, then living in Japanese-occupied Shanghai, helped with the war effort as best he could. He found food for refugees, interceded on behalf of clergy who had been detained, worked in an ambulance corps, collected and buried the war dead, and performed other relief work. At the same time, he became active in broadcasting, establishing his own Buddhist radio station, which featured dharma-talks, lectures on sutras, sutra-recitations, and even broadcasts of "Release of the Burning Mouths" ceremonies. However, the station did not last long. The Japanese authorities monitored its programs closely; and when Baisheng was asked to broadcast some anti-Chinese propaganda, he refused, closed the station, and burned the equipment. The year was 1940.

During the same period, he took on a heavy administrative load. After closing the radio station, he left Shanghai and went to Hangzhou, where he was the abbot of two temples and the director of two Buddhist societies. By 1944, the strain began to wear on him, and he decided to drop most of his administrative duties and return to doctrinal study full time. For the following year he again accompanied Yuanying on a lecture tour, and produced some short books.

However, victory over the Japanese in 1945 brought more administrative and relief work. The government asked Baisheng to go to Shanghai to reorganize the Shanghai Buddhist Association, and he took over as its acting president. He began restoring temples razed during the war, and led a protest against plans by the Shanghai Department of Civil Affairs to requisition temple property for government use. He also accepted an invitation to take over the abbacy of the Jing'an Temple after its abbot and prior had been arrested and banished for collaborating with the Japanese. Here he met and worked with several monks who would later become active in the BAROC on Taiwan, including Shengyan and Liaozhong.[9] He worked for a time to establish a number of social and charitable projects at this temple, including a Buddhist seminary, an elementary school, and a proposed Buddhist university.

As noted earlier, the president of the Taipei City Chapter of the BAROC, the layman Zeng Puxin, introduced Baisheng at the Shipu Temple in Taipei in 1948. Later in the year, seeing the rapid deterioration of the situation on the mainland, Baisheng decided to move to Taiwan permanently. Because he had arrived ahead of the wave of refugees who came when the government retreated to Taiwan, he was in a position to offer hospitality to over ten eminent monk-refugees, including Nanting, Zhiguang, Daoyuan, Jiede, Moru, and Miaoran. These monks, he says, "brought a new atmosphere to Taiwan Buddhism."

As we have seen, Baisheng was involved with the BAROC on Taiwan from the time he arrived in 1948, interceding for Cihang and all the monks in jail, arranging temporary office space in the Shipu Temple, and serving on its standing committee. When the Fourth National Congress finally opened on August 28, 1960, the delegates voted to resume the office of the presidency; and the standing committee asked Baisheng to fill the post (*1992 Gazetteer*:149). He obliged, and served out a three-year term. However, in 1963 he decided that, at the age of sixty, he needed to lay down his burdens and devote himself once again to study and practice. Consequently, the Fifth National Congress, held on December 22, 1963, elected Daoyuan president. As we have seen, Daoyuan is the monk who first invited Baisheng to come and meet Yuanying, and the two monks had been close associates ever since. Thus, even though Baisheng was no longer in the post of president, the conservative faction was still in control.

Baisheng came out of retirement to resume the presidency at the Sixth National Congress, held on March 15, 1967 at the Shandao Temple; and he won reelection at the Seventh National Congress on December 5, 1971. At the Eighth National Congress on October 5,

1974, the BAROC again decided to abolish the presidency and rely on a nine-person standing committee for leadership. This did not, however, signal another period of retirement for Baisheng, since he was one of the committee members (*1992 Gazetteer*:149–150). During the Ninth Congress, held in the BAROC headquarters on October 17, 1978, the BAROC again decided to resume the presidency and asked Baisheng to fill the post again. From then on, he held the post continuously until 1986.

At that time, he called a joint meeting of the directors and supervisors to announce his intention to retire due to poor health. After some discussion, the boards agreed to accept his resignation and proposed that the BAROC charter be amended to permit the creation of an office of honorary president *(mingyu lishizhang)* for him (*Zhongfohui Kan* [*BAROC Newsletter*] 53 [June 30, 1987]:2). Another monk was installed as acting president of the BAROC. In April 1986, the first meeting of the Eleventh National Congress elected Wuming, a very spiritual and much-loved senior monk, as the next president (*Zhongfohui Kan* [*BAROC Newsletter*] 42 [May 8, 1986]:1).[10]

In April of the next year Baisheng retired as abbot of the Linji Chan Temple in Taipei (*Zhongfohui Kan* [*BAROC Newsletter*] 51 [April 30, 1987]:2), and in May 1988 he handed the abbacy of the Shipu Temple over to his disciple (and later BAROC president after Wuming) Jingxin (*Zhongfohui Kan* [*BAROC Newsletter*] 63 [May 20, 1988]:4). Baisheng received one final honor from the Nationalist party when, in July 1988, he was named to the party's central advisory committee (*Zhongfohui Kan* [*BAROC Newsletter*] 65 [July 30, 1988]:1). However, his health continued to decline, and on April 3, 1989, he passed away in Taipei at the age of eighty-five.

At this point, we will shift our focus away from Baisheng himself and look in more detail at the activities of the BAROC during and after his long tenure.

Internationalism under Baisheng

Baisheng was a monk whose international vision sprang from various motives. On the mundane level, with his conservative, pro-Nationalist sentiments, he thought the ROC should use whatever means were available to maintain its presence in the face of increasing diplomatic isolation and the government's failure to retake the mainland. This view was not unusual for monks of his generation. As Welch observed, "Among refugees from the Mainland today, Buddhist monks are the most uncompromising of the anti-Communists" (Welch 1968; 159). Baisheng was also genuinely distressed by the divisions that he saw in world Buddhism, and he worked to establish international contacts among Buddhists to effect a reconciliation. Activities carried out both by him personally and by the BAROC under his direction include ordinations of foreign monks, involvement in international Buddhist organizations, and open advocacy of the ROC abroad.

Ordinations of Foreign Monks. Baisheng was very interested in missionary work in the West, and in neighboring East Asian and Southeast Asian regions. To this end, he occasionally transmitted lay precepts to Western believers, the monastic precepts to foreign ordinands, or the dharma of the Linji Chan lineage to foreign monks. For example, in 1961 he conferred the complete monastic precepts upon an American novice and then went with him on a tour of the island. (Unfortunately, the tour was cut short when both of them were injured in a traffic accident.) Later, he conferred the Three Refuges to an American Naval officer, and the bodhisattva precepts to an American layman who was attending a Buddhist conference. This, he says, marked the starting point for the transmission of the Chinese Buddhist precepts to the West (Chen Huijian 1994:93–94). At the same time, he also accepted the request of a Korean monk to transmit his dharma-lineage. Baisheng records that he traveled to Korea twice, and on one of these trips he participated in a full monastic ordination ceremony with over one thousand people receiving both lay and monastic precepts (Chen Huijian 1994:94).

Involvement in International Organizations and Advocacy of the ROC. In addition to the individual contacts occasioned by the ordination of foreign clergy, Baisheng also involved the BAROC in several international Buddhist organizations: the World Fellowship of Buddhists, the World Buddhist *Saṅgha* Council, and the World Chinese

Buddhist *Saṅgha* Council. In examining the history of the BAROC's involvement with these groups, we will also see how the BAROC advocated the cause of diplomatic representation for the ROC at international meetings and congresses.

World Fellowship of Buddhists (WFB). The BAROC's involvement in the World Fellowship of Buddhists *(Shijie Fojiaotu Youyi Hui)* actually predates Baisheng's election as BAROC president. This organization dates back to its first meeting in Colombo, Sri Lanka (then Ceylon) in 1950. Chinese Buddhism was represented at this first meeting by Fafang, a monk who had been teaching there as an exchange professor since 1940 (Chan 1953:58). The next general conference took place in Tokyo in 1952; and this time the delegates included the Zhangjia Living Buddha and Yinshun, who had just arrived in Taiwan from Hong Kong. Problems began with the Third General Conference, which took place in Rangoon, Burma in 1954. At this time, the BAROC delegation was not allowed to attend because of poor relations between Burma and the ROC. However, this was a matter external to the WFB, and so there was no impetus to reexamine the BAROC's status within the organization.

The BAROC did not attend the 1956 Fourth General Conference in Nepal, either; but this time the BAROC itself boycotted the meeting because the Nepalese government had invited a delegation from the PRC. The BAROC decided that the two delegations could not attend together, and so kept its representatives home. This evidently suited the PRC delegates, who agreed that there could only be one delegation from China. Later, in 1957, the head of the Chinese Buddhist Association, Zhao Puchu, went to the interconference executive committee meeting in Colombo and offered five thousand Sri Lankan rupees to the WFB on the condition that the BAROC be expelled from its seat. The move succeeded, and the BAROC was not even notified of the Fifth General Conference (Bangkok, 1958) or the Sixth General Conference (Phnom Penh, 1961). The BAROC protested but received no response.

At this point the central government of the ROC decided to involve itself in the issue and protested through diplomatic channels.

These efforts bore fruit in 1964, when the BAROC's membership was reinstated and it accepted an invitation to send delegates to the Seventh General Conference (India, 1964). From this meeting on, the BAROC has kept its membership, although poor governmental relations have sometimes raised difficulties. For instance, the Tenth General Conference (1972) again took place in Colombo, Sri Lanka; and the Sri Lankan government refused to grant entry visas to the BAROC delegation, forcing it to stay home. It may not be coincidental that the previous year, the ROC lost its seat in the United Nations to the PRC.

The ROC's loss of its United Nations seat continued to affect BAROC efforts at participation in the WFB. The next crisis came in 1980, when the WFB was preparing to hold its thirteenth General Conference in Bangkok. This time, the PRC took advantage of its membership in the United Nations and the WFB's UNESCO membership to convince the United Nations to write a letter to the fellowship's headquarters requesting that the BAROC yield its seat to the CBA. The letter went to the WFB Executive Committee for deliberation; in the end, they decided to let the BAROC retain its membership as before (the above synopsis of the BAROC's history with the WFB prior to 1984 is taken from *Zhongfohui Kan* [*BAROC Newsletter*] 29 [August 11, 1984]:1). The competition between the BAROC and the mainland CBA has continued to the present day, with no definitive resolution.[11]

As we look at the BAROC's involvement in other international bodies, we will not explore the struggles that have taken place in these arenas in the same detail; and so we will pause here to consider the implications of the BAROC's direct advocacy on Taiwan of the ROC. Both Chan and Welch have given accounts of Taixu's earlier efforts at internationalization as part of his endeavor to reform Chinese Buddhism. He was instrumental in setting up many international Buddhist groups, all of which were short-lived. Thus, such participation in and of itself is nothing new in Chinese Buddhism (Chan 1953:58–59; and Welch 1968:55–64).

However, there are several differences between Taixu's internationalism and that which developed after 1949 under the BAROC's auspices. First, whereas the conservative faction under Yuanying generally stayed out of Taixu's efforts, Taiwan Buddhism's international involvement after 1949 intensified under the patronage of Yuanying's conservative allies and disciples. Second, in post-1949 Taiwan, a new set of circumstances furthered the pursuit of internationalism: Taixu's organizational efforts and personal international tours gained government patronage because Chiang Kai-shek's Nationalist government wanted China to be internationally recognized as a world power to be reckoned with, rather than a colonial territory to be exploited. After 1937 the government was also seeking aid and sympathy in its war against Japan. Taixu was able to play on this by promising that his efforts would draw the world's attention to China's great cultural and religious heritage; incidentally, these efforts would also draw attention to him personally and enhance his prestige within Chinese Buddhism. The conservatives' agenda at that time was simply to forestall government encroachments on temple properties, and they did not see how Taixu's international ventures would help.

After 1949, the BAROC's task on the international scene was different. While the ROC held its seat in the United Nations, the BAROC saw its task as calling attention to the Communist government's depredations against Buddhism: temples destroyed; clergy beaten, killed, and laicized; books burned. After the ROC lost its U.N. seat in 1971, and as the central government relied more and more on representation in nongovernmental organizations to press its cause on the world stage, the task became more urgent. In this setting, it is understandable that the BAROC delegations to successive WFB general conferences could not remain silent about even so small a matter as the name given to their nation on their placard.[12]

Thus, whereas Taixu and his reformists had engaged in international organizations in order to enhance China's image, the conservatives under Baisheng took the initiative to call international diplomatic attention to Communist abuses against Buddhism on the mainland, and to help the ROC gain a voice after it lost its seat at the United Nations. With that, we will look briefly at some of the other international organizations in which the BAROC holds some influence.

World Buddhist Saṅgha Council (WBSC). The BAROC's involvement in this organization is much more a direct result of Baisheng's initiative than its participation in the WFB.

The World Buddhist *Saṅgha* Council (WBSC) was not originally as connected with the ROC on Taiwan as it would become under Baisheng's leadership. It was founded in Sri Lanka in 1966, the date of its first meeting. Its second meeting was in Saigon, Vietnam in 1969; but after this meeting, the Sri Lankan monk who provided the impetus for the organization passed away, and the council itself faded into dormancy (*Zhongfohui Kan* [*BAROC Newsletter*] 32 [February 15, 1985]:1).

It was Baisheng who impelled the WBSC's revival some twenty-two years later. In 1980, Baisheng and another BAROC associate, Wuyi, were in Bangkok, Thailand attending the WFB's thirteenth General Conference. Baisheng began holding private discussions with clerical leaders from various parts of the Buddhist world to revive this international monastic body, he says, to fulfill three purposes: to celebrate the seventieth anniversary of the ROC, to counter Communist schemes for domination, and to turn the ROC into "a mainstream service center for the Buddhist world." He received enough encouragement at the WFB meeting to proceed with further negotiations to hold the WBSC's Third Congress in Taiwan; and so he went to Hong Kong directly after the Bangkok meeting to confer further with the leaders of the Hong Kong Buddhist Federation (*Xianggang Fojiao Lianhehui*) and signed an agreement with them for aid in planning the meeting. Next, he and Wuyi went to consult with government officials in Taiwan, and received two directives: First, since the WBSC was originally a Sri Lanka-based organization, they should obtain the express permission of Buddhist leaders there to hold the Third Congress in Taiwan. Second, they had to keep the plans for the congress secret in order to avoid trouble with the mainland, and to avert the possibility that the CBA might try to plan its own meeting to compete with the one in Taiwan.

Accordingly, Baisheng, Wuyi, and other Chinese Buddhist leaders from Hong Kong and Malaysia traveled to Sri Lanka in April 1981 to make formal plans for the meeting. The participants accepted the proposal for a congress in Taiwan, and elected Baisheng himself to serve as acting president of the council until a proper election could be held at the congress. Upon returning to Taiwan, Baisheng deputed Wuyi to act as secretary for the Third Congress, and placed him in charge of all the arrangements. Work proceeded quickly, and a final international planning committee meeting took place in Malaysia in October to arrange for guests of honor, set the agenda, and settle on the theme, "Buddhism and World Peace."

The Third Congress took place from December 1 to 6, 1981, and received representatives from Indonesia, Australia, Malaysia, Burma, England, Taiwan, Sri Lanka, Singapore, the Philippines, and many other countries. Taking advantage of an international conference in its home territory, the ROC government dispatched several officials to address the congress in plenary session: the interior minister, the chief of the Control Yuan, and the vice-president all welcomed the delegates and touted the ROC's atmosphere of religious freedom. Baisheng himself, a witness to the horrors of war, gave an impassioned plea for Buddhist clergy to take the lead in political activism on behalf of world peace and nuclear disarmament.[13]

When the Third Congress held its elections, Baisheng easily won the post of president of the council, and Wuyi won the post of Chinese secretary (the congress also elected an English secretary from among the delegates from Sri Lanka). The delegates also voted to move the headquarters of the WBSC from Sri Lanka to Taipei. Thus, we can see that the ideals proposed by Baisheng the previous year all came to pass: The BAROC by its hard work succeeded in locating itself in the mainstream of global Buddhist affairs, to the extent of bringing the leadership and headquarters of a major Buddhist international organization to Taiwan itself, and in so doing it could sneer at the Communist government, whom, it was noted, had often tried to invite foreign and overseas Chinese clergy to activities on the mainland "without receiving the slightest response" (*Zhongfohui Kan* [*BAROC Newsletter*] 7 [January 20, 1982]:4). The leadership and headquarters have remained in Taiwan at the Linji Chan Temple in Taipei ever since.

World Chinese Buddhist Saṅgha *Council.* The founding of the World Chinese Buddhist *Saṅgha* Council (WBCSC) was a cooperative venture between the BAROC under Baisheng's leadership and the ROC central government. The first meeting took place November 5 through 11, 1965, in Taipei and was timed to coincide with the one-hundredth anniversary of the birth of Dr. Sun Yat-sen. The BAROC provided the organizational leadership, and the government provided funding for the first conference. The First Conference elected a nine-member domestic chairmanship composed of Baisheng, Nanting, Daoan, Yinshun, Daoyuan, and other monks from the BAROC leadership; and a ten-member foreign chairmanship composed of delegates from the twelve participating countries. Baisheng was also elected as secretary-general.

This organization appears to have been more casual at its inception than the other two examined above. The second conference did not take place until five years later, and then only because the Hong Kong Buddhist Federation had invited Chinese clergy from several countries to attend the opening ceremonies for its newly completed hospital. The BAROC delegation to this event suggested that a second conference of the WBCSC could be held at the same time. The Hong Kong Buddhist Federation agreed, and the second conference was scheduled for April 5, 1970. Because the preparations had been made in such haste, the proceedings were not as smooth as desired; but the delegates carried on with new elections, and Baisheng again won the post of secretary-general to the organization (*Zhongfohui Kan* [*BAROC Newsletter*] 7 [January 20, 1982]:1). Beyond this point, however, the council appears not to have been very active.

Other Foreign Contacts. Apart from membership in these international Buddhist organizations, the BAROC has been active in many informal international contacts. Every year, the board of director's report to the BAROC National Congress contains items concerning foreign delegations entertained at the BAROC offices, and BAROC delegations going abroad. In addition, for many years the BAROC has been an active member of the Sino-Japanese Buddhist Cultural Exchange *(Zhongri Fojiao Wenhua Jiaoliu),* which cooperates with its Japanese companion organization, the Japanese-Chinese Buddhist Cultural Exchange *(Nika Bukkyō Bunka Kōryū)* in hosting the annual meetings in rotation (*Zhongfohui Kan* [*BAROC Newsletter*] 57 [October 31, 1987]). Such exchanges with Japan have flourished even more under the encouragement of the current BAROC president, Jingxin, who speaks fluent Japanese and received his bachelor's degree from Bukkyō Daigaku in Kyoto in 1977 (*Jingxin Da Fashi Wuzhi Huadan ji Pushan Guangdesi Shiwu Zhounian Jinian Zhanji* 1978:4–5).

Continuation of the Struggle to Regain Possession of Japanese-Era Temples

In the above section, we looked at the primary activities of the BAROC during the period of its dominance under the leadership of Baisheng. In the course of this investigation, we have seen that the BAROC frequently works closely with the government in several areas. However, BAROC–government relations have not always gone smoothly; and we will be looking here at one major area of conflict: the disposition of Japanese temples in Taiwan after 1945.

The question of what to do with Japanese temples was not a problem peculiar to Taiwan. During the 1930s and 1940s, Japan also controlled large areas of the Chinese mainland throughout which it established temples, and sent chaplains to minister to the local Japanese and to do missionary work. When the war ended in 1945, the central government of the ROC had to settle on a policy with regard to Japanese properties, including temples. The first law was promulgated in 1945 in Chongqing [Chungking] by the Ministry of the Interior and was called "Articles for Attention in the Takeover and Disposition of Japanese Temples and Shrines by Local Governments" *(Difang Zhengfu Jieshou Chuli Riren Simiao Ciyu Zhuyi Shixiang)*. Here the central government left the actual takeover and management of temple properties to the provincial governments, who were accountable to the central government in reporting and getting approval for how they handled these cases. This 1945 directive clearly intended that any Chinese citizen whose home had been taken over as a Japanese temple should get his or her property back, and all Chinese temples should revert to their former governing bodies. Only Japanese temples built during the occupation could be taken over for government use.

In theory, this directive ought to have provided for an orderly and equitable process of disposition, with public lands going to the local government and private lands being returned to their owners. However, the actual situation in the streets and fields of post-Retrocession Taiwan was anything but orderly. George Kerr, in his book *Formosa Betrayed,* describes what he saw as an American diplomat in Taiwan after 1945: Armed gangs of military officers simply took whatever houses and other properties they wished, and government agencies summarily requisitioned larger-scale Japanese-era buildings for office space. A report in the inaugural issue of *Chinese Buddhism Monthly* shows that this problem affected Buddhist temples as well; and that as early as 1948, the BAROC was submitting petitions to the central government requesting the return of these temple properties (*Zhongguo Fojiao Yuekan* [*Chinese Buddhism Monthly*] 1, no. 1 [March 1, 1954]:7). This problem became especially acute when the Nationalists retreated to Taiwan in 1949, and the central government needed buildings quickly. At the beginning of this chapter, we saw that even Chinese-built and -populated temples had to deal with the forced billeting of soldiers. However, after a time this problem was resolved with BAROC intervention. The situation of Japanese-built temples, however, proved more intractable.

Although the BAROC identified a total of sixty-six Japanese-era temples that had yet to be given back to Buddhists for religious use by the mid-1960s, most of the controversy related to a fairly small group of temples in Taipei: the Nishi- and Higashi-Honganji, the Donghe Chan Temple, the Shandao Temple, the Shipu Temple, and the Fahua Temple.[14] During the early phase of the conflict, the primary issue was the government's failure to hand over the temples in accordance with the provisions of the 1945 directives. Nine years later, the BAROC began losing patience with government inaction and became more aggressive in submitting petitions to the Executive Yuan requesting that existing laws be enforced, military and government agencies that occupied temples be asked to leave, and the properties be given directly to the BAROC for management. The results were spotty. A communiqué to the BAROC from the Executive Yuan dated December 12, 1954, indicates that the Yuan was willing to consider returning the Donghe Chan Temple, but not the Nishi-Honganji (*Zhongguo Fojiao* [*Chinese Buddhism*] 1, no. 10 [January 1955]:15).

The dispute took on a new dimension in 1957, when the Executive Yuan passed the "Measures for the Disposal of Special National Properties in Taiwan Province" (*Taiwan Sheng Guoyou Tezhong Fangwu Dichan Qingjie Chuli Banfa*). The second article of this act stipulated: "The Taiwan Provincial Government, in cooperation with the concerned agencies, shall draft measures [for the management of] temples and shrines belonging to the Japanese, which shall be reviewed by the Executive Yuan before they go into effect" (quoted in "Zhongguo

Fojiao Hui Qingyuanshe ji Fujian" 1965:21). This law meant that the government intended to take over the management of these temples permanently as "special national properties" rather than return them for use as religious institutions. Underlying the government's classification of these temples as "special national properties" was a question of their identity: Were they Chinese or Japanese temples? If they were Japanese, then they could be considered as property abandoned by the enemy in the "recovered territories" at the end of the war, and the government could take them over with impunity. Shintō shrines fell easily into this category, but the situation of Buddhist temples was not as clear.

The BAROC thought it obvious that Buddhist temples ought to be classified as Chinese temples; and in a petition submitted to the Executive Yuan on October 13, 1957, it laid out its reasoning (*Zhongguo Fojiao Yuekan* [*Chinese Buddhism Monthly*] 10, no. 2 [October 1965]:21). The first argument was one that it deployed frequently, and which dated back to its earliest petitions in 1948. This was that, although the temples were in the care of Japanese abbots and subordinate to Japanese lineages of Buddhism, the funds used to construct, maintain, and staff them came from native Taiwanese (that is, ethnic Chinese) devotees. The Executive Yuan agreed to this proposition as far back as October 1948, when it issued a directive on the implementation of the 1945 Five Articles, which stated, in part:

> The second of the Five Articles for the Disposition of Japanese Temples says, "All Japanese temples and shrines should be taken over by the local government, which should register and take care of them." However, temples that were built with funds donated by Taiwanese natives should not be considered Japanese property. The local Buddhist association should compile a list of these temples and present it, along with the proper legal documents, to the provincial government, which should then deliberate on their return (Executive Yuan directive [37], no. 47179. Reproduced in *Taiwan Fojiao* [*Taiwan Buddhism*] 19, no. 10 [October 1965]:7).

As its second argument, the BAROC reminded the government that the provisions of the 1929 "Law for the Supervision of Temples" [*Jiandu simiao tiaoli*], still the law of the land as of this writing, appeared to support the BAROC's case (The text of this law is reproduced in Chu Hai-yüan 1990:113–139). Article six of this law states: "All property and religious paraphernalia pertaining to a temple are the property of that temple, under the management of the abbot." Article eight set limits on the abbot's authority, specifying that he or she could not sell, alienate, or make alterations to temple property without permission both from the local government and the larger religious organization to which the temple belonged (Chu Hai-yüan 1990:124). Under these provisions, the BAROC asserted that *(a)* temples could not be considered the private property of abbots, whether Chinese or Japanese, because they did not exercise ownership rights over them; *(b)* many former Japanese temples now had new Chinese abbots, who under the law, should be in charge of these temples; and *(c)* the BAROC, as the only nationwide organization of Buddhists in the ROC, logically ought to be considered the "larger religious organization" to which these temples belonged, and so ought to have at least a consultative role in their disposition.

The third argument was based on a legal opinion issued by the Ministry of Justice on March 2, 1950. This opinion stated that if any Japanese-era social welfare organization re-incorporated under a Chinese board of directors after Retrocession, then it should be allowed to retain all of its former property. The BAROC asserted that many former Japanese temples had done just that, and that the ruling should apply to these temples as well as to other social welfare agencies.

The BAROC's fourth and final argument appealed to the government to consider how the failure to return these temples to religious usage would affect the government's image and relationships, both abroad and domestically. On the foreign front, there were two issues: First, how could the government criticize the Chinese Communist Party regime's desecration and destruction of temples if it engaged in similar behavior at home? Second, the failure would affect relations with Japan. The BAROC cited the disappointment of a Japanese delegation that had come to deliver the bone relics of Tang-dynasty Buddhist pilgrim and translator Xuanzang, at not being able to visit these former Japanese properties, and at hearing how the temples had become dilapidated through neglect.

On the domestic front, the BAROC reminded the government that, in terms of the overall national budget, any value gained from the sale or use of these temple properties would be negligible; but the loss of public confidence, particularly among Buddhist devotees, would be immeasurably greater.

The BAROC did not depend solely on the persuasive power of these petitions and communiqués; it also relied upon the influence of highly placed allies within the government. In the same month that the BAROC submitted its 1957 petition, legislative committee members Chen Cheng and Jiang Shaomo submitted an interpellation before the Legislative Yuan. Besides repeating many of the arguments submitted by the BAROC, this interpellation is noteworthy for its documentation of individual cases of abuse. In some cases, the failure of the provincial government to return temples for religious use could be blamed on mere foot-dragging; Chen and Jiang cite the Shandao Temple as a case of this. As of the time of the interpellation, this temple had done the requisite survey of all its land and assets, registered them with the Taipei District Court, and been issued a temple registration certificate. Having fulfilled all these legal requirements, the temple should have gone into the control of the BAROC. Nevertheless, the central government's conscription office and the Taipei City Police Administration's traffic unit were still operating out of this temple's property. Chen and Jiang also turned up cases of outright abuse of authority, as in the case of an employee of the Taiwan Land Bank who expropriated the Fahua Temple, of which the bank was the trustee, and attempted to sell it and keep the profits.

Nothing happened as a direct result of these interpellations, and more petitions and communiqués passed between the BAROC and the central government. Meanwhile, two more laws went into effect and complicated the affair by providing different and contradictory mechanisms for the return of temple properties. The "Act for the Disposition and Handling of Japanese Temples Taken Over by Taiwan Province" (*Taiwan Sheng Jieshou Riren Simiao Caichan Qingjie Chuli Banfa;* November 22, 1959) called for the provincial government to set up a deliberative panel to handle each case, while the "National Properties Management Act" (*Guoyou Caichan Chuli Banfa;* February 23, 1961) gave this responsibility to a committee on national property management within the Executive Yuan Council (*Taiwan Fojiao* [*Taiwan Buddhism*] 19, no. 10 [October 1965]:7; and *Zhongguo Fojiao Yuekan* [*Chinese Buddhism Monthly*] 10, no. 2 [October 1965]:26). Despite the confusion and further delays occasioned by these two acts, their intent was clear: Both stated that the government was to take over temple properties for safekeeping and eventual return.

The final phase of this crisis came about on May 3, 1965, when the BAROC learned of the Executive Yuan's intention to raze the Nishi-Honganji, then one of the largest and most ornate temples in Taiwan, to make room for apartments. Shortly thereafter, on June 8, 1965, it heard through the press that the Higashi-Honganji was also slated to be put on the market. The BAROC acted quickly to communicate its shock at this decision; but the Executive Yuan, in its reply, declared that this temple did not meet the conditions for return to religious use, and that the property, "located in a thriving city center where the property values are very high," needed to be handled as a special case. This was the final decision, and it asked the BAROC not to raise the matter with them again (*Taiwan Fojiao* [*Taiwan Buddhism*] 19, no. 10 [October 1965]:7; and *Zhongguo Fojiao Yuekan* [*Chinese Buddhism Monthly*] 10, no. 2 [October 1965]:19).

But the BAROC did raise the matter again, this time submitting a petition signed by Daoyuan, then the BAROC president, to the Legislative Yuan, the Control Yuan, and the National Assembly, dated September 20, 1965. Appended were all of the previous petitions, interpellations, laws, government directives, rulings, and communiqués accumulated during the previous twenty years. They repeated all of the arguments already cited above. All seemed clearly to support the BAROC's contention that it, as the body representing all Buddhists in the ROC, should be given control of these two temples so that they could be restored to their former glory and resume functioning as places of religious activity. As before, the BAROC also asked allies within the Legislature to submit interpellations on its behalf.

Evidently, however, other interests were at work within the government. In a 1967 critique of the BAROC, Shengyan brings up the unsatisfactory conclusion of this dispute as an example of the BAROC's lack of any real authority. Despite the BAROC "expending nine oxen and two tigers' worth of effort" in the matter, the Higashi-Honganji was sold in June 1967 to a merchant for a large sum of money (Zhang Mantao 1979b:171).

As for the other contested temples, I have found no documentation of how their cases were finally resolved. The 1967 sale of the

Higashi-Honganji Taiwan Branch Temple appears to have been the final episode in this long-running conflict, and my impression is that temples in Taiwan today are much more secure from government seizure. However, this case is instructive in showing that there are limits to the influence that the BAROC holds within government circles, contrary to the popular criticism of the organization as a KMT organ.

This is not the only criticism that has been leveled against the BAROC over the years.

Criticisms of the BAROC

In his examination of the BAROC's history on the mainland prior to 1949, Welch observed that there seemed to be a perennial gap between "paper and practice." He says:

> Branches were supposed to carry out any orders received from national headquarters, but in fact they often ignored them. Chapters were supposed to remit four tenths of their membership dues to the branches, and the branches were supposed to remit half of these four tenths to the national headquarters. In practice such remittances were exceptional. Therefore, the association 'was constantly in financial difficulties and asking for money from the provincial branches,' as the head of one provincial branch tells us. ... According to its regulations, all of the monks and nuns in China were supposed to join. In fact, many did not. ... The large number of abstentions is evidence, perhaps, that its help and protection were not as effective as they were supposed to be (Welch 1968:49).

It would seem that given Shengyan's 1967 critique of the BAROC, twenty years on Taiwan had not brought any improvement.

Even before this critique, we see evidence of financial and organizational difficulties. Nanting, in a 1954 article in *Rensheng* magazine assessing the BAROC's first six years on Taiwan, complains that even though the BAROC's special committees have some of the most eminent names in Taiwan Buddhism on their rosters, most of these members fail to show up for meetings (Nanting 1954:308). The January 1955 issue of the BAROC magazine *Chinese Buddhism Monthly* contains a call for all local chapters to pay all their back dues before holding elections for their boards of directors and supervisors (*Zhongguo Fojiao Yuekan* [*Chinese Buddhism Monthly*]1, no. 10 [January

1955]:15). Thus, the lack of participation and lack of financial support are apparent shortly after the BAROC's move to Taiwan.

Thirteen years later, Shengyan echoed and elaborated upon these complaints. The BAROC office staff consisted of three elderly laypeople, and the secretary-general had to expend much energy on finding ways to meet office expenses. The reason was that, of the estimated six to eight million Buddhists in Taiwan, only forty-five thousand actually belonged to BAROC; and many of them did not pay their dues for years on end. Similarly, because of the lack of participation, almost all of the workload fell upon a small group of activists centered around Baisheng. Consequently, this handful of monks was constantly trying to do too much at once, and not doing anything well. Baisheng himself did everything from receiving international delegations to painting the eyes on Buddha-images at every small temple. His greatest asset, Shengyan says, was his ability to fall asleep at will, and work through the night.

The root problem, according to Shengyan, was a vicious circle: The lack of moral and financial support from the local chapters crippled the BAROC's ability to do anything concrete for Chinese Buddhism. Because the burdens of financing and work fell by default to such a small group of people, it was unable to do very much to benefit the average Buddhist, who consequently got the impression that the BAROC was ineffective and not worth supporting, and so withdrew further (Zhang Mantao 1979b:171–173).

Another criticism that one commonly hears in Taiwan even today is that the BAROC is too closely allied with conservative KMT politics, and so cannot represent the interests of all Buddhists in Taiwan, particularly the native Taiwanese. Yang goes even further, reporting that in 1955, the party actively interfered with the Third National Congress: It took advantage of the need to have delegates from all of the provinces of mainland China, and planted government and party supporters among the delegates, and even had them represent more than one province to cast more than one vote.[15] The result was that, in the elections held during that congress, Li Zikuan and the other more progressively minded heirs of Taixu's reform movement lost all power within the BAROC, and all the positions of real influence went to the heirs of Yuanying's conservative faction. The government and ruling party were evidently interested in using the BAROC as a tool for unifying the island (Yang 1991:35–36).

Yang goes on to say that similar party interference marred the elections held during the Eighth National Congress in 1974. According to a report filed by Zhiming in the journal *Haichaoyin*, the KMT compiled and submitted the list of candidates for the boards of directors and supervisors, and only those with money and government connections won posts. It will be recalled that this was one of the occasions on which the BAROC decided to abolish the presidency and resort to governance by the standing committee as a whole. Whether there is any connection between this and the interference Yang cites, I do not know. The result, he says, is that the BAROC is dominated by two types of leaders: those who work for the ruling party, and those only out for themselves. Nowhere did he find any concern for the common Buddhist cleric or layperson (Yang 1991:35–36. Zhiming's report is found in *Haichaoyin* 55 [November 1974]:6).

If the BAROC failed to become the unifying force for Taiwan Buddhism that it might have, I suspect that the most basic cause is that it has always consisted, at the national level at least, of only a very small, closed group of people with actual decision-making authority. Since Baisheng first took over as president, the presidency has always devolved upon either him or those within his circle. When he first gave up the office, Daoyuan, his close friend from his mainland days, won the election. When Daoyuan finally retired, Wuming, another longtime friend and associate, took over. The current president of the BAROC, Jingxin, is Baisheng's direct dharma disciple, and was the president of the Taiwan Branch Association for many years. In looking through BAROC publications from the 1950s through the 1990s, one finds the same twenty or so names appearing in every office, commission, or committee. That the BAROC leadership is such a closed shop may explain why energetic younger monks such as Shengyan and Xingyun eventually became inactive in the organization and began building their own enterprises. Their efforts, along with other factors, led to the loss of the BAROC's hegemony and ushered in a new period of pluralization, to which we will turn in the next chapter.

— ·∽∾∾∽· —

CHAPTER 6

THE PERIOD OF PLURALIZATION

For the first two decades after Retrocession, the BAROC almost completely monopolized the field of Buddhist organizations. This is no longer the case. The *World Directory of Buddhist Organizations*, updated annually and published by the Dharma-Wheel Publishing Group *(Falun Zazhi She)*, has seventeen entries under the rubric "Nationwide Buddhist Organizations"; and four of these are marked as revised entries since the previous year's edition *(Shijie Fojiao Tongxun Lu* 1994:261–262). The BAROC appears in this list as first among equals, and one notices many groups whose names suggest functions similar to those fulfilled previously by the BAROC alone. For instance, one may see the "Chinese Buddhist Temple Federation" *(Zhonghua Fosi Xiehui),* the "Buddha's Light International Association, ROC" *(Guoji Foguang Hui Zhonghua Zonghui),* the "Contemporary Buddhist Studies Association of the ROC" *(Zhonghua Minguo Xiandai Fojiaoxue Hui),* the "Chinese Buddhist *Saṅgha* Association" *(Zhongguo Fojiao Sengqie Hui,* not to be confused with the World Chinese Buddhist *Saṅgha* Council discussed earlier) and so on. Some list high BAROC officials as their chief executives, but many do not.

Such a situation would have been impossible only a short time ago. This chapter will be concerned with when and why this pluralization *(duoyuanhua)* took place, and what it means for Buddhism in Taiwan. After these general considerations, we will examine the two largest alternative Buddhist organizations on the island: Fo Kuang Shan, and the Buddhist Compassion Relief Tzu Chi Association (BCRTCA).

BACKGROUND

What does the term "pluralization" signify? Superficially, it refers to the proliferation of Buddhist organizations and groups other than the BAROC on Taiwan after Retrocession, particularly those that directly challenged the BAROC's hegemonic claim of representing Buddhists in the ROC nationwide. Looking below the surface, the term refers to the divergent ideals that these organizations represent; and here one distinction becomes apparent. Some groups, represented in this chapter by Fo Kuang Shan, do not necessarily deviate from the ideals promoted all along by the BAROC, but merely provide an alternative route for their realization. Others, represented here by the BCRTCA, articulate a new vision of Buddhist life and practice that has been explicitly adapted for Taiwan's current social and religious needs.

Chronology

Many scholars in Taiwan follow the lead of the sociologist Yao Lixiang in dating the "period of pluralization" to the early 1970s, which is when these two largest and most important rival groups were founded.[1] Although this periodization may be useful in some respects, one must use it cautiously for two reasons: First, one must not infer that the BAROC enjoyed complete hegemony over Buddhist affairs before 1970. As we shall see, at least one splinter organization pre–dates 1970, albeit by only a few years. More importantly, one must bear in mind the complaints raised by Dongchu and Nanting about the grudging participation and dues delinquency that plagued the BAROC during the early years. This indicates the presence of a significant population of Buddhists before 1970 for whom the BAROC was irrelevant, despised, or both.

Second, Yao wrote on the subject of Buddhist pluralization before some very important political developments of the late 1980s occurred and opened the floodgates for the establishment of alternative organizations. In Yao's articles, "pluralization" generally refers to the existence of a handful of rival organizations. Because of these political developments, which will be discussed below, the years since 1987 could be said to represent a new phase of increased pluralization. It would be more useful to take dates such as 1970, 1987, and 1989 as signposts demarcating periods of increasing intensity in the process of pluralization. The early complaints of the BAROC leadership indicate that the seeds of this phenomenon were present from the early 1950s, but remained underground because of such factors as poor communications, political turmoil, economic uncertainty, and martial law. The tendency towards pluralization first came to concrete expression in 1968 with the appearance of the first alternative organization, the Chinese Buddhist Layman's Association, that gathered steam during the 1970s when Fo Kuang Shan and the BCRTCA took root, and matured in the late 1980s and early 1990s with the establishment of groups that competed directly with the BAROC in all spheres.

Factors that Contributed to Pluralization

Several factors combined to break the BAROC's monopoly as an organization. Some of these factors existed within the BAROC itself; others were external.

Internal Factors.   In a real sense, the BAROC contributed to its own loss of hegemony in several ways, some of which were discussed in the previous chapter. For example, we have seen that the BAROC charter explicitly excludes the laity from occupying more than one-third of the leadership positions, whether in the National Congress, the board of directors, the board of supervisors, or any other subunit of the BAROC (BAROC charter, Section 4, Article 23. The charter is reproduced in

Lin Jindong 1958:233–239).[2] This regulation was founded on Buddhist traditions of hierarchy and deference, which place laymen above lay-women, nuns above laity, and monks above everyone. However, one of the hallmarks of Buddhism in the twentieth century has been the increased involvement of laity in spheres of activity previously reserved for clergy, and many laity now demand greater participation in the life and vision of the Buddhist religion.

Another internal factor already noted above is the extremely closed circle of leadership at the top of the BAROC hierarchy. As the years went by, and it became increasingly clear that only a small clique enjoyed access to real executive authority, more and more of the rank and file became disaffected and sought other avenues for activity.

Coupled with these two factors built into the very structure of the BAROC, there were other, more amorphous influences. Yao reports that, after the electoral improprieties of the Eighth National Congress in 1974 many Buddhist clergy resigned their membership in the BAROC (Yao 1988:243; see also Yang 1991:36). Another factor was the continued tension between "Taiwanese" and "mainlanders" in society. As we shall see, many of those who flocked to join the BCRTCA were drawn by the founder's humble origins in Taiwan village society and her appeal to nativist sentiments.

External Factors. While the above factors presaged schism within Taiwan Buddhism from an early date, pluralization really flowered only in the late 1980s, when the government made two decisions that transformed the political landscape within which Buddhism operated. The first was the lifting of martial law in 1987, and the second was the passage of the Law on the Organization of Civic Groups in 1989.

Lifting of Martial Law. For over fifty years, martial law was a feature of life in the ROC. Initially declared in 1934, it was applied over Taiwan in December 1949 by order of the Executive Yuan and acti-vated by an emergency decree issued by Chiang Kai-shek. Martial law superseded the ROC's constitution during the period of mobilization against the Communist rebellion, and effectively put the civilian gov-ernment under military supervision. In 1970, the Defense Ministry promulgated further restrictions, among which were the suspension of the rights to a free press, privacy of correspondence, free speech, free assembly; and to petition the government, give academic lectures, and practice religion. Enforcement of these provisions fell to the Taiwan Garrison Command, which acted upon this extraconstitutional authority to regulate travel to and from Taiwan, manage customs inspections, and enforce the above restrictions on political rights and freedoms (Tien Hung-mao 1989:110–112).[3]

As detrimental as all this may seem to the free practice of religion, it actually worked to the BAROC's advantage. As we saw in the previous chapter, the government looked to the BAROC until 1989 for verification of clergy wishing to study abroad, which gave the organization effective control over the clergy's access to higher education in America or Japan. Since the BAROC and other eminent monks in Taiwan during the period from the 1950s to the 1970s saw no benefit from foreign study, very few clergy went; and the majority of these found their own way.[4] Again, since the government looked to the BAROC to certify all applications for clergy wishing to travel abroad for any reason, the BAROC exerted tremendous control over Taiwan Buddhism's international image. In all areas of activity, the BAROC maintained a unique role as the official liaison between the Buddhist world and the government. It is no wonder, then, that during the tenth National Congress held in December 1982, the delegates passed a resolution that condemned calls for the lifting of martial law and the legalization of new political parties as "ridiculous" (*Zhongfohui Kan* [*BAROC Newsletter*] 18 [January 1, 1983]:1).

1989 Revised Law on the Organization of Civic Groups. While the lifting of martial law in 1987 undermined the BAROC's rights to act as a liaison between Buddhists and the ROC government, and paved the way for Buddhist temples, lecture halls, and individuals to bypass it and deal with the government directly, the 1989 Revised Law on the Organization of Civic Groups had the complementary effect of permitting other groups to form that could compete with the BAROC to fulfill its traditional functions. This law, originally intended to allow for the organization of opposition political parties, opened the way for organizations in other spheres of social and civic life to proliferate; and religion was no exception (Copper 1993:xxv, 71).

Before this bill was passed, ROC law had stipulated that there could be no more than one organization filling any "niche" in society. In other words, only one organization could exist with any given set of functions, area of jurisdiction, or sphere of membership. Thus, under the old system, no other organization could compete with the BAROC to be a nationwide organization of Buddhist temples and individuals, intermediate with the government, hold nationwide ordination sessions, or recruit members among Buddhists throughout the ROC. In addition, because the BAROC was also organized at the provincial, county, and metropolitan levels, no other group could compete in these more limited jurisdictions. As a result, while martial law gave BAROC certain necessary functions as a liaison between Buddhists and their government, the old restrictions on civic organizations ensured that *only* the BAROC could legally fulfill those functions.

The revised law changed the situation drastically. After 1989, the central government gave up the task of restricting the establishment of civic groups and political parties; the only remaining requirement was that such groups register with the Ministry of the Interior. The government no longer forbade the establishment of new groups based on the preexistence of another group fulfilling the same functions in the same geographical area and recruiting members from among the same constituency. The result of this law was even more dramatic than the ending of martial law, and has engendered a rapid expansion in the number of Buddhist groups in Taiwan, some of which have narrowly defined purposes, and some of which compete directly with the BAROC in all its functions (Jiang 1994).

With this background in mind, we will now turn our attention to three examples of organizations that arose and flourished on Taiwan since the late 1960s. The two largest and most influential of these, Fo Kuang Shan and the BCRTCA, arose before the lifting of martial law and the passage of the Revised Law on Civic Organizations, and so we will pay particular attention to the strategies they employed to justify their existence under the old system.

First, however, we will look at the earliest organization to challenge the BAROC's hegemony: the Chinese Buddhist Lay Association (CBLA).

THE CHINESE BUDDHIST LAY ASSOCIATION (*ZHONGHUA FOJIAO JUSHI HUI*)

This organization came into being as a protest against the exclusion of laity from BAROC power. As we have already noted, this exclusion was deliberate, and authority was concentrated in the hands of a small, closed group. However, many BAROC members were laypersons of proven administrative ability and leadership qualities, and these members quickly tired of being kept out of decision-making circles. One, a retired head of the National Police Administration named Li Qian, led a group of like-minded laypeople out of the BAROC to form their own organization in 1968 for laypeople only.

Although the CBLA was intended as another nationwide organization of Buddhist devotees, it stayed within the restrictions of the law by aiming its recruitment exclusively at laypeople. (One may speculate that the founder also had the high-level connections necessary to ensure smooth relations with the government.) Over the years, the CBLA has appealed mainly to active and retired government workers, and has devoted its energies primarily to social welfare work (Yao 1988:242–243; Nakamura et al. 1976:181).

The BAROC was not happy with this situation. Besides its firm belief that Buddhist laity ought to be subordinate to the clergy in all matters, it resented the competition for membership. While it is true that the two organizations, both corporate members of the World Fellowship of Buddhists, could cooperate in combating PRC influence within that international body, relations remained cool at home. In 1982 the *BAROC Newsletter* reprinted an editorial by the layman Tang Xiangqing concerning the CBLA. Despite the editor's disclaimer that this opinion piece did not necessarily represent the views of the editorial board, it still holds interest because of the sharpness of its criticism of the CBLA. The article decries the CBLA membership's unwillingness to subordinate themselves to clerical leadership and warns that the CBLA could fall into heresy in the name of "liberation" from clerical oversight (Tang Xiangqing 1982:4).

Li Qian and his followers constituted the vanguard of groups that sought new ways to practice Buddhism in Taiwan. Fo Kuang Shan and the BCRTCA followed, and attained nationwide influence during the period of martial law. We will now turn our attention to these two alternative organizations.

FO KUANG SHAN

Biography of Xingyun

In order to understand either Fo Kuang Shan or the BCRTCA, one must begin with their founders, as it is their vision, energy, and charisma that enabled their respective organizations to grow and elaborate as they have. The founder of Fo Kuang Shan is the Ven. Xingyun (or Hsing-yun), a monk of extraordinary fame and popularity under whose leadership a single temple in the southern part of Taiwan developed into a worldwide network of subtemples, foundations, social welfare agencies, and other auxiliary organizations. We encountered him once already in chapter four, writing of his struggle to find lodging as a young refugee monk in Taiwan in 1949. We will now look closely at his life and work.

Xingyun was born in Jiangdu, Jiangsu Province in 1927, the third child of a very poor family. This was the time of the Northern Expedition, in which Chiang Kai-shek's Nationalist forces subjugated the local warlords and unified China. Because of this and the subsequent War of Resistance against the Japanese, Xingyun's childhood was spent almost entirely among the stresses and uncertainties of war. In scattered autobiographical remarks, he tells of eating almost nothing but rice gruel with sweet potatoes day after day, both before and after joining the *saṅgha* (Xingyun 1994:206). Worse by far, however, was that in 1937, his father disappeared without a trace (Fu Chi-ying 1997:27). Xingyun believes these continuous hardships tempered him for a life of work and struggle, and at the same time imbued his character with a spirit of generosity and charity.

Xingyun left the household life in 1937 at the age of eleven to study under Zhikai of the Dajue Temple on Qixia Mountain near Nanjing, a very famous and illustrious Buddhist site. He went on to receive the full precepts there in 1941, and remained at Qixia Mountain to study at the Qixia *Vinaya* School *(Qixia Lüxue Yuan)*. Later he went for further study to the Jiaoshan Buddhist Studies Institute *(Jiaoshan*

Foxue Yuan). After completing his courses, he embarked on a busy career of educational, journalistic, and administrative work, in rapid succession becoming a magazine editor, high school principal, and abbot of the Huazang Temple in Nanjing.

In 1949, the fall of the mainland impelled him to leave Nanjing for Taiwan; and, as recounted earlier, he struggled for the first few months until he found lodgings. At first he stayed at the Yuanguang Temple in Chungli with Cihang; and, after the collapse of the latter's school, he followed Cihang in the search for shelter. Along with Cihang, Xingyun was one of the group of monks arrested and detained for twenty-three days (Fu Chi-ying 1997:83).

Nevertheless, as time went on, his fortunes improved; as more people within Buddhist circles learned of his seemingly boundless energy and capacity for hard work, he found himself more in demand to take on various projects and responsibilities. He worked for a time as editor-in-chief of *Rensheng,* Dongchu's Buddhist periodical, for which he contributed articles under the pen name "Mojia." In 1951 he was named chief of educational affairs for the Taiwan Buddhist Lecture Society. In 1952 he relocated to the eastern coastal town of Ilan to live in the Leiyin (Sound of Thunder) Temple; and during his tenure there he organized a Buddha-recitation society, a dharma-propagation society, a Buddhist choir, and a Buddhist student's association. At the same time he helped to establish a Buddhist Sunday school, a kindergarten, and Taiwan's first Buddhist dharma-propagation radio program (FG 3837c). Most surprising to him was his election to the BAROC board of directors and its standing committee after the Second National Congress in 1952, which he declined out of embarrassment over his own perceived youth and inexperience. He was twenty-five years old at this time (Xingyun 1952:2–3).

His activism on behalf of Buddhism enabled him to develop many contacts and gather many disciples, and he quickly began receiving invitations to preach and lecture from all over Taiwan. His followers began asking him to found permanent institutions closer to their homes, and so in 1955 he founded the Kaohsiung Buddhist Hall; in 1957 the Buddhist Cultural Services Center in Taipei; in 1962 he returned to Kaohsiung to found the Shoushan (Longevity Mountain) Temple, in which he also established the Shoushan Buddhist Studies Institute (the forerunner of the present-day Eastern Buddhist College) (FG 3837). He eventually accepted election to the BAROC board of directors standing committee, and held this position into the early 1990s. Although he attended meetings and participated actively, he does not appear to have regarded this body as a significant part of his endeavors.

The Founding and Elaboration of Fo Kuang Shan

The turning point in Xingyun's career came when, using some of the royalties from his publications, he purchased a bamboo-covered mountain overlooking the Ta Shu Rural District in Kaohsiung County in order to construct a new temple to be called Fo Kuang Shan, which he hoped would serve to fill Taiwan's need for a true "public monastery" *(shifang conglin)*. Within a short time, Xingyun put the new temple on a firm financial basis by diversifying sources of income:

1. royalties from his own publications;

2. agricultural rental income;

3. surplus donations to his social welfare enterprises;

4. income from dharma-meetings *(fahui youxiang);*

5. surpluses collected at Fo Kuang Shan's subtemples;

6. surplus contributions to Xingyun personally or any of Fo Kuang Shan's managers;

7. voluntary donations from domestic and overseas devotees;

8. membership dues (Foguangshan Zongwu Weiyuanhui 1979:43).

From its official founding *(kaishan)* on May 16, 1967, Fo Kuang Shan has continuously expanded. The original temple now covers the entire mountain and serves as a pilgrimage site for Buddhists from all over Taiwan, and its facilities house an enormous range of activities: Buddhist studies institutes offering courses in Chinese, English, and Japanese; a high school; a public library; several bookstores and gift shops; conference facilities capable of accommodating large-scale international gatherings; a museum; audiovisual and multimedia facilities;

classrooms for teaching flower arranging, martial arts, vegetarian cooking, and calligraphy, in addition to traditional Buddhist subjects; places for intensive Buddhist practice such as Seven Day Buddha-Recitation Retreats and other forms of group cultivation, as well as individual practices such as meditation and sealed confinement; the list goes on and on.

In addition to the original temple, Fo Kuang Shan has branched out to establish subtemples all over Taiwan and in several foreign countries. Xingyun recounts that new subtemples arose not from his own desire to extend his religious empire, but from his continuing island-wide popularity. For example, he tells the story of an engineer whom he had engaged to help design the Great Shrine Hall at Fo Kuang Shan. This engineer, a member of the Hakka minority, one day burst out, "Why do you only build temples in Hokkien areas? Why don't you build any in Hakka areas?" Xingyun resolved to begin seeking ways to establish a branch temple around Taoyuan, Hsinchu, Miaoli, and Toufen counties, areas of high Hakka concentration. Local devotees, who would benefit directly from the presence of the temple, provided the necessary funding (Xingyun 1994b:7–8). This was the way, Xingyun states, that all Fo Kuang Shan subtemples were founded, even the overseas branches. As of 1992, the organization had a total of fourteen temples around Taiwan, along with twenty-two lecture halls and lay practice establishments. In addition, it has thirty-seven overseas branches in Japan, Hong Kong, the Philippines, Malaysia, India, the United States, Canada, Brazil, the United Kingdom, Germany, France, Australia, New Zealand, and the Republic of South Africa. (Fo Kuang Shan Committee on Religious Affairs 1991:46–47 contains a directory of all branches.)

In addition, Fo Kuang Shan sponsors social welfare activities throughout Taiwan. One of the earliest programs was the Fo Kuang Clinic, founded at Shoushan in 1976 and moved to Fo Kuang Shan itself two years later. This facility offers free medical care, primarily to residents of Fo Kuang Shan but also to indigent members of the local community. In 1985, the organization established the "Cloud and Water Mobile Clinic," a system of vans equipped with medical supplies, driven by trained staff who deliver regular medical care to remote areas. Fo Kuang Shan also sponsors an annual "Winter Relief

Program," an emergency aid program, a "Friendship and Care Brigade" that visits residents of its senior citizens' home, an organ donor bank, a children's home, a retirement home for Fo Kuang Shan's retired staff and supporters, a cemetery, and the "Kuan Yin Life Conservation Group" for purchasing and freeing captured fish and birds (Fo Kuang Shan Committee on Religious Affairs 1979:43–44; 1992:32–35).

All of these activities took root during the period of martial law and prior to the liberalization of the laws on civic organizations. During this time, Xingyun managed to establish a large Buddhist organizational network by adapting to the prevailing legal environment. Even during the most repressive periods of the ROC's history on Taiwan, the government has never actively interfered with the establishment of Buddhist temples; it has only regulated the proliferation of civic organizations. Thus, by concentrating on founding temples, subtemples, and lecture halls, all of which existed as discrete organizations and were registered as corporate members of the BAROC, there was no danger of running afoul of the pre-1989 laws.

Developments in Fo Kuang Shan after 1989

The passage of the Revised Law on Civic Organizations in 1989 opened the way for Fo Kuang Shan to expand its activities in two ways: It could now compete more directly with the BAROC, and it could begin setting up a single, large-scale Buddhist umbrella organization.

The most obvious example of competition with the BAROC is in the staging of monastic ordinations. Soon after its foundation, Fo Kuang Shan entered the rotation for the annual BAROC-sponsored ordination, and held its first ordination session in 1977. The next ordination did not take place until 1990; however, after that the pace quickened tremendously, with other sessions in 1991, 1992, and 1993. In keeping with Xingyun's desire that Fo Kuang Shan emulate the mainland public monasteries of the past and with his early training at the Qixia *Vinaya* School, the ordination sessions at Fo Kuang Shan have generally been longer than the BAROC sessions, and have exposed the ordinands to more teachers and elders. For example, in contrast to the standard four-week BAROC period, the 1991 Fo Kuang Shan session lasted over three months. However, BAROC leaders do not seem to have been alienated by the competition, as many of them participated in this session, either standing alongside Xingyun as ordaining elders or aiding in the training of the ordinands (*Zhongfohui Kan* [*BAROC Newsletter*] 96 [May 15, 1991]:4).

In fact, this new competition may have spurred the BAROC to institute some reforms in its own ordinations. During the 1993 ordination session at the Guangde Temple in Kaohsiung County, the monk Jingxin was simultaneously the BAROC president, abbot of the host temple, and preceptor, which gave him an unusual opportunity to control the proceedings. He took advantage of this opportunity to introduce six specific reforms into the ordination intended to provide better training within a more solemn and religious environment. Two of these reforms were to lengthen the ordination session to six weeks, and to hold separate sessions for monks and nuns, rather than housing and training them together (*Zhongguo Fojiao Yuekan* [*Chinese Buddhism Monthly*] 37, no. 10 [October 1993]:8–9). I speculate that these reforms were inspired at least in part by the increased competition made possible by the dissolution of the BAROC's monopoly on monastic ordinations.

The second change that the 1989 law brought was that Xingyun now had a free hand to unify his many followers and organizations into a single, large-scale, nationwide body, a privilege previously reserved to the BAROC under the old, "one niche, one organization" rule. Accordingly, Xingyun began the very next year to plan for this new body. He called a meeting at the Fo Kuang Shan subtemple in Taipei, the Pumen Temple, on August 10, 1990, in order to choose a name and discuss the proposed organization's objectives and regulations. After the groundwork had been laid, the founding meeting of the Buddha's Light International Association, ROC (BLIA) took place on February 3, 1991, in the Sun Yat-sen Memorial Hall in Taipei.

Chapters of the BLIA rapidly arose in all countries where Fo Kuang Shan branch organizations existed, and more were proposed in other countries such as Holland, Thailand, and Singapore. With this rapid expansion, the leadership decided to hold a second organizing conference to include representatives from countries other than the ROC. This second meeting took place in October 1991 at Fo Kuang Shan, and there it was decided that the first BLIA General Conference should take place outside the ROC. Accordingly, this conference convened May 16–20 at the Los Angeles Music Center. The second General Conference was held October 16–20, 1993, back at Fo Kuang Shan (Fo Kuang Shan Committee of Religious Affairs 1991:45; Buddha's Light International Association 1992:7–8).

"Fo Kuang Buddhism" as a New Form of Chinese Buddhist Sectarianism

Pluralism is not just a matter of institutions competing for members and resources. From a religious standpoint, the concrete growth and elaboration of Fo Kuang Shan as an institution is less significant than the vision that drives it. This vision, which Xingyun refers to as "Fo Kuang Buddhism," marks Fo Kuang Shan as an example of pluralism within Taiwan Buddhism, and inspires believers to join and contribute. Fo Kuang Buddhism has two aspects: the rationalization and standardization of Buddhist life and practice, and the articulation of the religious beliefs and values that inspire this life and that these practices enact.

Standardization. Some modern critics of Taiwan Buddhism have identified one of its main problems as lack of unity. For example, Lan Jifu, a prominent historian of Buddhism in Taiwan, claims that the absence of a centralized structure of discipline and authority impeded Buddhism from adapting to the rapidly changing conditions of Taiwan society in the 1970s and 1980s. Because the BAROC has no coercive authority over any of its members in matters of practice and ideology, all individual and corporate members are free to pursue their own goals and ideals, with no need to cooperate. Even when faced with gross misconduct on the part of clerical members, the most that the BAROC can do is revoke their ordination certificates (if they were ordained at a BAROC ordination session) and expel them from the organization, a move that hardly amounts to laicization. Furthermore, the BAROC has no authority whatever to oust such members from their temples, or to compel their disciples to seek spiritual guidance elsewhere. In the case of lay members, the BAROC has no recourse other than to revoke their membership (Lan 1987:51).[5]

The complex of temples, organizations, and activities subsumed under the name Fo Kuang Shan constitutes a different kind of organization from the BAROC. The BAROC is an umbrella organization providing government liaison and other services to its members. Fo Kuang Shan, it may be argued, is a religious order based on the thought and charisma of Xingyun. Like the Chogye Order of Korea or any of the Japanese schools of Buddhism, members subscribe to a more detailed ideal of the Buddhist life than do BAROC members; and Fo Kuang Shan, through a variety of sanctions, can enforce adherence to this ideal more effectively. Fo Kuang Shan has thus been able to achieve a much greater degree of unity than has Taiwan Buddhism as a whole.

This unity operates at a variety of levels. A simple example: Every so often, debates arise about standardizing monastic garb throughout the ROC (see, for example, the opinions collected in *Zhongguo Fojiao Yuekan* [*Chinese Buddhism Monthly*] 9, no. 9 [May 1965]:10–25.) However, these debates invariably prove inconclusive because there is no agreed-upon body to set and enforce standards. Therefore, to this day monks and nuns may wear clothing of any cut or color, constrained only by the provisions of the *vinaya* and the need to be recognized as clergy by their fellow citizens. At Fo Kuang Shan, on the other hand, monastic robes have been standardized to the extent that they function as uniforms. Once one knows the system, one may know whether a monk or nun is a novice, a student, or a fully ordained cleric simply by looking at his or her robes.

Another example of this standardization on a higher systemic level is the ranking of clergy. Because Fo Kuang Shan is a large, complex organization involving hundreds of clergy, such human resource issues as the maximum utilization of each cleric's skills and talents, evaluation of job performance, and individual advancement cannot be left to the vagaries of personal relationships and recommendations. The possibilities for factionalism and grievances would be too great. Therefore, Fo Kuang Shan relies on more modern, impersonal management techniques. The clergy are divided into grades and ranks based partly upon seniority, but also on "personal cultivation, job skills, and scholastic achievement, with consideration given to contribution and attitude" (Fo Kuang Shan Committee of Religious Affairs 1991:43–44). The board of directors holds an annual evaluation meeting in which it decides whom to promote. As with the military, eligibility for certain jobs within the Fo Kuang Shan system depends upon attaining a certain rank. For instance, the Senior Monastics Department has supervisory authority over all activities within Fo Kuang Shan. Only clergy of grade three or higher may vote in the elections to this department (Fo Kuang Shan Committee of Religious Affairs 1991:43). In this way, Fo Kuang Shan attempts to provide a fair, impartial, and open forum for deciding upon issues of evaluation and promotion.

In and of itself, this approach is not an innovation; the great public monasteries of the past, facing similar needs for order and fairness, also divided resident clergy into ranks that determined the jobs they could legitimately volunteer for, as well as their order of precedence in seating and processions. Furthermore, the senior monks of these temples met twice annually to recommend certain clerics for promotion (Welch 1967:36–46). However, Fo Kuang Shan uses a different system of grades and ranks than did the old public monasteries, dispensing with the traditional division into "eastern" and "western" ranks and inventing a new terminology. From bottom to top, these are:

1. Pure grade *(qingjing shi):* six ranks altogether, each rank one year

2. Study grade *(xue shi):* three ranks altogether, each rank three years

3. Practice grade *(xiu shi):* three ranks altogether, each rank four years

4. Open rank *(kai shi):* three ranks altogether, each rank five years

5. Master *(da shi)* or elder *(zhanglao)* (Foguangshan Zongwu Weiyuanhui 1994:94)

More substantively, the Fo Kuang Shan system relies upon a formal board that decides on promotions based upon recommendations received from below and evaluated according to standard written policies, whereas the old system relied upon a more informal gathering of senior officers who based their decisions upon personal observation. In this sense, the Fo Kuang Shan system operates more like a military review board than like the monastic system of the past.

Religious Dimensions. However, Fo Kuang Buddhism is more than just a matter of organization and standardization; it is also a religious vision. Over the years, Xingyun has articulated a set of principles for producing a Buddhism able to operate within the modern world. These principles have been collected in a book entitled *How to Be a Fo Kuang Buddhist* (Xingyun 1987. In this section, page numbers in parentheses refer to this work). Some of the most important of these principles are:

1.   The Fo Kuang Buddhist commits him- or herself completely to the organization and to wider society. In opposition to the "cloud and water" monk of the past, he or she accepts Fo Kuang Shan's vision of the Buddhist life and remains within the system loyally to the end. He or she places the *saṅgha,* the work of the temple, and the cause of Buddhism above the self.

2.   "Fo Kuang Buddhism" aims at this-worldly goals rather than at goals in other worlds or future lives. In elaborating upon this topic, Xingyun takes as his starting point the Mahayana Buddhist doctrine of the Two Truths, the worldly (Skt: *saṁvṛti-satya*) and the absolute (Skt: *paramārtha-satya*). The first of these refers to truth as conventionally perceived by ordinary consciousness, the second to the realization that all of these conventional perceptions have no absolute basis or permanence, but rather are constructed from the ever-changing causes and conditions of the mind and the world it regards—a subject and its objects which themselves are not ultimately separate and distinct. Through the ages, realization of the second truth comes only with enlightenment, and so it has received more emphasis as an object of philosophical reasoning and meditation. However, Xingyun seeks to revalue conventional truth in order to enable the Fo Kuang Buddhist to act effectively and compassionately within the present world. He explicitly rejects pessimistic evaluations of this world as a "flaming house" or a prison. He says:

> Undeniably, the main cause of the decline of Buddhism today is its excessive concern with attaining supramundane liberation and its failure to reach out to the people. Consequently, people mistakenly believe that Buddhism is negative and pessimistic and do not know that the spirit of Mahayana Buddhism is to serve society (p. 12).

Based on this line of reasoning, Xingyun urges his monks and nuns to become active within society, and to pursue training in service occupations such as medicine and teaching. Liberation from the cycle of birth and death must be held as a long-term goal to be achieved gradually through thorough study and practice; the immediate goal is to develop the virtues of compassion and morality (pp. 15–16).

Coupled with this emphasis on the conventional world over the transcendent is a stress on the present life over future lives. This is a direct effort to reorient Chinese Buddhism. During Xingyun's childhood and early years as a monk, Chinese Buddhist monks and nuns frequently found themselves drawn more and more into the business of conducting funerals; some became quite dissolute because their religious cultivation was stymied by the amount of time they devoted to this lucrative pursuit (Chen-hua 1992:14–16, 80–88). Many early reformers, such as Taixu and Yinguang, as well their later heirs in Taiwan such as Yinshun and Zhenhua, decried this practice as a major cause of Buddhism's poor image and its decline into mere commercialism. Consequently, under the banner of "Buddhism for Human Life" *(rensheng)* or "Buddhism in the Human Realm" *(renjian),* they called for a new orientation towards the teaching and transformation of living human beings rather than dead ones.

Xingyun, who quotes both Taixu and Yinguang in support of his vision of Buddhism, echoes them here as well. Funerals, when performed correctly in form and spirit, can be of benefit to both the deceased and their survivors. However, a greater portion of a Fo Kuang Buddhists's time and energy must go into improving the life of the living, in terms of both their present material needs and their spiritual edification (p. 14).

3.   Privatism in any form is another target of Xingyun's reform ideals. As noted earlier, one of his goals in founding Fo Kuang Shan was to recreate a public monastery for Chinese Buddhism worldwide. The distinguishing feature of a public monastery is that it serves as an ordination center for the *sangha* as a whole. In order to keep the system impartial, a public monastery of the past on the Chinese mainland did not permit its resident clergy to privately accept disciples (Welch 1967:132). We have already seen that, at an ordination, the BAROC prevents the development

of any possible tonsure-family nepotism by providing the ordaining masters and training personnel itself, effectively turning the host temple into a temporary public monastery. Xingyun, in founding Fo Kuang Shan and then moving to establish it as an permanent ordination center in its own right, needed a different solution. Thus, although Fo Kuang Shan technically should be considered a hereditary temple, Xingyun has decreed that its monks and nuns may not privately accept disciples, in conformity with the great public monasteries of the past.

In passing this rule, Xingyun's intent was to raise the quality of both monastic and lay disciples at Fo Kuang Shan. He cites the early Republican-period reformer Yinguang, who thought that the ease with which monks accepted disciples was a cause of Buddhism's moral decline. In order to remove this cause, Xingyun insists on a collective system of accepting disciples based strictly on seniority. Thus, if any layperson comes to a member of the Fo Kuang Shan clergy wishing to seek tonsure or to become a lay disciple, that cleric may grant the request, but only on behalf of the most senior clerical member of his or her generation. That entire generation then becomes the collective master of the new disciple.

Besides the prevention of favoritism during ordination sessions, this system has several other effects. It keeps clergy from competing for disciples; it prevents undue attachments between individual masters and disciples, or cliques based on master–disciple alignments, from forming; finally, it reinforces the idea that the *saṅgha* as a whole is a source of refuge representing the third of the Three Jewels, and not just one individual master, however charismatic (pp. 20–21).

Xingyun inveighs against other forms of privatism as well. He forbids his clergy to save money privately, except for specific purposes, and then only in their temple's treasury. Otherwise, all their income is to be used freely toward the propagation of Buddhism. He does not allow clergy to build their own temples, as this would entangle them too much in the pursuit of funding and then administrative work, with little time for study, cultivation, or dharma-propagation. Finally, he discourages his clergy from becoming involved in special relationships with any devotees or donors, as this would also encourage selfishness and cliquishness (pp. 21–27).

4. Xingyun has sought in many ways to involve the laity more deeply in the Buddhist life, frequently blurring the distinction between the clerical and lay realms. Thus, not only are laypeople involved in the day-to-day operation of Fo Kuang Shan in specific jobs as secretaries, janitors, hosts, gift shop clerks, and so forth; but the temple also houses an order of lay female celibates as well (Fo Kuang Shan Committee of Religious Affairs 1991:3). While Fo Kuang Shan shares these characteristics in common with other temples in Taiwan, it does have one program that is, to my knowledge, unique: the "Short-term Novitiate Program," in which interested persons may live the monastic life for a specified period of time without committing themselves to remain in the *sangha* for life, as is usually the expectation within Chinese Buddhism (Fo Kuang Shan Committee of Religious Affairs 1991:26–27).

In the heading to this section, I called Fo Kuang Buddhism a new form of Chinese Buddhist sectarianism. While Fo Kuang Buddhism does not qualify as a "sect" in the technical sociological sense,[6] I use the term "sectarianism" to indicate a consciousness that, within the overall context of Chinese (or even just Taiwan) Buddhism, the ideals and practices of one's group are unique to it, and that these are not transplantable to or practicable within other Buddhist groups. Thus, one may view Fo Kuang Shan as a sectarian phenomenon based on the following considerations:

(1) It is based upon a comprehensive religious vision as articulated by its founder, Xingyun. Furthermore, both he and his followers see this vision as sufficiently different from Buddhism as practiced elsewhere in Taiwan that it may only be actualized within the context of Fo Kuang Shan or one of its subsidiaries; one may not practice "Fo Kuang Buddhism" in other temples; (2) Disciples join the system because of their conviction of the value of this vision, and they generally remain within Fo Kuang Shan for life. Although there are cases of clergy ordained there who subsequently go their own way, such instances are rare;[7] (3) It breaks with many aspects of traditional Chinese Buddhism in order to adapt to modern circumstances, such as in the rationalization of the evaluation and promotion system,

and the deliberate blurring of boundaries between the clergy and the laity.

Conclusions

The visitor or pilgrim to Fo Kuang Shan is struck by a number of things: the immense thirty-two-meter Buddha-image overlooking the plain below the mountain, the Pure Land Cave with its life-sized diorama of the preaching of the Lotus Sutra complete with statues of the 1250 arhats in attendance, and the sheer size of the temple community. A somewhat closer examination reveals the complex and highly ramified organizations and enterprises administered within the sprawling facilities and satellites. However, I believe that Fo Kuang Shan's real significance within Chinese Buddhism lies in its articulation of a religious vision rooted in Taixu's earlier reforms, and in its establishment of a monastic/lay cooperative structure to actualize that vision within a society that is rapidly moving from the industrial to the information age. The casual visitor may be impressed by the amount of money and resources required to construct and maintain Fo Kuang Shan's physical plant and corporate infrastructure, but I suggest that it is impossible to understand how the temple can command such a high level of contributions without understanding the vision that motivates people to give. This vision, combined with Xingyun's personal energy and charisma, has allowed Fo Kuang Shan to grow and diversify to an astonishing extent, both during and after the period of martial law.

THE BUDDHIST COMPASSION RELIEF TZU CHI ASSOCIATION

The second of the two great successes of the period of pluralization is the BCRTCA *(Fojiao Ciji Gongde Hui),* founded by the nun Zhengyan (Cheng-yen). This organization is larger than Fo Kuang Shan, and it occupies a very different niche in the modern world of Taiwan Buddhism. However, like Fo Kuang Shan, it cannot be understood apart from its founder, and so we will begin our discussion with a consideration of her life.

Biography of Zhengyan[8]

In 1937, a young girl was born in Qingshui village, Taichung county, to a family named Wang; and her parents named her Jinyun. She was the first child born to the household; and as other brothers and sisters arrived, she helped care for them. Her mother ran the house but was ill much of the time; her father operated several movie theaters, which took him away from the house for long periods. Jinyun's early childhood coincided with the Sino-Japanese War and World War Two, and she quickly learned to run for cover when she heard the air raid sirens.

She was a model filial daughter, but also prone to visionary experiences. Once in 1952, her mother fell seriously ill with a perforated ulcer and needed emergency surgery. For three days, Jinyun prayed to Guanyin and vowed that, in order for her mother to recover, she would trade twelve years of her own life and begin eating a vegetarian diet. During the three nights, she dreamed the same dream: She saw a small Buddhist temple with a large door in the middle and a smaller door on either side. There was an altar with a large Buddha-image upon it, and her mother lay stretched out on a bamboo pallet in front of it. Jinyun saw herself kneeling by a small fire near the pallet, attempting to prepare some medication. As she did so, she suddenly felt a warm breeze coming from one of the smaller doors; and when she looked up, a beautiful woman seated on a white cloud floated into the temple. Jinyun instinctively knelt in front of the woman, who tipped a bundle of medicines from a bottle into Jinyun's outstretched hands. Jinyun took the bundle, opened it, and gave it to her mother, at which point the dream faded. After three days of prayers and vows and three nights of this dream, her mother recovered completely without surgery. Jinyun subsequently kept her vow and began eating a Buddhist vegetarian diet.

Sometime prior to 1960, the family moved from Qingshui to Fengyuan; and as Jinyun continued to grow, she divided her time between helping run the household and traveling with her father as he attended to his theaters. As she helped him balance the books and collect accounts, she acquired some competence in business. However, in 1960 her father suddenly collapsed in his office, complaining of a severe headache. She arranged for a car to take them along a bumpy

road to their home. A doctor came and found his blood pressure exces-
sively high, and her father died before any treatment could be given.

Jinyun was torn by his death for a long time. On the one hand, she
blamed herself for making him endure the rough ride home instead of
seeking medical help immediately. On the other hand, as she contem-
plated his corpse and realized that he was no longer there, a persistent
question formed in her mind: "Where is my father?" She asked herself
this question over and over for many days, until her maternal grand-
mother finally took her to see a shaman (jitong), who told them he had
descended to the "Hell of Those Who Died Wrongful Deaths"
(wangsicheng; on this term, see Morohashi 1984, 6:222c). This answer left
her unsatisfied. Later, she picked up a book on Buddhist doctrine from
a local temple and read the words, "Where there is birth, there is also
death," and this answer solved the question for her.

To resolve her feelings of guilt, she performed repentance rituals at
the Ciyun Temple in Fengyuan. Afterwards, she visited this temple frequently and became friendly with Xiudao, a nun who had studied in
Japan during the Japanese colonial period. Her contact with Xiudao
and the other nuns led her to consider for the first time the possibility of seeking ordination herself, and that year, she made her first
attempt to leave the household life. After obtaining a recommendation
from Xiudao, she boarded a train heading north and went on to the
Jingxiu Hall in the Taipei suburb of Hsi-chih (which, as the reader may
recall, had also been the refuge of Cihang). However, within three days,
her mother found her and compelled her to return home.

Even as she resumed her household responsibilities, Jinyun continued to frequent the Ciyun Temple near her home. She found herself more and more dissatisfied with the nuns' reliance on "funeral
Buddhism" for their livelihood, and made another set of vows that, if
she were ever ordained, she would observe: First, she would accept no
alms from lay supporters, but would instead live by Baizhang Huaihai's
ancient dictum, "A day without work is a day without food." Second,
she would find ways to extend the spirit of Buddhism to all levels of
society.

She finally left the household for good in 1961. One day, while har-
vesting rice alongside the nuns of the Ciyun Temple, Xiudao abrupt-
ly asked her, "Do you want to go seek ordination?" Jinyun was so star-

tled that she could only stare at the nun. Xiudao continued, "Certainly you do, and right now!" At that point Jinyun's resolve strengthened, and she agreed, "Yes, right now!" They dropped their tools; and Jinyun, without returning home first and carrying nothing but the clothing, jewelry, and money she had at that moment, went with Xiudao to the train station. They took the first train, which happened to be southbound, and proceeded to the southeastern city of Taitung. They settled for a while in a Japanese-era shrine on a mountain nearby, performing austerities and gleaning local fields for their sustenance. During this time, two of Xiudao's disciples from the Ciyun Temple found them; and the four women resided together.

With only two sets of clothing between them and the weather getting colder, the two knew that they needed to find more secure lodgings; but rather than return to the Ciyun Temple, as Xiudao's two disciples wished them to do, Xiudao and Jinyun went to the Qingjue Temple in the resort town of Zhiben (Chih-pen). The disciples, disappointed, returned to Fengyuan and informed Jinyun's mother of her whereabouts. Her mother promptly came with one of Jinyun's uncles and demanded that she return home. This time, Jinyun refused. She removed all her jewelry; and, keeping only a wristwatch and her dress, she gave everything back to them and told them she would remain in the temple. Thus she finally broke with her family and former responsibilities.

After a time in Zhiben, some devotees invited Jinyun to go to Hualien, a town on the east coast known mainly for its marble quarries and attractive scenery. She stayed for seven days, and then returned to Taitung briefly; but by 1962 she had returned to Hualien. Although she did not know it at the time, she would make this town her home thereafter.

On her second visit, she went to a small temple called the Puming (Universal Brightness) Temple that honored the bodhisattva Kṣitigarbha (Ch: *Dizang*). To her amazement, this was the temple Jinyun had seen in her dream many years before when her mother was ill. A member of the committee of laypeople who managed this temple, Mrs. Xu, developed an affection for Jinyun, and arranged to have a small room built for her onto the back of the building. She witnessed as Jinyun shaved her own head and picked for herself the dharma-name Xiucan.

In early 1963, the annual BAROC ordination session was to take place at the Linji Chan Temple in Taipei; and Jinyun felt that the time had finally arrived for her to become a nun. She took the train to Taipei and arrived at the temple during the registration period. However, during her registration interview, a problem arose: She did not have a tonsure-master, having shaved her own head, and so was ineligible. Dejected, she went to the Huiri Lecture Hall, thinking that she would buy a set of *The Collected Works of Taixu* to take back to Hualien.

It so happened that Yinshun, an active participant in many BAROC ordinations, was residing at the lecture hall at the time. He greeted her and learned of her situation, for which he offered his sympathy. As she was preparing to leave, she suddenly turned to the cleric who was to drive her to the train station and begged him to ask Yinshun to be her tonsure master. The cleric declared this was impossible, as Yinshun did not know her, and had only taken four disciples his entire life. She persisted and went to Yinshun with the request; and he consented, saying that he felt a strong sense of affinity with this young woman. As he tonsured her, he gave her an exhortation that has been her maxim ever since: "At all times do everything for Buddhism, everything for sentient beings!" *(Shishikeke wei fojiao, wei zhongsheng)*. He also gave her a new, official dharma-name: Zhengyan. She raced back to the Linji Chan Temple, arrived during the last hour of registration, and was ordained at the end of the thirty-two day session. At this time she took three more vows for herself: not to be a dharma-master *(fashi)*, not to be the abbess of any temple, and not to take tonsure disciples. She was twenty-six years old.

The newly ordained Zhengyan returned to Hualien and took up residence in her room behind the Puming Temple. During the next few years she engaged in a serious study of the Lotus Sutra, as well as in the practices of copying it over by hand and of burning incense scars on her forearm, dedicating the merit to living beings. Her life was especially difficult at this time because of her vow not to accept alms. She began a brief career of lecturing on the sutra at various venues, and attracted a core group of thirty female lay devotees who loved her earnestness and compassion.

Beginning in May 1963, she again took up the practice of austerities, eating only one meal a day and worshipping the Buddha. At this time, a strange phenomenon was noted: Every night, from the police dispatcher's station behind the temple, a light could be seen coming from the roof of her small room and around the doorframe. Zhengyan was unaware of the controversy this was causing among the temple's lay committee. Some were disturbed by the light, and attributed it to demonic influences. Others thought that her room ruined the geomantic properties (*fengshui*) of the temple site. When Zhengyan finally did find out about the disputes within the committee, she voluntarily moved out of the temple and took a room at Mrs. Xu's house. She did, however, maintain contact with the temple, often leading groups of devotees back there for religious practice. Besides her vow not to accept alms, she developed three more guiding principles for her emerging community: not to perform funerals, not to put on dharmameetings (*fahui,* a major source of income for most temples), and not to seek donations. She and her disciples took up manufacturing candles and baby booties in order to support themselves.

The seeds for the BCRTCA were sown in 1966 by two events that altered the course of Zhengyan's life. On her way out of a small private hospital in Fenglin where she had been visiting an ill disciple, she saw a pool of blood on the lobby floor. She asked where it had come from, and was told that it was the blood of an aboriginal woman who had had a miscarriage. The woman's kinsmen had spent eight hours transporting her to the clinic, but the doctor refused to see her unless they could pay a deposit of N.T. $8000 (about U.S. $200 at that time). They did not have the money, and so had no choice but to take the woman back out again. She subsequently died of the blood loss.

While thoughts of this incident were still preying upon Zhengyan's mind, three Roman Catholic nuns came to see her in order to convert her. They talked about many things, but the most significant topic for Zhengyan was that of social action. The nuns pointed out that while Christian groups in Taiwan were engaged in many different kinds of social-welfare work, Buddhism appeared to be doing nothing to benefit people in society. Zhengyan gave a lot of thought to the plight of the poor in eastern Taiwan and to the nuns' words.

She decided to leave Hualien and go to Yinshun's temple in Chiayi in order to be with him for a time. However, when her disciples heard of her plans, they came in a group and begged her to stay. After some discussion, she agreed to stay on the condition that they help her to carry out an idea. They should each get a bamboo cylinder to use as a kind of savings bank. Every day, before they went to the market to buy food, they were to put five Taiwan cents (about one-fifth of an American penny) into the bank for the poor. At the same time, everyone would make one extra pair of baby booties each day, and set aside the proceeds to add to the fund. She hoped in this way to raise enough money each month to be able to put up the deposit required for one indigent person to receive medical attention. Her followers agreed, and Zhengyan consented to stay in Hualien.

These thirty followers put the plan into action, and word of their activities quickly spread among their friends in the market. Other people liked the idea, and they also began to participate. Sensing the need for an organization to collect and administer the funds, Zhengyan met with all the participants on March 24, 1966, and formally organized the Buddhist Association for the Merit of Overcoming Difficulties and Compassionate Relief *(Fojiao Kenan Ciji Gongde Hui)*. All monies collected were subsequently deposited under the association's name. (The current name of the Association [the BCRTCA] was made official in 1980, when it registered as a civic organization with the government.)

At this point, Zhengyan's story becomes the story of the association, and so it is appropriate to pause and note how the patterns of her early life have influenced the association's growth and orientation.

First, Zhengyan had the opportunity in her youth to develop some business skills. She began early in her childhood to help her father manage his movie theater business, which she took over completely after his death. This put her in a good position to run her temple's cottage industries, and to attend to the management of the association in its early phase.

Second, many of her most formative experiences had to do with issues of medical care. At different points in her early life, she was traumatized by her mother's illness, her father's sudden death and her attendant grief and guilt at not having gotten him to a doctor in time, and the death of the anonymous aboriginal woman whose family lacked the funds to obtain treatment. The dream she dreamed for three consecutive nights during her mother's illness involved her futilely attempting to prepare medicine on her own and then receiving medicine directly from a Guanyin-like figure.

Third, she was given to making and keeping a series of difficult vows, and she showed herself willing and able to undertake severe ascetic practices. She also made the very filial prayer that she would exchange twelve years of her own life for her mother to recover from her ulcer. These things demonstrate Zhengyan's remarkable ability to deny her own gratification in the pursuit of larger goals, as well as her determination to achieve them.

Finally, she appears surprisingly modern in several respects. Even while she was so attracted to Buddhism, she actively rebelled against many aspects of traditional Chinese Buddhism that she found distasteful, such as the excessive dependence on funeral rites and alms. It is also significant that when she wanted to purchase reading materials for further study at the time when she thought she would have to delay her ordination, she chose the works of Taixu, and that she felt such a deep (and mutual) affinity for Taixu's direct disciple Yinshun. In later years she, like Xingyun of Fo Kuang Shan and many others, has made use of Yinshun's modification of Taixu's "Buddhism for Human Life" *(rensheng fojiao)* into "Buddhism in the Human Realm" *(rejian fojiao)* as a slogan and a guiding principle.

The Development of the Association

After the founding meeting in 1966, the association grew quite rapidly; and within a year the Puming Temple proved too small to handle the stream of devotees who came to visit, the business of administering the association, and the work of publishing its monthly newsletter. Thus, in the fall of 1967, Zhengyan approached her mother directly to purchase the land necessary for the foundation of a new temple, to be called the Still Thoughts Pure Abode *(Jingsi Jingshe)*. The main shrine hall was completed in 1969.

This may appear to be a breach of her vow not to solicit donations; however, the success of the association had forced her to rethink many of her previous vows. Rather than abrogate them completely, she decided that she would be willing to do things on behalf of the association and its work that she would not do for herself or her temple.

For example, the association attracted many young women who asked her to take them as tonsure-disciples. She consented to this on the strict condition that they join the association and participate actively in its work. All of her disciples, lay and ordained, take as their motto, "The Master's resolve is my resolve, the Buddha's mind is my mind" *(Yi shi zhi wei ji zhi, yi fo xin wei ji xin)*. Similarly, the founding of the Still Thoughts Pure Abode was for the purpose of giving the association adequate space to manage its operations, and Zhengyan became its abbess for the sake of the association. She and her nuns still refuse all donations for their own upkeep, opting instead to pursue their livelihood through handicrafts. They have also steadfastly refused to perform funerals or hold dharma-meetings.

The association took its first client in April 1966, a mainland Chinese widow who was unable to walk and had no one to take care of her. Deciding on a policy of providing complete relief services, the association sent volunteers to clean her house, take her to medical appointments, and provide for her until she died. As collections increased, the association took on more clients, providing them the same level of service and the same promise not to cut off aid halfway.

Another turning point came in 1978, when Zhengyan suffered her first attack of angina pectoris. At this time, friends advised her to make out her will and put her affairs in order; and from then on she needed to keep medication close at hand at all times. The following year, she had another attack in the middle of the night and was unable to find her medication, an event that led her to realize that she might die at any moment and that the association was not prepared to carry on its work without her. Thus, she began thinking about ways to put the association on a firmer foundation for the future.

She decided that the solution was to have the association collect funds to construct its own hospital in Hualien. In the first place, Hualien had no modern medical facilities, and many of the people the association sought to serve died during the long and uncertain trip to Taipei. In the second place, the association was locally dependent on small and dingy clinics that required large deposits and could not provide adequate care. In the third place, the association was often forced to send patients to Christian missionary hospitals, which raised the possibility of losing the patients to Christianity. With its own hospital, the association could avert this possibility, in addition to which there would be no further need to waste resources supporting inferior facilities, and more money could be ploughed back into supporting the association.

Thus, when Yinshun came to spend the summer in 1979, Zhengyan broached the idea with him, and he agreed to serve as the chairman of the board to direct the enterprise. The first donation, fifteen *liang* (.5625 kg.) of gold, came from a professor at Tung Hai University; and Zhengyan also received a lot of aid from sympathetic government officials, especially then-provincial governor Lin Xianggang, in surveying possible sites and expediting the paperwork. At one point, a Japanese businessman offered to donate eight billion New Taiwan dollars, the equivalent of U.S. $200,000,000, which would have been enough to complete the project without further fundraising. However, for reasons that will become clear, Zhengyan refused the offer, insisting that her followers in Taiwan raise the money themselves.

After the association had raised enough money to begin work and had settled on a site, it held the formal groundbreaking on February 2, 1984, with Zhenhua as master of ceremonies, and several government officials in attendance, including Lee Teng-hui, the future president of the ROC. Lee, although a Presbyterian, was sufficiently impressed with the organization's work that he made a donation and joined the association on the spot.

However, the hospital was far from complete, and further difficulties lay ahead. The association had, over the five years since Zhengyan conceived the project, raised only N.T. $30 million of the estimated N.T. $800 million needed. More seriously, the military unexpectedly intervened and declared the site of the groundbreaking a security zone, and no amount of intervention by friends in the government could persuade them to permit construction to proceed. The association moved quickly to find another site, and the second groundbreaking took place on April 24, 1984. The excitement generated by the formal commencement of construction stimulated increased donations; and the first building, a five-story medical facility with 250 beds, was completed two years later. In 1987, the association broke ground for a second building with an additional 350 beds.

Since then, Zhengyan has augmented the hospital with other projects. The Buddhist Tzu Chi Nursing School opened its doors in 1989;

and of the first graduating class of one hundred, about one-half joined the hospital staff. After that, Zhengyan proposed the construction of a medical school, which broke ground in March 1992, and opened in 1994. It currently enrolls about 200 students. The association is now planning to construct an entire university around the medical school, which will offer a complete educational curriculum for the people of the east coast.

Since its founding in 1966, the growth of the association has been staggering. At its inception, it had thirty members; and it raised N.T. $28,788 (about U.S. $720) during the first year. By 1986, the numbers had grown to over 80,000. By 1990, the association broke the one-million-member mark; and, by 1992, this number had more than doubled. As of 1994, the BCRTCA has about 3,500,000 members, including those in its international branches in the United States, Japan, Canada, England, Malaysia, and Singapore, with the U.S. branch the fastest-growing. This means that in Taiwan, about one-tenth of the population belongs to the association (Lu 1992:6–7). The relief fund in 1994 stood at N.T. $1.7 billion (Lu 1994:5).

The Association as a Lay Organization

As noted above, Fo Kuang Shan is primarily a large temple housing thousands of monks and nuns; and it is administered as a large, highly diversified corporation. Its most conspicuous symbol is the large, gold Buddha-image visible from all of the surrounding countryside. The BCRTCA, on the other hand, is not especially identified with the Still Thoughts Pure Abode, which has not grown appreciably since its establishment in 1967. The only expansions it has undergone have been in order to accommodate the association's increased need for workspace and the greater number of overnight lay visitors. The main shrine hall is still very small and simple, and the small group of resident nuns continues to support itself through handicrafts. When the association establishes branches in other cities or countries, they are uniformly lay associations, not branch temples. Far from being a corporation, the association functions as a family.

The center of the family is Zhengyan herself, who, I believe, to a greater degree than Xingyun, relies on her own charisma to lead.

Scholars in Taiwan have offered various explanations to account for her appeal. Jiang points out that she is an extremely eloquent speaker in the Taiwanese (or Hokkien) dialect, which would make her the only national-level Buddhist leader in Taiwan (at least until 1989, when Jingxin became president of the BAROC) to embrace Taiwanese culture (Jiang 1993a:94). Lu points out that Zhengyan's grassroots support comes almost entirely from the native Taiwanese and Hakka populations, and that the success of her association engenders pride in the people's ability to dispense with foreign (particularly American) aid in favor of self-help.

While acknowledging Zhengyan's appeal to native Taiwanese cultural pride, Lu goes further and presents a very detailed analysis of her charisma and leadership style as a way of understanding her broad attraction. At the base of her appeal Lu pinpoints two elements: her appropriation of archetypal parental imagery, and her unquestioned moral integrity. (The following considerations are summarized from Lu 1994:9–13; 1992:8–11.)

As to the first of these factors, Lu cites several testimonials culled from the association's publications that show that many people, far from simply joining the organization, may be said to convert to it. For example, one man who had spent much time in and out of prison came to the Still Thoughts Pure Abode and heard Zhengyan speaking gently about the association's need for help in bearing its heavy responsibilities. He immediately began crying and confessing his faults. Afterwards, he gave up smoking, drinking, and gambling, and went into business selling fruit by the roadside. He contributed to the association from his profits, and subsequently introduced over five thousand new members into it.

In another case, Zhengyan was visited by a woman from a wealthy home who, by her own account, found no satisfaction in all that she had, but was perpetually unhappy. Zhengyan advised her to accompany an association member while she went to call upon poor families. As they proceeded, this woman too broke into tears and realized that she had never known how fortunate she was and how little she had cared for the needs of others. She later credited Zhengyan with "cleansing her heart," and went on to say, "I am grateful to the Master that a group of disreputable women like me, who only knew how to gossip and hang around department stores, could become useful people giving ourselves to social work" (Lu 1994:11).

The reason Zhengyan has this effect on people, according to Lu, is that she simultaneously embodies the strict father and the kind mother. On the one hand, she is uncompromising in challenging greed and materialism, and in calling for people to open their hearts to those unrelated to them. On the other hand, she speaks in soft, kind words and exhibits an unaffected concern for even the most wayward visitor. According to several association members, meeting her is like finding a long-lost relative, or someone in whom one can take refuge for life. One male disciple, who had been dissolute and had no interest in listening to Buddhist lectures, acquired a tape of Zhengyan lecturing and listened to it sixty or seventy times. He said, "The Master speaks softly and gently, like a mother calling her lost child to come home" (Lu 1994:11). Stories such as this are far from rare.

The second factor, her absolute moral integrity, is another key element in her leadership style. Considered objectively, she has very little upon which to base her credibility. Even though she came from a middle-class family, she is still a village woman by upbringing and temperament, and she has received little education. She has studied the Lotus Sutra as indicated above, and she has a solid basis in Confucius and Mencius, but beyond that she has very little in the way of Buddhist education—peculiar for a disciple of Yinshun, arguably the most influential Buddhist intellectual in Taiwan.

However, her integrity allows her to lead by example, and her compassion allows her to affect people deeply with few words. Because she supports herself through handicrafts rather than donations, lives simply, works very hard on behalf of the association, and makes and keeps many vows, she elicits immediate trust. The fact that despite physical frailty and the handicap of being a woman, she has accomplished so much inspires followers to exert themselves to the utmost. Perhaps more than any other Buddhist leader in Taiwan, her followers seek to emulate her, in accordance with her dictum, "The Master's resolve is my resolve, the Buddha's mind is my mind." Many identify with her to the extent that they value their relationship with her more than with their own families, and some make vows to follow her from one rebirth to the next.

Her charisma is such that deliverance from calamity and the healing of physical or mental illnesses are frequently attributed to her.
Accounts of her early austerities and supernatural displays of light are
well known, adding credibility to these attributions, although she herself credits such phenomena to the effects of following her program,
and not to any personal power. All of the above considerations point
to a leadership style that relies very heavily on Zhengyan's personality
and character, and presage problems when she passes from the scene.

Below her in the organizational structure are three vice-presi-
dents, all laypeople, each with responsibility over one of three aspects
of the association's work: medical care, education, and cultural work.
Below them is a group simply called "the Committee," which currently consists of about four thousand members scattered throughout
all the branches. They form the nucleus of the association. The committee evolved from the original thirty women who agreed to join
Zhengyan in her charitable work and, during the early stages of the
association's growth, tended to consist of homemakers aged forty and
above. However, after construction of the hospital started, men began
joining (many introduced by their wives), the average age dropped, and
the average educational level rose. Today, the committee is still about 75
percent female, and takes care of such diverse activities as fundraising,
preaching, giving talks on the association and its work, recruiting new
committee members, accompanying people to the Still Thoughts Pure
Abode or the hospital, volunteering at the hospital, and so on. Before
the founding of the men's auxiliary, they also handled traffic and security for the Still Thoughts Pure Abode and the hospital. For many of
these people, their work within the association amounts to a full-time
job (Lu 1994:14).

The men's auxiliary, called the "Compassion Sincerity Team"
(cichengdui), was formed in 1989 in response to the increasing work of
the association and the greater number of male members. The
Compassion Sincerity Team's role within the organization is not as
great, for the simple reason that men have less free time to devote to it.
Nevertheless, the association has channeled the men's available energy
and time into traditionally male tasks such as directing traffic, maintaining security, and the kind of hospital volunteer work that requires
more strength and stamina than compassion and kind words.

From the above description, it is apparent that the BCRTCA organizational scheme is considerably simpler than that of Fo Kuang Shan. This is because it has a much more clearly focused mission than the latter. Whereas Fo Kuang Shan attempts to provide a comprehensive program with opportunities for all aspects of Buddhist work and cultivation, the BCRTCA engages primarily in medical and social welfare work, and in encouraging the virtue of giving. Accordingly, it does not require the complex organizational infrastructure necessary at Fo Kuang Shan.

The BCRTCA is equally clearly a lay Buddhist association. Although Zhengyan provides the leadership even more emphatically than Xingyun, the backbone of the organization is still the lay members. As far as I can determine, the nuns of the Still Thoughts Pure Abode are few in number and primarily occupied in their handicraft industries and with seeing to the needs of the visitors to the temple. In addition, the Pure Abode itself is very small and does not serve as the main symbol of the organization; that role is reserved to the white marble hospital buildings.

Finally, the association found a way to thrive and grow even during the period of martial law. It did not compete with the BAROC as a general-purpose service organization for Buddhists, but found its own niche as a nationwide social-service agency. Some critics have also stressed that the association posed no challenge to the government or the social order, but provided an outlet for rich industrialists to salve their consciences with their contributions (Jiang 1993a:95). Still, it is clear that the association located an unfilled need in society and filled it with great success. Also, like Fo Kuang Shan, it is apparent that the association's growth accelerated greatly after the lifting of martial law and the liberalization of the law on civic groups, although in this case the connection may not be significant.

The Religious and Moral Vision of the Association

As with Fo Kuang Shan, the BCRTCA relies upon the religious and moral vision of its founder to provide a rationale for its members' continued involvement beyond the effect of Zhengyan's personal charisma. This vision is articulated in her speeches and articles, and has been synthesized in a book entitled *Still Thoughts.* (Zhengyan 1991. Page numbers in the text will refer to this edition.) This book is reminiscent of the "recorded sayings" genre in Chinese Buddhist literature, and its influence has been enormous: As of 1992, it had been through one hundred printings; and in 1990 was number three on the Taiwan best-seller lists (Lu 1992:5). In addition, many elementary and middle school teachers use it as a supplementary text on ethics (Lu 1994:22).

Zhengyan's ethical-religious synthesis is a blend of Confucianism and Buddhism, the traditional and the modern. As noted above, she is familiar with both the *Analects* of Confucius and the *Mencius;* and her thinking reflects Confucian concepts in two primary ways: in the exaltation of the virtue of filial piety *(xiao),* and in her belief that individual moral rectification leads outward to rectification of the family, society, and nation.

Zhengyan's teachings on filial piety go beyond evoking traditional injunctions. In response to the recent prevalence of the nuclear family over the extended family, she emphasizes marital harmony as one of the foundations of true filial piety. Many members of the association reform their own attitudes after engaging in its work among the poor and hearing her words. They then report that their spouses notice the difference in their demeanor, and are thus introduced into the association. The result is frequently the ending of affairs; or husbands spending more time at home, often going so far as to help with household chores. Sometimes the entire family will join the association (Lu 1992:22).

On individual morality as a way to deal with social problems, Zhengyan has written:

> Every woman with a spiritual philosophy should cultivate her mind and body so she is like the moonlight, merciful and soft. ...Illuminate the whole family, or even the whole society and everyone who comes in contact with you, like the cool and refreshing moonlight. This way, we can create a world where mutual love and care exist (p. 51).

Like Confucius and his followers, Zhengyan believes that the key to solving the ills of society lies in the personal cultivation of the individual. As we have seen above, this frequently does lead to concrete improvements in the moral atmosphere of the family; and Zhengyan believes this leads in turn to the rectification of the society and the world. Because of this, Zhengyan's critics sometimes point out that the association never advocates structural changes to right the injustices of society, but contents itself with exhorting members to live righteously.

In terms of specifically Buddhist teachings, Zhengyan takes social work as both metaphor and method to reinterpret traditional Buddhist teachings, and to prescribe new practices suited to contemporary lay society. For example, the term *daochang* traditionally denotes a temple or meditation hall where one works on spiritual cultivation. However, in *Still Thoughts,* Zhengyan calls upon her disciples to think of their everyday workplace as a *daochang,* a "place of the way" (p. 119). When her followers take the work of the association and export it far and wide, she praises this as "expanding their *shentong,*" using a Buddhist term that normally refers to supernormal powers acquired as the fruit of spiritual practice. When one has rendered charitable service to the poor and needy, the happiness one brings them and the sense of ease one feels are "dedicating the merit" (Lu 1994:8).

In order to emphasize that hers is a path of practical action as opposed to study or meditation, Zhengyan points out that the scriptures of Buddhism embody the way *(dao),* and the way is a road that must be trodden (Lu 1994:6). Thus, wisdom is not to be found by study and meditation, but by realizing the nonduality of the donor and the recipient in the transactions of charity. Meditative stabilization (Skt: *samādhi*) may be attained not only in seated meditation, but in going about one's work with a mind concentrated upon the recipient of one's good deeds. In consonance with this emphasis on practical action, the Still Thoughts Pure Abode offers no program of religious practice or cultivation beyond holding morning devotions; apart from this, there are no liturgical observances, no space set aside for meditation practice, no lecture hall.

In a similar manner, Zhengyan interprets the traditional six perfections of Buddhism in light of the association's social welfare work. One begins with the perfection of giving by setting aside one's resources of time and money in an attitude of love. In this way, giving becomes religious self-cultivation. This is why Zhengyan refused the offer of the Japanese businessman to completely underwrite the construction of the hospital; if taken, such an offer would rob association members of this opportunity for religious practice. Likewise, this is why she stressed from the outset of her work setting aside a small amount each day, as opposed to giving a larger sum once a month or once a year. By giving smaller amounts each day, one develops the mind of charity and enhances its constancy.

However, the real perfection of giving involves the other perfections as well. Businessmen who donate millions of N.T. dollars to the association still work in the hospital carrying trash or directing traffic, and many members at large collect funds for the association by going to local trash heaps and picking out items for recycling. By enduring the opprobrium that Chinese society still attaches to such work, one develops the perfection of forbearance. Keeping to one's vow to set aside money daily and to do the work of the association develops the perfection of discipline. Maintaining one's cultivation over a lifetime develops the perfection of effort. As pointed out above, concentrating one's mind while serving the poor or working at one's daily occupation encourages the perfection of concentration. Finally as one engages in compassionate bodhisattva conduct and slowly lets go of all afflicted thoughts, one develops the perfection of wisdom. The perfection of wisdom completes the circle, for once one goes to perform one's charitable work with the purified mind of wisdom, giving is also perfected (Lu 1992:11–21).

Zhengyan has also consciously adapted traditional Buddhist precepts for the needs of modern society. When men join the association, they typically take on the traditional Five Lay Precepts of Buddhism: not to kill, steal, engage in sexual immorality, lie, or drink intoxicating beverages. However, to these Zhengyan adds five more: They are to give up smoking, chewing betel nut, and gambling (which includes video games and the stock market); they are to be filial sons and good family men, and they are to buckle their safety belts when driving cars or wear helmets if riding motorcycles (Lu 1992:16).

The final piece of this brief sketch of Zhengyan's religious-ethical synthesis is her insistence that one approach life from a basic stance of perfect gratitude and perfect love. Of the first, she says, "Feel grateful when confronted with adverse circumstances" (p. 63), and "Others scold me, misunderstand me, slander me; and I am grateful. I thank them for giving me a state of cultivation" (p. 67). The love she advocates is neither romantic nor particularistic, but the expansive, pure love of the Buddha:

> A man who was suffering because of love asked, "Can love be ended?" The Master said, "Love is difficult to end. The Bodhisattva path is to realize love, not to end love. The Buddha also does not end love, but the Buddha's love is universal and undefiled. While personal love and personal desires bring suffering to living beings, only great and long-term love can liberate living beings from pain" (p. 191).

As an example of how important these basic attitudes are, one may look at her advice to a woman whose life was torn by her husband's long-standing affair: Zhengyan instructed her to feel gratitude for this opportunity to reflect upon impermanence, and to generate pure love, not only for her husband but for his mistress as well (Lu 1992:19).

The above represents only a brief look at the religious and moral underpinnings of the BCRTCA's work and rapid growth. It shows Zhengyan as very skilled at taking traditional Confucian and Buddhist moral teachings and reinterpreting them not only for modern society, but specifically for the needs of the laity who make up the backbone of the organization and its mission.

The BCRTCA as a Women's Religious Phenomenon

Finally, we must consider the significance and special features of the phenomenal success of this organization founded by a group of women, headed by a woman, and still predominated by women.

According to Lu, who has observed the association both as a woman scholar and as a member of the organization, its success among women in Taiwan rests upon a paradox. The association clearly gives women meaningful work to do outside the confines of the traditional Chinese home, and women's dominance in the organization gives them a sense of ownership uncommon among civic organizations in Taiwan. One may see this from the fact that, unlike most civic groups run by men with a "women's auxiliary" playing a subordinate role, the BCRTCA has a men's auxiliary in the Compassion Sincerity Team.

However, the association has achieved this level of success by not threatening traditional conceptions of men's and women's roles in society. While women in the organization have the opportunity to work outside the home, their work reflects moral values traditionally associated with women: caring, compassion, humility, gentleness, and harmony. Members do not call for any fundamental reforms either in gender roles or in socioeconomic relations. On this point, Zhengyan and her association have sometimes been criticized by those who advocate a more thoroughgoing modernization of Taiwan Buddhism (For example, see Yang 1993:34).

However, it is clear that the BCRTCA provides a refuge and place of healing for women who are comfortable with these traditional values, and whose lives have been transformed by the technological and social changes that give them increased leisure time and discretionary income. In the association they find a group modeled after the ideal family, with Zhengyan as both mother and father. Zhengyan in turn gives them teachings that not only help them to develop wisdom in the Buddhist sense, but also to reconcile to and fulfill their traditional roles. For example, *Still Thoughts* has an entire section devoted to a perennial problem of Chinese women, that of poor relations between mothers- and daughters-in-law.

The association has also given its female members a sense of unity of purpose, and led them to a previously unheard-of level of empowerment through the pooling of resources. All women in the organization are aware that what is now an international body that moves vast sums of money to bring help where it is needed began as a group of thirty village women who decided to donate a pittance each day. Because of this sense of unity and empowerment, many women have found an escape from the dissatisfaction of living in a materialistic, selfish culture, and have learned to find happiness in giving up their own ego-gratifications for a larger religious purpose. This is what Zhengyan, through her charisma and vision, has brought about for them.

OTHER NEW BUDDHIST ORGANIZATIONS

This chapter has been devoted primarily to a consideration of the two largest organizations that emerged during what Yao characterizes as Taiwan Buddhism's "period of pluralization." However, as I indicated at the beginning of the chapter, this period has brought about a multitude of new Buddhist groups, especially since the lifting of martial law and the liberalization of the laws on civic organizations.

For example, Shengyan (one of those monks who achieved eminence in Taiwan since Retrocession), has recently been expanding and promoting Dharma Drum Mountain, a planned complex near the northeast seacoast that, when completed, will include the Chung Hwa Institute of Buddhist Studies, a university, a high school, an international Chan meditation center, a scholarly publishing and translation bureau, international conference facilities, and a temple. Working through a network of lay people incorporated as the Dharmapala Organization of Dharma Drum Mountain, Shengyan hopes to raise the N.T. $580 million (over U.S. $23 million) necessary to bring the project to fruition. Besides benefiting from the open climate for new civic groups, the establishment of the Dharma Drum complex also takes advantage of the recent liberalization of the education laws.

This organization, along with the BAROC and the two examined in detail in this chapter, appear to be the most stable and well supported as of this writing. New Buddhist organizations are being founded at a great rate, which means that the hopes harbored by some that Taiwan Buddhism may one day achieve some measure of unity seem to be farther away than ever. It may be that such diversification is inevitable when a society makes the transition from authoritarian rule under a dominant, Leninist-style party to a true representative democracy; but I tend to believe, ever since the Buddha on his deathbed refused to name a successor as Master of the Teachings and instructed his disciples to be lights unto themselves, that Buddhism has always lacked a mechanism to achieve institutional unity. What unity Buddhism in Taiwan has enjoyed since 1945 has been artificial, fostered in the environment of martial law and KMT rule. As democratization proceeds, I believe we will see further pluralization until a new equilibrium is achieved.

CHAPTER 7

—✸—

CONCLUSIONS

One of the projects that I had originally envisioned as an integral part of this study was to see if there was any intrinsic value in writing a regional history of Chinese Buddhism such as this. What would such a study reveal? Would it demonstrate any significant regional variations in Chinese Buddhism such that Western scholars would have to question their conception of "Chinese Buddhism" as a single, monolithic phenomenon? Or would the alternative viewpoint prove true, namely that there is nothing so very unique or remarkable about Buddhism in Taiwan, and that scholars are consequently free to generalize their findings about Buddhism from one part of the empire to another?

My conclusion runs along the lines of the first assertion: Buddhism in Taiwan has developed along unique lines. To be sure, one can find similarities in some aspects of Taiwan's historical circumstances with other parts of China. For example, Taiwan was surely not the only frontier area lacking in qualified clergy during the Ming/Qing period, and so we may conclude that nothing particularly new or different happened then. At a somewhat different level, developments in Taiwanese Buddhism exhibit a distinctiveness shared by Buddhism in all parts of the Southern Fujianese cultural sphere. For example, when the Han-Taiwanese first began staging monastic ordinations during the Japanese period, it followed the model of the combined public monastery/hereditary temple found at the Yongquan Temple on Gushan in Fujian province, described by Welch as atypical in Chinese Buddhism. Dongchu, in his report to the BAROC, lamented the lack of public monasteries such as he had been used to in his own home region, and also noted the construction of Buddhist temples in Taiwan as following traditional Fujianese architectural models. In these cases, what is unique is not Taiwan Buddhism, but Southern Fujianese Buddhism.

But let us now turn our attention to aspects of Buddhism in Taiwan that are indeed unique to the island. Taiwan was not the only part of China occupied by Japan before and during World War II, but three factors distinguish the Taiwan experience from that of other occupied areas: First, China freely ceded Taiwan to Japan long before Japan overran other areas of China by force; second, Japan claimed Taiwan as an integral part of the empire (albeit with some ambivalence towards her native inhabitants) for fifty years; and third, by the time of Retrocession, very few of the Han-Taiwanese ever expected to be anything other than Japanese citizens. On the mainland, we read that Buddhists (especially Buddhist clergy), contributed greatly to the effort to oust the Japanese occupational forces. In Taiwan the resistance took a subtler form as the Buddhist establishment steered a path between the Scylla of complete Japanization with the concomitant loss of their Chinese Buddhist identity, and the Charybdis of asserting their heritage too much and risking repression. One can only marvel at the political and diplomatic skills of monks such as Benyuan, Shanhui, and Jueli as they instituted Chinese-style ordination ceremonies and maintained Chinese monastic discipline without incurring the suspicion of the governor-general even as they worked alongside Japanese Buddhist missionaries as members of the Sōtōshū and Rinzaishū.

In addition to maintaining this "dual citizenship," one must notice again that the Buddhists' survival strategies also included joining island-wide religious organizations with *zhaijiao*. Given the hostility that the government-approved forms of institutional Buddhism have traditionally shown to any form of White-Lotus millenarian Buddhism, their cooperation in this period is quite remarkable. One possible explanation for this is that, with both branches of Buddhism living under a non-Chinese regime, the distinction between "government-approved" and "seditious" became meaningless, especially since the governor-general took *zhaijiao*'s sectarian histories, which represented them as direct descendents of Southern Chan Buddhism, at face value. Another factor may be that institutional, monastic Buddhism had no umbrella organization such as the BAROC to give it a unified identity over lay Buddhism; the South Seas Buddhist Association was the only such organization available with Japanese approval, and it included both forms of Buddhism under its aegis.

This alliance was undoubtedly remarkable, but was it unique? Before we assert an unqualified answer in the affirmative, more studies in regional forms of Buddhism are necessary. We must remember here that we are comparing the situation in Taiwan with what we know of Buddhism from previous scholarship, which tends to concentrate on monks who lived and worked around the capital or the provincial seats of the empire and had a good deal of traffic with the imperial bureaucracy. However, an alternative picture emerges from de Groot's regional study of the Xiantian Sect in Fujian Province, which shows that local Buddhist temples and monks on the mainland did interact and cooperate with *zhaijiao* in the late nineteenth and early twentieth centuries. It could be that the situation on Taiwan is merely the tip of the iceberg, and that scholars need to reassess the relationship of monastic and folk Buddhism in areas other than the imperial capital as new evidence emerges from such regional studies.

Another important clue to the uniqueness of Taiwan Buddhism lies in the fact that the mainland monks themselves noticed (and lamented) differences between the Buddhism they had known at home and that which they found in Taiwan. We have already seen that Dongchu, when making his tour of the island, objected the to Fujianese-style architecture of Taiwanese temples. The mainland monks also decried the heavy involvement of laypeople in the ownership and administration of temples, the too-cozy relationship between "orthodox" Buddhism (or what they identified as such in Taiwan) and *zhaijiao,* and the absence of public monasteries to serve as centers for ordination. Their immediate response was to begin planning how they might take the Buddhism they found in Taiwan and re-create it in a form with which they were more familiar and comfortable. All this goes to indicate that even within the confines of Chinese Buddhism itself, people noticed differences between regional forms of Buddhism and they considered these differences significant.

Subsequent to the arrival of the mainland Buddhist establishment in 1949, what has been most striking about the development of Buddhism in Taiwan has been its response to the economic boom of the 1960s and 1970s. The "Taiwan miracle" meant that Buddhist laypeople, both mainlander and Taiwanese, had vastly increased resources for giving donations to Buddhist clergy and institutions. The subsequent construction of large and elaborate temple complexes, construction of Buddhist seminaries and universities, increased investment in publication and mass media enterprises, and other manifestations of conspicuous consumption all form part of a larger picture of developments in the general religious situation in Taiwan at this time.

All of this put together means that, speaking strictly at the level of the phenomena addressed in this study—the institutional development of Buddhism in Taiwan and its relationships with the various governments under which it has lived—Taiwan Buddhism holds a unique place in the overall history and development of Chinese Buddhism. From this we may extrapolate the conclusion that it is indeed worthwhile to engage in regional studies of religion in China, and that, wherever we turn our gaze, we may expect to find unique stories that will enrich our understanding of the subject.

In concentrating exclusively on the question of the uniqueness (or otherwise) of Taiwan Buddhism, there is a danger that we may overlook its other significant features. For example, we can look at the development of Taiwan Buddhism's relationships with the secular government as the culmination of the struggle between Buddhism and the state over the *sangha*'s place in civil society that began in the fourth and fifth centuries C.E. It is well known among scholars of Chinese Buddhism that, from the time of Huiyuan (344–416) on, the government tried, sometimes successfully and sometimes unsuccessfully, to impose restrictions on the growth and activities of the monastic order. (Ch'en 1964:75–77) The fact that such a struggle could ensue in the first place arose from the imperial government's assumption of authority over religious matters. Thus, it might concede special rights to monks and nuns, such as exemption from tax, military conscription, and corvée labor, while at other times imposing regulations upon the community, such as restricting travel or requiring government certificates prior to ordination.

However, the adoption of the Nationalist government's constitution, with its separation of church and state, created a new atmosphere. On the one hand, the government gave up the authority to regulate ordinations and monastic activities. On the other hand, the *saṅgha* lost any privileges that it once had vis-à-vis ordinary citizens. The biographies of Shengyan and Zhenhua make clear that monks were no longer exempt from military service; and, in contemporary Taiwan, even young boys who join the order face the same two years of mandatory military service as any other male citizen. In addition, the government no longer even recognizes the adoption of a monastic name as a legal name-change. One Buddhist monk of my acquaintance showed me his passport, which was still issued to him in his secular name, and informed me that the government still kept all his files under that name. It is clear, therefore, that in Taiwan the *saṅgha*'s historical struggle for "extraterritoriality" has come to an end, with Buddhist clergy now treated as ordinary citizens with all the rights and responsibilities that entails.

Another area in which developments in Taiwan represent a continuation of trends already present in Chinese Buddhist history is the increased involvement in social welfare projects. While the activities of the BCRTCA and Fo Kuang Shan (among many, many others) appear remarkable, a glance at Welch's *The Buddhist Revival in China* shows that Buddhists have long engaged in disaster relief efforts, running orphanages, and social welfare. The difference in Taiwan is one of degree, not of kind. In addition, one can see similar movements worldwide in what has come to be described as "Engaged Buddhism," in which Buddhism's formerly other-worldly outlook is being replaced by a concern for this present world with its political struggles, natural disasters, and social problems. In this respect, Buddhism in Taiwan is simply part of larger trends already underway in Chinese and world Buddhism.

In conclusion, I will beg the reader's indulgence in permitting me to rehearse some of the issues that presented themselves to me during the course of my research on this book and urge that those more qualified than I to deal with these topics consider pursuing them in the future.

First, Buddhist attitudes towards social issues and social action are clearly changing. The fact that some clergy are performing ceremonies for the spirits of aborted fetuses similar to the practice of *mizuko kuyō* in Japan has sparked heated controversies over both the appropriateness of the practice itself and of abortion as a means of birth control. Both the BCRTCA and Fo Kuang Shan promote the ideal of charitable social work as a means of creating a "pure land on earth," and emphasize concrete action in society as a way of exercising the bodhisattva's compassion. Many Buddhist temples, seminaries, and lecture halls, especially in urban areas, have also taken on the extreme environmental degradation of Taiwan, providing a Buddhist rationale for environmental protection, and taking steps themselves to promote these values: exchanging polystyrene bowls and disposable chopsticks for reusable substitutes, recycling, and so on. At the extreme edge of the political spectrum, small groups of Buddhists advocate confrontational political action such as street demonstrations, emphasizing that they do so *as Buddhists.* Back issues of the magazine *Buddhist Culture (Fojiao Wenhua)* provide a rich source of information on these more radical movements.

From the sociological point of view, Buddhism in Taiwan is clearly struggling with issues of identity and status. As we have seen, Taiwan is in step with the rest of the Buddhist world in that laypeople are taking over responsibilities that in the past were the province of ordained clergy, and that some of the clergy find this regrettable. The decline in the overall numbers of ordinations demands analysis, and certainly the prevalence of women in the monastic order as an unprecedented phenomenon of the contemporary situation calls for research from those versed in women's studies theories and methods. I have already published elsewhere an analysis of the way that status is conferred and understood among lay Buddhists (Jones, 1997), but more could be done in this area as well.

One book cannot pretend to say everything that there is to say on a topic so broad as Buddhism in Taiwan. If I have done my job well, then those readers who specialize in the study of Chinese Buddhism should find their appetites whetted, not sated. Perhaps we may see other studies in the future that will look at the subject from other angles and cast new light on areas neglected here. Only then can we say that the study of Buddhism in Taiwan has reached maturity.

NOTES

On Romanization and Pronunciation

1. This dictionary neatly sidesteps the political implications of adopting the pinyin system by calling it the "United Nations phonetic transcription system."

Introduction

1. Vuylsteke 1994, 14.

2. Vuylsteke 1994, 8.

3. See, for example, Murray and Hong 1991. Murray and Hong question the notion that American researchers in history and anthropology could look at Taiwan for examples of Chinese society and culture from the late Qing period, when the Japanese viceregal government had done all it could do to destroy Chinese culture on the island for fifty years. Most especially, Murray and Hong fault most (though not all) researchers for not recognizing the fact that Taiwan itself is a cultural unit that deserves study on its own terms.

4. Welch's own statement of the aims, methods, and sources of his research may be found in his Preface, Welch 1967, v–x.

5. Kubo 1984, 47–71.

6. Yoshioka 1974, 31–45. This work is primarily an account of Yoshioka's trip to Taiwan in the early 1970s.

7. Nakamura et al., eds. 1976, 129–188.

8. See his various works listed in the bibliography.

9. Vuylsteke 1994, 12–14.

10. Vuylsteke 1994, 10.

11. Chang 1994, 29.

Chapter One: The Qing-Dynasty Period

1. The reader should also be aware that anthropologists working in Taiwan have found many villages that were in fact dominated by a single surname, which means that one should not generalize Lin Hengdao's assertions to all towns and villages in Taiwan. Lawrence Crissman, for example, found that single-surname settlements were common along the coast, less common in the interior. See Crissman 1981:96.

2. That is to say, lay Buddhism, white robes being the traditional garb of the laity in Indian Buddism.

3. In her 1985 article on White Lotus Sects in late imperial Chinese history, Susan Naquin organizes such sects into two kinds: sutra-recitation and meditation sects. The first kind emphasizes collective gatherings of all local sect members for sutra-recitation and other works of merit. The second is more private, has much less organizational infrastructure, and emphasizes vertical teacher–pupil lineages rather than horizontal member–member fellowship. The three major sects examined in this section clearly fall into the first type. It is possible, though not certain, that the "Gate of Emptiness" sect is of the second type, and thus would not have left traces of a well-articulated organization. See Naquin 1985:255–291.

Chapter Two: The Early Japanese Period

1. The reader should be aware that this is not the only way in which to divide the important relationships and lineages obtaining during the Japanese period. Two works, the *1992 Gazetteer*:127–145, and Liang and Huang 1993:241–250, both speak of only three "Great Dharma-lineages" at this time. Both base this on the statement that Yongding of the Chaofeng Temple and Benyuan of the Lingyun Chan Temple both came out of the Kaiyuan Temple in Tainan, and therefore both of their temples should be assimilated to the Kaiyuan Temple lineage. Although this is true enough for Yongding, who was in fact the abbot of the Kaiyuan Temple for a time, I find no indication in my other sources that Benyuan spent any time at all in that temple. Jiang Canteng, who provides the most detailed account of Benyuan's life that I have seen, makes no mention of any connection; and these two books provide no further information beyond the assertion that he is part of the Kaiyuan Temple system in some unspecified way.

2. All of the material in this section, unless otherwise noted, is condensed from Jiang Canteng 1993a:49–62.

3. The major source for the life of both monks is Shi Chanhui 1981. This work will subsequently be referred to as *"Annals"* in the text.

4. He may or may not have made the acquaintance of Miaoguo during this first stay in Taiwan. According to the *Biography of Ven. Miaoguo (Miaoguo Heshang Zhuan)*, Jueli stayed in the Lingyun Chan Temple in 1902, a date that is even less credible; and Miaoguo, still a layman at this time, went to visit him there. Miaoguo's *Biography* is quoted in Shi Chanhui 1981, p. 132. However, as the editor notes, Jueli's own autobiographical statement places his first visit to Taiwan in 1909. See Shi Chanhui 1981:119.

5. One might also argue that Jueli, in providing educational opportunities for nuns, actually set in motion one of the primary factors enabling them to become important.

6. It should be noted that this dichotomy of corrupt Japanese/pure Chinese Buddhism, a common theme in materials relating to Buddhism in Taiwan, cannot be taken at face value; it is simply not the case that all tendencies towards liberalizing the monastic precepts to allow for clerical marriage and the abandonment of vegetarianism stemmed from Japanese influence. The monk Lin Qiuwu, a resident of the Kaiyuan Temple in Tainan during the Japanese period and a firm anti-Japanese partisan, advocated these very things on Marxist grounds. See Li Xiaofeng 1991 for Lin's biography.

7. That the Fayun Chan Temple was able to derive significant income from its land-holdings controverts historian Lin Hengdao's assertion, quoted earlier in this chapter, that the Japanese expropriated all such lands.

8. The *Foguang Dacidian* (6:5283a) confuses things further by saying that the temple was founded in 1763 by Shaoguang.

Chapter Three: Buddhist Associations and Political Fortunes during the Late Japanese Period

1. Literally "amulet-spell-water." This is the practice of inscribing magical spells on a paper amulet, burning it, mixing the ashes in water, and giving it to the client to drink in order to cure illness.

2. The editors of the *1971 Gazetteer* note that this clause refers specifically to the Xilai Hermitage conspirators.

3. This account is based on *1971 Gazetteer*:60a–60b. However, a memoir written by Lin Delin, the treasurer of the Daxian Temple in Chiayi, presents a variant reading of the events. In his account, the event grew spontaneously as people discussed the desirability of having a religious event in connection with the fair. Eventually, he and some other representatives met with Ōishi Kendō, the head of the Sōtōshū mission in Taiwan with the idea, and gained his support. Ōishi helped get financing and set up a planning committee that included Shanhui, Benyuan, Huang Yujie, Lin Delin, and others. The lectures lasted thirty-five days (not forty), and Lin's account makes no mention of Lin Puyi, Chen Taikong, or Shibata Kiyoshi. See Lin Delin 1934:23–25.

4. Again, there are discrepancies between the *1971 Gazetteer*'s account of these events and Lin Delin's. Lin mentions nothing of formal negotiations between Ōishi Kendō of the Sōtōshū and the representatives of *zhaijiao*. According to him, someone simply hung a banner behind the speaker's platform which read, "Taiwan Buddhist Youth Association Lecture Meeting" *(Taiwan Fojiao Qingnian Hui Da Jiangyan Hui)* for no other reason than that it sounded good and did not have sectarian overtones. The appearance of the banner prompted people in the audience to wonder what this organization was, and momentum soon gathered for the actual creation of an organization with this name. See Lin Delin 1934:26–27.

The reason I chose to emphasize the *1971 Gazetteer*'s account and relegate Lin Delin's memoirs to the notes is that Lin, although an eyewitness to the events, wrote down his recollections some twenty years later without checking any documentation; and his account is full of lacunae, lapses, and humble petitions to the reader to forgive his faulty memory. However, I did feel it appropriate to include his presentation for the sake of balance.

5. This refers first to the Russo-Japanese War of 1904–05, and second to Japan's nominal entrance into World War I as an ally of Britain. See Reischauer 1970:148–151.

6. This bias can be quite blatant and manifest at times. See for example Chen Xiaochong 1991:513:

> What is worth noting is that many people, without looking at some aspects of the period of Japanese colonial rule such as the Japanization Movement, still hold beliefs that seem true but really aren't. For example, there are people who think that Japanese rule brought with it law and order, without seeing that behind this lurked a totalitarian government and an unchecked police force; or some people say that Taiwan's current economy was built upon a foundation laid by the Japanese, failing to see that the Japanese raised this Taiwanese "cow" intending to keep all the "milk" for herself; still others say that the Japanese instituted universal education on Taiwan, without understanding that this was colonial education in the Japanese language to enslave and so on.

7. That is, if one counts the Japanese Buddhist priesthood as true Buddhist clergy, something many Chinese Buddhists are not willing to grant. However, I suspect that the submission to an official Buddhist establishment outside of *zhaijiao* circles still entailed a significant loss of self-determination for *zhaijiao* adherents.

8. It is not clear to me what his status with Sōtō was. Zheng Zhiming merely says that in 1903 he "received the precepts" from a Sōtō missionary. He does not say what this missionary's status was, nor does he say which precepts Su received. The fact that Su was married is no clue, since Japanese monks could and did marry.

Chapter Four: Retrocession and the Arrival of the Mainland Monks

1. Welch uses the term "Chinese Buddhist Association" as his English rendering of this organization's name. However, the BAROC itself uses the term "Buddhist Association of the Republic of China" in order to distinguish itself from the corresponding organization in the PRC, the *Zhongguo Fojiao Xiehui*, which calls itself the "Chinese Buddhist Association" in its official English communications.

2. Baisheng had been a longtime friend and assistant to Yuanying on the mainland. See Chen Huijian 1994, 88–89. Yuanying himself was still alive at this time but had remained on the mainland. He had even been elected to head the newly formed Chinese Buddhist Association (*Zhongguo Fojiao Xiehui*) under the Communist government, but died in 1953 before he had a chance to take office. See Dongchu 1974:2/803–805.

3. The meaning of this statement is unclear. It might mean "could claim to have received the pure precepts." Alternatively, there might be a typographical error, and the word "received" *(shou)* should have been the word "transmit" (also pronounced *shou*). Given his next statement, the first choice makes more sense.

4. These are monasteries that, in theory, belong to the *saṅgha* as a whole. They are opposed by "hereditary temples" *(zisun miao),* which are the property of the abbot. In traditional mainland Chinese Buddhism, aspirants to ordination normally received tonsure and entered the *saṅgha* only at hereditary temples but could receive full monastic ordination only at public monasteries. This was to prevent from taking root in public monasteries the cliquishness and nepotism that might arise from the quasi-familial rela-

tionships among a disciple and his or her tonsure-master and fellow disciples, and to provide an impartial, standard education in monastic rules and decorum for all ordinands. Dongchu appears to be saying that the ubiquitous lack of decorum, and standardization of such basic things as monastic garb and the liturgy of morning and evening devotions, stemmed directly from the lack of public monasteries and the standardized education they provided.

5. See, for example, "Tongyi Sengqie Fuse Zhufang Yijian Jijin" 1965, 10–28 for a wide variety of opinions on the matter of standardizing monastic robes.

6. "Sunning the scriptures" means taking the collection of scriptures from the temple library and spreading them in the sun once a year to dry them and prevent mildew.

7. Jianzheng points out later in his study that apologists for Yinguang find his emphatic insistence on filiality difficult to reconcile with his leaving home to become a monk, and even more with the story that he expressed delight when he heard the news that his last brother had died childless, thus ending his family line. Yinguang opined that this was a good thing because it closed off one more conduit for the continuation of the cycle of suffering. See p. 68.

8. This refers to a debate among several of the disciples of Hōnen (1133–1212), the founder of the Jōdoshū, or Pure Land School, in Japan. Some of them, such as Ryūkan, thought that the believer needed to recite Amitābha Buddha's name constantly in order to be in the necessary state of mind to attain rebirth at the moment of death. Ryūkan himself recited the name 84,000 times daily. Others, such as Kōsai, thought that one chanting of the name, done with proper faith, sufficed. See Matsunaga and Matsunaga 1976:2/74–78.

9. As for Yinguang inventing this technique, this is recounted by his monastic follower Huizhou. Huizhou says that he searched the Pure Land scriptures for this technique without success, and later went to Yinguang to ask where it had come from. Yinguang laughed and said he invented it by modifying the Chan practice of counting breaths. Shi Huizhou, "Dashi Jiao Wo Nianfo Fangfa" ("The Great Master Teaches Me the Method of Reciting the Buddha's Name"), in Yinguang 1991:7/472–473.

10. Several of Yinguang's letters to Li Bingnan (addressed to him under his dharma-name Deming) are contained in Yinguang 1991:3/369–375.

11. Yinshun was not the first to propound this theory. In the west, several European scholars noted the affinities that Amitābha and his retinue had with Indian and Persian solar deities; and, drawing upon Max Müller's theories of common Indo-European roots for European and Indian language and culture, theorized a direct derivation. One such presentation is found in de Mallmann 1967:85–95. It is possible that Yinshun was influenced by these theories; but if he was, he does not acknowledge it, and he claims not to be able to read any European language. See Yinshun 1985:2.

12. For example, Fujiyoshi points to this part of Yinshun's presentation as the root cause of his subsequent troubles. See Fujiyoshi 1968:740. Also, Yang points to this as one of the two most offensive parts of Yinshun's *Treatise*. See Yang Huinan 1991:20.

13. My experience in Taiwan has shown that, if this relationship was lost during Yinshun's early adulthood, it has since been recovered. Many Pure Land events and dharma-meetings that I attended included invocations of Bhaiṣajya-rāja as well.

14. This was the case, for instance, at the Nongchan Temple in the northern Taipei suburb of Peitou. The founder of this temple was Dongchu, author of the report on Buddhism in Taiwan examined above, and a member of Taixu's reform group. The current abbot, Dr. Shengyan, is Dongchu's disciple.

Chapter Five: The Buddhist Association of the Republic of China

1. He died before actually taking office. See the entry under 1953 in the *Fojiao Shi Nianbiao* 1986:344. Also see Dongchu 1974:2/805. For a synopsis of the struggle between Taixu's reformers and Yuanying's conservatives, see Welch 1968, chapters two and three.

2. According to Dongchu, this means that he was one of the four lamas representing Tibet (the Dalai Lama and Panchen Lama), Inner Mongolia (the Zhangjia Living Buddha), Outer Mongolia (the Rje-bstun Dam-pa Living Buddha), and Qinghai Province (the Dalai Lama and Panchen Lama) (Dongchu 1974:1/386).

3. This is not the only time that one of the ordaining elders was also the abbot of the host temple. The 1955 ordination was held at the Shipu Temple with Baisheng as the preceptor. This appears to vitiate the purpose of this system of ordination in keeping personal tonsure relationships from influencing the course of the ordination session; but it is probably unavoidable, since most of the BAROC leadership at all levels consists of clergy who have one or more temples in their charge. See *1992 Gazetteer*, 159–162 for a list of the host temples, ordaining elders, and numbers of ordinands for ordinations held in Taiwan between 1953 and 1981.

4. I say "technically" because there are no *fully ordained* nuns in the Theravāda lineages due to a lapse in the line of nuns qualified to ordain novices. Recently, scholars have documented the phenomenon of women shaving their heads and leaving the householder life, but without taking full ordination. See Gombrich and Obeyesekere 1988 and Bartholomeusz 1994.

5. Tsung found that, in her small sample of fifty-one nuns, only a miniscule number went into the monastic life from an authentic sense of vocation. Most saw it as an escape from various troubles, restricted options, and so on.

6. According to both the *1971 Gazetteer* and the *1992 Gazetteer*, this June 1957 meeting was the Third National Congress; neither source even mentions the 1955 meeting or the Zhangjia's reelection. However, I am inclined to give more credit to Daoan's report, partly because he is an eyewitness source closer in time to the events, and partly because a 1955 Congress would have been in line with the BAROC's practice of holding new elections every three years. There may be a way to resolve this contradiction if the 1957 National Congress did not involve new elections. In this case it would still count as the Third National Congress.

7. Most of the information in this section, except where noted, comes from Chen Huijian 1994, 81–96.

8. As Welch notes, the whole practice of "transmitting the dharma" is complicated; and the significance of Yuanying's transmission to Baisheng may have any number of meanings. At the very least it certifies that the two men were "of one mind" in matters pertaining to their understanding and experience of Buddhist doctrine and prac-

tice. Since Baisheng specifies that it is the dharma-lineage of two particular temples, it may also have given him the right to be called to either temple as abbot at some point in the future. Also, as the *Foguang Dacidian* points out, the practice is prevalent within the Chan and Esoteric traditions, which emphasize the transmission of an experiential understanding of their teachings. See Welch 1967, 156–158, and FG 2551a,b.

9. Shengyan has been intermittently active in BAROC affairs, but has been increasingly occupied with his own projects both in Taiwan and America. As of this writing, Liaozhong has been the secretary-general of the BAROC for many years. Both of these monks went into the army shortly after this time.

10. Wuming (1911–), a native of Jiangnan province, left the household life at the age of fourteen with his family's blessing. Like Baisheng, he associated with many conservative monks during the 1930s, including Cihang, Yuanying, and the Pure Land revivalist Yinguang. He too engaged in relief work during the war. He is primarily known for his devotion to Guanyin, whom he has seen in meditative visions, and his practice of reciting the Great Compassion Mantra 108 times each day. After coming to Taiwan, he became active in the BAROC, participated in the first ordination at Daxian Temple in 1952, founded temples and Buddhist seminaries, founded an orphanage, engaged in publishing activities, and led international missions abroad. To this day he commands great love and respect among Buddhists on Taiwan and elsewhere. See Chen Huijian 1994, 121–141.

11. Jones 1996, 295–300 contains a detailed account of the conflicts between the two groups at the fourteenth General Conference in Sri Lanka.

12. At the fifteenth WFB meeting in Nepal, the mainland CBA delegation insisted that the BAROC's placard read "Taiwan, China" rather than "Republic of China." The BAROC delegation walked out of the meeting, and the General Conference organizers finally resolved the resulting impasse by removing the placards of *all* the delegations. See Jones 1996, 300.

13. The full text of Baisheng's opening and closing speeches, and the speeches of the above-mentioned government officials, are all reproduced in *Zhongfohui Kan (BAROC Newsletter),* 6 (December 30, 1981), 1–3.

14. Despite the fact that BAROC members had purchased the Shipu and Shandao Temples, it appears that the government continued to place offices on their premises.

15. I believe this accusation needs to be investigated further before it is accepted. Yang's only quoted source for this scenario is Daoan's diaries, which report much "confusion" and "corruption" at the pre-Congress organizational meeting. The diaries' publishers left several blanks in his manuscript for names of people and temples guilty of acting in bad faith, and Yang "guesses" that four of these blanks should be filled with the word "party," i.e., the KMT. See Yang 1991, 35.

Chapter Six: The Period of Pluralization

1. Yao Lixiang 1988, 236–237. Yao divides post-Retrocession Taiwan Buddhist history into three periods: (1) the Period of Japanization, 1945–1952, during which the BAROC was occupied with putting its own infrastructure in place and had not yet effected the de-Japanization of Taiwan Buddhism; (2) the Period of Rebuilding,

1953–1970, during which the BAROC pursued its reformation of Taiwan Buddhism as the sole institutional agency representing Buddhism on the island; and (3) the Period of Pluralization, 1970–present, in which other groups arose to compete with the BAROC for loyalty, representative authority, resources, membership, and vision for the future.

2. As late as 1985, this was still perceived by the BAROC leadership as a problem. The *BAROC Newsletter* at this time carried a report of a meeting of the Youth Committee in which the BAROC secretary-general Liaozhong complained of excessive lay leadership among Buddhist youth and called for more clergy to take over the top positions. See *Zhongfohui Kan (BAROC Newsletter)* 36 (August 26, 1985), 4.

3. Scholars of modern Chinese history note that another set of laws, called the "Provisional Amendments for the Period of Mobilization of the Suppression of Communist Rebellion" (or "temporary provisions" for short) and passed on the mainland in 1948, gave the president sweeping emergency powers and contributed as much as martial law to the repressive political situation before 1987. As of 1993, these provisions were still in effect (See Copper 1993, 91). However, I have come across no evidence that these laws had any effect on either the BAROC's early hegemony or on the pluralism of the later period; and so I have chosen not to discuss these provisions here.

4. For example, Ven. Hengqing (Heng Ch'ing), now a member of the Philosophy Department at National Taiwan University, originally went to America as a layperson to study education. She was ordained a nun in Los Angeles under the Chinese Buddhist missionary monk Xuanhua (Hsuan Hua) in 1975 after she had already earned a master's degree. She remained in America and earned a doctorate in Buddhist Studies at the University of Wisconsin in 1984, and then returned to Taiwan. Since she went to study abroad as a layperson, she applied for foreign study through the Education Ministry as an ordinary citizen and not through the Ministry of the Interior as all "religious figures" were required to at the time. For her story, see Lan Jifu 1993a, 47. Another example is Shengyan, who went to Japan for further study in 1969 with no support from the BAROC, his home temple, or his master. He went, he says, "almost as a protest." See Zhang Shengyan 1993, 96–97.

5. It should be noted that, about two years before this article was written, the BAROC decided to take a more proactive stand by establishing a subcommittee to investigate applicants for BAROC membership in order to prevent heretical or fraudulent groups from gaining admittance under the guise of orthodox Buddhism. See *Zhongfohui Kan (BAROC Newsletter)* 36 (August 26, 1985), 1. Also, in the matter of individual clergy, we have already seen that the BAROC scrutinizes ordinands closely during their ordination sessions and eliminates those whom it feels would harm Buddhism by their conduct or views.

It might also be argued that this criticism is groundless simply because Buddhism has never had a central authority exercising coercive power in matters of doctrine and discipline, in accordance with the Buddha's refusal to name a successor to head the *saṅgha* after he died. The highest level of control that any Buddhist group can exercise is expulsion from the group, which does not amount to expulsion from Buddhism or even from the monastic order.

6. According to Bryan Wilson, there are eight such conditions: (1) sects are exclusive and do not admit of dual allegiances; (2) they claim to have a monopoly on truth; (3) they are lay organizations with an antisacerdotal bias; (4) they reject any spiritual "division of labor"; (5) they are voluntaristic, meaning that members choose to join and must meet certain criteria before they are accepted; (6) they set standards for members and provide sanctions for the wayward or inadequate; (7) they demand total allegiance; and (8) they originate as protest groups. See Wilson 1982, 91–92. It is clear that Fo Kuang Shan may not be considered a sect according to these criteria.

7. For example, the Ven. Xindao (Hsin Tao) left Fo Kuang Shan, spent several years in ascetic practices, and subsequently attracted many followers, who built him a temple in the Fu Lung area of the northeast coast of Taiwan. See Hsin 1992, 2–3.

8. The material for this section comes from the following sources: Chen Huijian 1994, 143–190; Jiang 1993a, 91–95; Lu 1994; Lu 1992; and Chen Meikuei 1994, 68–79.

GLOSSARY OF CHINESE CHARACTERS

Aiguo Fojiao Hui 愛國佛教會
Amoy *see* Xiamen
an 庵
Andō Rikichi (Jpn) 安藤利吉
Anqing (city) 安慶

baibai 拜拜
Baijiaoling 白角嶺
Baisheng, Ven. 白聖法師
Baiyi Fojiao 白衣佛教
Baiyun Temple 白雲寺
Baoguo Temple 報國寺
Baohai, Ven. 寶海法師
Baohua Temple 寶華寺
baojuan 寶卷
Baotong Temple 寶通寺
Beitou 北投
"ben 'zong' zhi yi 'jiao' ren" 本宗旨以
　教人
benshan 本山
Benyuan, Ven. 本圓法師
Benzhong, Ven. 本忠法師
benzun 本尊
betsuin (Jpn) 別院
Bishanyan Temple 碧山巖寺
Biyun Chan Temple 碧雲禪寺
Bunkyō-kyoku (Jpn) 文教局
butsudan (Jpn) 佛壇

butsuji (Jpn) 佛寺

Cai Quan 蔡權
Cai Wenju 蔡文舉
Cai Yunchang 蔡運昌
Cai Zhang (Ven. Xuanjing's lay name)
　蔡漳
Cai Zhenren 蔡真人
caijiao 菜教
Caituan Faren Zhongguo Fojiao
　Wenhua Jiaoyu Jijinhui 財團法人中
　國佛教文化教育基金會
caiwu 財務
Canche, Ven. 參徹法師
Caodong (Xiantian patriarch) 曹洞
Chang Shaosong 常少松
Changuang, Ven. 禪光法師
Chang-hua (town) 彰化
changzhai 長齋
Changzhou 常州
Chanhui, Ven. 禪慧法師
Chanmen Risong 禪門日誦
Chanqi 禪七
chanzong fayao 禪宗法要
Chaofeng Temple 超峰寺 *see also* Old
　Chaofeng Temple *and* New Chaofeng
　Temple
Chen (Ven. Benyuan's lay surname) 沈

235

Chen Cheng 陳成
Chen Taikong 陳太空
Chen Ying (lay name of Pulie) 陳英
Chen Yonghua 陳永華
Chen Yunrong 陳運榮
Chengsheng, Ven. 澄聲法師
Chengyi, Ven. 成一法師
Chen-hua, Ven. 真華法師
chengming 稱名
Chewu, Ven. 徹悟法師
Chiayi (town) 嘉義
chicaijiao 吃(喫)菜教
Chih-pen (town) 知本
Chinnan Gakurin (Jpn) 鎮南學林
Chishan 赤山
chō (Jpn) 廳
Choushe Fojiao Daxue Cujin Weiyuanhui
　籌設佛教大學促進委員會
"chuansu bu chuanseng" 傳俗不傳僧
Chung Hsing University 中興大學
Chung-li (town) 中壢
Cichengdui 慈成隊
Ciguan, Ven. 慈觀法師
Cihang, Ven. 慈航法師
Ciyun Temple 慈雲寺
Conglin Xueyuan 叢林學院

da bei chan yi 大悲懺儀
Dadun 大墩
Dagang Mountain 大岡山
Dagang Shan Benshan Famai Lianyihui
　大岡山本山法脈聯誼會
Dajue Temple 大覺寺
dangki (Hokkien) 童乩
Danshui (town) *see* Tamsui
dao 道
Daoan, Ven. 道安法師
daochang 道場
daojieshi 導戒師
daoshi 導師
Daoyuan, Ven. 道源法師
dashi 大士
Daxian Temple 大仙寺
Daxing, Ven. 大醒法師
Da-Zhuan Xuesheng Foxue Lunwen Ji
　大專學生佛學論文集
Dehua Hall 德化堂

dejie heshang 得戒和尚
Derong, Ven. 德融法師
Deshan Hall 德善堂
Deyuan Chan Temple 德源禪寺
Difang Zhengfu Jieshou Chuli Riren
　Simiao Ciyu Zhuyi Shixiang 地方
　政府接收處理日人寺廟祠宇注意
　事項
dinghang 頂航
Dinghui Temple 定慧寺
Dizang Pusa 地藏菩薩
Dong Yingliang 董應亮
Dongchu, Ven. 東初法師
Dongda Temple 東大寺
Donghai Daxue 東海大學
Donghe Temple 東和寺
Dongwu Daxue 東吳大學
dou (measure of capacity) 斗
duoyuanhua 多元化

Er Er Ba Shi Bian (Jian) 二二八事變(件)

fadan xitong 法擔系統
Fafang, Ven. 法舫法師
Fagu Shan 法鼓山
Faguang Fojiao Wenhua Yanjiusuo
　法光佛教文化研究所
Faguang Foxue Jiangxiban 法光佛學
　講習班
Faguang Temple 法光寺
Faguang Wenhua Jiaoyu Jijinhui 法光
　文化教育基金會
Fahua Temple (Taipei and Tainan)
　法華寺
fahui 法會
fahui youxiang 法會油香
Falun Zazhi Hui 法輪雜誌會
fangsheng yigui 放生儀軌
fapai 法派
fashi 法師
fawu 法務
Fayun Chan Temple 法雲禪寺
Fayun Chansi Tong Jie Lu 法雲禪寺同
　戒錄
Fayun Foxueshe 法雲佛學社
Fayun Nüzhong Yanjiuyuan 法雲女眾
　研究院

fei (bandit) 匪
fei wa shu 飛瓦術
Fengshan 鳳山
fengshui 風水
fenhui 分會
Fo Guang 佛廣
Fo Kuang Shan 佛光山
Fo Shuo Ba Daren Jue Jing 佛説八大
  人覺經
Fo zai ren jian 佛在人間
Fo Zheng 佛正
Foguang Dacidian 佛光大辭典
Foguangshan *see* Fo Kuang Shan
Fojiao Ciji Gongde Hui 佛教慈濟功
  德會
Fojiao Kenan Ciji Gongde Hui 佛教克
  難慈濟功德會
Fojiao Wenhua (periodical) 佛教文化
Fojiao zhi Tese yu Jiazhi 佛教之特色
  與價值
Fomen Bibei Kesongben 佛門必備課
  誦本
Foqi 佛七
foshi 佛事
Foxue Shetuan 佛學社團
foxueyuan 佛學院
fuchi 副敕
Fujian Province 福建省
fukyōjō (Jpn) 佈教所
fulu 附錄
Fuquan Temple 福泉庵
fusi 副寺
Fuxin Hall Branch (Fuxin Tangpai) 復
  信堂派
fuzhoushui 符咒水

ganshi 幹事
Ganyuan Hall 乾元堂
Gaomin Temple 高旻寺
genben yishi 根本意識
gengzhe you qi tian 耕者有其田
guaiseng 怪僧
Guan Wuliang Shou Fo Jing 觀無量壽
  佛經, T.365
Guangde Temple 光德寺
Guangdong (province) 廣東省
Guangfu (Retrocession) 光復

Guangming (Wang Zuotang's monastic
  name) 光明
Guangming Shijie 光明世界
Guangwen, Ven. 廣聞法師
Guangzhou 廣洲
Guanyin Ma 觀音媽
Guanyin Pusa 觀音菩薩
Guanyin Shan 觀音山
Gubo (town in Xiamen [Amoy]) 鼓波
guhun yi 孤魂儀
Guiyi Dao 歸一道
guiyishi 皈依師
gun (Jpn) 郡
Guoji Foguang Hui Zhonghua Zonghui
  國際佛光會中華總會
Guomindang (Nationalist Party) *see*
  Kuo Min Tang
guoshi 國師
Guoxingye (Koxinga) 國姓爺
Guoyou Caichan Chuli Banfa 國有財
  產處理辦法
Gushan 鼓山
guwen 顧問

ha (Jpn) 派
Haichaoyin (periodical) 海潮音
Haichuang Temple 海幢寺
Haihui Temple 海會寺
Haiming Chan Temple 海明禪寺
Haiming Foxueyuan 海明佛學院
Haining (town in Zhejiang Province)
  海寧
Haiyin Temple (Quanzhou, Fujian
  Province) 海音寺
Han Tong 韓同
Hanyang Hall 漢陽堂
Hanyang Hall Branch 漢陽堂派
Hao Baicun *see* Hau Bei-tsun
Hau Bei-tsun (Hao Baicun) 郝柏村
He Liaoku 何了苦
Hengqing, Ven. 恆清法師
heshang 和尚
Higashi-Honganji (Jpn) 東本願寺
Hokke-ha (Jpn) 法華派
Hongjing (Ven. Yongding's style) 宏淨
Hongluo Mountain 紅螺山
hongyi 紅姨

Hongyi, Ven. 弘一法師
honzan (Jpn) 本山
Hsi-chih (town) 汐止
Hsinchu (town) 新竹
Hu Bikang (Baisheng's lay name)
　胡必康
Huairang 懷讓
huaitai ernü 懷胎兒女
Hualien (town) 花蓮
Huang Changcheng 黃昌成
Huang Dehui 黃德輝
Huang Jian 黃監
Huang Shanshi 黃善士
Huang Yujie 黃玉階
huanqiu 圜丘
Huashan Hall 化善堂
Huawen, Ven. 化聞法師
huayan yi 華嚴儀
huayuan 化緣
Huazang Temple 華藏寺
huazhai 花齋
Huguo Renwang Xizai Fahui 護國仁
　王息災法會
Huiji Temple 慧濟寺
Huikong, Ven. 慧空法師
Huimin, Ven. 惠敏法師
Huineng 惠能
Huiquan, Ven. 會泉法師
Huiri Lecture Hall 慧日講堂
huiji 會籍
huixiang 迴(回)向
hujiao weiguo 護教衛國
Huoshan 火山

Ikoma Takahisa (Jpn) 生駒高堂

jia (measure of land area) 甲
Jiandu Simiao Tiaoli 監督寺廟條例
Jiang Canteng 江燦騰
Jiang Ding 江定
Jiang Qingjun (Ven. Shanhui's lay name)
　江清俊
Jiang Shaomo 姜紹謨
Jiang Yunxun 蔣允焄
jiangtang 講堂
Jianning (town in Fujian province) 建寧
Jiantan Temple 劍潭寺

jianyuan 監院
jiao 醮
Jiaoshan 焦山
Jiaoshan Foxue Yuan 焦山佛學院
jiaoshoushi 教授師
Jiasheng (town) 嘉盛
Jiayi (town) see Chiayi
jiby ō seiri (Jpn) 寺廟整理
jie shifu 戒師父
jie xiongdi 戒兄弟
Jiede, Ven. 戒德法師
Jiliunü (alt. name for Fo Guang) 機留女
Jinchuang Sect 金幢派
Jing'an Temple 靜安寺
Jingfeng, Ven. 景峰法師
Jingjin Foqi Yigui 精進佛七儀規
Jingjue Foxueyuan 淨覺佛學院
Jingsi Jingshe 靜思淨舍
jingtu chan 淨土懺
Jingtu Famen Shuoyao 淨土法門說要
jingtu wen 淨土文
Jingtu Xinlun 淨土新論
Jingxin, Ven. 淨心法師
Jingxing, Ven. 淨行法師
Jingxiu Yuan 靜修院
Jingye Monastery 淨業叢林
jinja (Jpn) 神社
Jinmu Niang Niang 金母娘娘
Jinshan Temple 金山寺
jitong 乩童
Jiuhua Shan 九華山
Jiuzhong, Ven. 鳩眾法師
Jōdoshū 淨土宗
Jōdoshū Seizan-ha (Jpn) 淨土宗西山派
Juejing, Ven. 覺淨法師
Jueli, Ven. 覺力法師
junzi 君子
Jushi Xuefo Hui 居士學佛會

Kaican, Ven. 開參法師
Kaihua Hall 開化堂
Kaihui, Ven. 開會法師
Kaiji, Ven. 開吉法師
kaishan 開山
kai shi 開士
Kaiyuan Temple 開元寺
Kaizhao, Ven. 開照法師

Kanakura Enshō, Prof. 金倉圓照
Kegon-shū (Jpn) 華嚴宗
kikeiteki nihonjin (Jpn) 畸形的日本人
Kimura Taiji (Jpn) 木村泰治
kochō (Jpn) 股長
kodō bukkyō (Jpn) 皇道佛教
Kogi Shingonshū (Jpn) 古義真言宗
kominka undō (Jpn) 皇民化運動
kongkong 空空
Kongmen Sect 空門派
Koxinga *see* Zheng Chenggong
Kubo Noritada 窪德忠
Kuo Min Tang 國民黨
kuxing 苦行
kyūkan jibyō (Jpn) 舊慣寺廟

Lan Jifu, Prof. 藍吉富
Laoguan Zhaijiao 老官齋教
Leiyin Temple 雷音寺
li (settlement) 里
Li Bingnan 李炳南
Li Changjin 李昌晉
Li Deming 李德明
li Fahua Jing yi 禮法華經儀
Li Jiancheng 李建成
Li Maochun 李茂春
Li Qian 李騫
Li Tianchun 李天春
Li Yuying 李玉英
Li Zikuan 李子寬
Lian Heng 蓮橫
liang (tael: measure of weight) 兩
Lianfang, Ven. 蓮芳法師
Lianfeng Temple 蓮峰寺
Lianhua Temple (Hubei Province)
    蓮華寺
lianyi zhongxin 聯誼中心
Liaozhong, Ven. 了中法師
Lin Delin 林德林
Lin Fanshu (Ven. Yongding's lay name)
    林蕃薯
Lin Hengdao 林衡道
Lin Huoyan (Ven. Baohai's lay name)
    林火炎
Lin Jiangmai 林江邁
Lin Jinmi 林金秘
Lin Jinshi (Ven. Jueli's lay name) 林金獅

Lin Laifa 林來發
Lin Li 林藜
Lin Meirong, Prof. 林美容
Lin Puyi 林普易
Lin Sen 林森
Lin Shaomao 林少貓
Lin Xiongzheng 林熊徵
Lin Xuezhou 林學周
Lingquan Chan Temple 靈泉禪寺
Lingyan Shan Temple (Suzhou) 靈巖
    山寺
Lingshan Jiangtang 靈山講堂
Lingyin Temple 靈隱寺
Lingyuan, Ven. 靈源禪師
Lingyun Chan Temple 凌雲禪寺
Linji Chan Temple 臨濟禪寺
lishi 理事
lishizhang 理事長
Liu Gan 劉乾
Liu Guoxuan 劉國軒
Liubu Chengyu Zhujie 六部成語註解
Longhu An 龍胡庵
Longhu Yan 龍胡巖
Longhua Hui 龍華會
Longhua Lianyi Hui 龍華聯誼會
Longhua San Hui 龍華三會
Longhua Sect 龍華派
Longshan Temple (Taipei) 龍山寺
Longshu Jingtu Wen 龍舒淨土文
Longyun Temple 龍雲寺
Lu Bing (Puyao's lay name) 盧炳
Luo Jun 羅俊
Luo Qing 羅清
Luojiao 羅教
Luye (town) 鹿野

Marui Keijirō (Jpn) 丸井奎治郎
Mazu Daoyi 馬祖道一
Mengdie Yuan 夢蝶園
Mengjia 艋舺
Mengjia Baoan Fotang Shuojiaochang
    艋舺保安佛堂說教場
Mengshan Shishi Yi 蒙山施食儀
miao 妙
Miaodi, Ven. 妙諦法師
Miaoguo, Ven. 妙果法師
Miaoji, Ven. 妙吉法師

Miaolin Pali Buddhist Graduate School 妙林巴利佛教研究所
Miaomi, Ven. 妙密法師
Miaoqin, Ven. 妙欽法師
Miaoran, Ven. 妙然法師
Miaoyuan, Ven. 妙圓法師
Mile Neiyuan 彌勒內院
mingyu daoshi 名譽導師
mingyu huiyuan 名譽會員
mingyu lishizhang 名譽理事長
minjian chuangjian 民間創建
Minnan Foxue Yuan 閩南佛學院
minzheng si 民政司
mitan 密壇
Mituo Temple 彌陀寺
Miyazaki Naokatsu (Jpn) 宮崎直勝
Miyuan Temple 彌院寺
Mojia (Ven. Xingyun's pen name) 摩迦
Moru, Ven. 默如法師
mu 畝
Myōshinji-ha (Jpn) 妙心寺派

Nagatani Jien (Jpn) 長谷慈圓
Naimukyoku (Jpn) 內務局
Nan'e Bukkyōkai (Jpn) 南瀛佛教會
Nanguang Nüzhong Foxueyuan 南光女眾佛學院
Nanting, Ven. 南亭法師
Nantou (town) 南投
Nanying Fojiao Hui see Nan'e Bukkyōkai
neidan 內丹
New Chaofeng Temple 新超峰寺
nianfo 念佛
nianzhu 念珠
Nichiren-shū (Jpn) 日蓮宗
Nika Bukkyō Bunka Kōryū (Jpn) 日華佛教文化交流
Nishi-Honganji (Jpn) 西本願寺
Nongchan Temple 農禪寺
"nüzi wu cai bian shi de" 女子無才變是德

Ouchuan, Ven. 藕船法師
Ōishi Kendō (Jpn) 大石堅堂
Old Chaofeng Temple 舊超峰寺

pai 派

Peitou see Beitou
Peiying Shuyuan 培英書院
Peng Shuide 彭水德
pu 普
Pu'an 普庵
Pubai 普柏
Pubu 普步
Puci 普賜
Pucong 普聰
Pude 普德
Pufang 普方
Pufo Yigui 普佛儀規
Pujie (Qing-era Zhaijiao figure) 普傑
Pujie (Ven. Shanhui's zhaijiao name) 普傑
Pujing 普經
Pujue 普爵
Pule 普樂
Pulie 普烈
Pumei 普梅
Pumen Temple 普門寺
Pumen Wenku 普門文庫
Pumiao 普妙
Puming Temple 普明寺
Puneng 普能
Puqian 普錢
Puqing 普青
Purong 普榮
Pushan 普善
Pusheng 普昇
Putao 普濤
Puti Shu (magazine) 菩提樹
Putong 普通
putong huiyuan 普通會員
Puxiao 普宵
Puyao 普耀
Puying 普應
Puyou 普有
Puyue 普月

qigong 氣功
qipao 旗袍
Qingcao (Dong Yingliang) 青草
Qingchao Yeshi Daguan 清朝野史大觀
qinggong 輕功
qingjing shi 清淨士
Qingjue Temple 清覺寺

qiqi nianfo yi 七期念佛儀
qiren 奇人
Qita 七塔
Qiushang Hanping 丘上漢平
Qixia Lüxue Yuan 棲霞律學院
Quanguo Huiyuan Daibiao Dahui
　全國會員代表大會

renjian 人間
renjian fojiao 人間佛教
renjian jingtu 人間淨土
rensheng 人生
Rensheng (periodical) 人生
rensheng fojiao 人生佛教
Rinzaishū (Jpn) 臨濟宗
Rinzaishū Taiwan Betsuin (Jpn) 台灣
　別院
Risshō Daigaku (Jpn) 立正大學
Rongfang, Ven. 榮芳法師
rouherenruyi 柔和忍辱衣
roushen 肉身
Ruxue, Ven. 如學法師

San Guan Da Di 三官大帝
Sanchong *see* Sanchung
Sanchung (town) 三重
Sanguan Hall 三官堂
Sanhsia (town) 三峽
Sanhua Hall 三華堂
Sanlun 三論
sanshi qizheng 三師七證
San Tian Gu Fo 三天古佛
Sanyi (Quanzhou prefecture, Fujian
　province) 三邑
sanzhi qipai 三枝七派
Sawaki Kōdō (Jpn) 澤木興道
Shajika (Jpn) 社寺課
Shakai-ka (Jpn) 社會課
Shandao Temple 善導寺
Shande Hall 善德堂
Shanhui, Ven. 善慧法師
Shanzhi, Ven. 善智法師
Shaoguang, Ven. 紹光法師
Shende Hall 慎德堂
shenhua 神化
shehui si 社會司
Shengkai, Ven. 聖開法師

Shengman, Ven. 盛曼法師
Shenguang 神光
Shengyan, Ven. 聖嚴法師
shenming hui 神明會
shentong 神通
Shenxiu 神秀
Shenzhai Hall 慎齋堂
shi (measure of weight) 石
Shi'an, Ven. 石岸法師
shi bo 師伯
shi di 師弟
shi gong 師公
Shi Jianzheng 釋見正
shi shu 師叔
shi xiong 師兄
shi zhi 師姪
Shibata Kiyoshi (Jpn) 柴田廉之
shi e 十惡
shi shan 十善
Shi'er Men Lun 十二門論, T.1568
shifang conglin 十方叢林
Shijie Fojiao Huaseng Hui 世界佛教
　華僧會
Shijie Fojiaotu Youyi Hui 世界佛教徒
　友誼會
Shingon-shū (Jpn) 真言宗
Shinshū Honganji-ha (Jpn) 真宗本願
　寺派
Shinshū Kibe-ha (Jpn) 真宗木邊派
Shinshū Ōtani-ha (Jpn) 真宗大谷派
Shipu Temple 十普寺
"Shishi keke wei fojiao, wei zhong-
　sheng" 時時刻刻為佛教，為眾生
Shizhu Piposha Lun 十住毘婆沙論,
　T.1521
shoshin shōten (Jpn) 諸神升天
shou (receive) 受
shou (transmit) 授
Shoushan Temple 壽山寺
shouzuo 首座
shū (Jpn—administrative unit) 州
shū (Jpn—religious school) 宗
Shuangxi Temple (Shaanxi Province)
　雙溪寺
Shude Hall Branch (Shude Tangpai)
　樹德堂派
Shulin (town) 樹林

Shuilu Fahui　水陸法會
shutchōjō (Jpn)　出張所
si (temple)　寺
si da zushi daochang　四大祖師道場
sishu　私塾
Song Yongqing　宋永清
Sōtōshū (Jpn)　曹洞宗
Sōtōshū Taiwan Betsuin (Jpn)　曹洞宗
　台灣別院
Su Zeyang　蘇澤養
Sun Zhenkong　孫真空
Sunzhang Qingyang, Miss　孫張清揚

Taibei Fojiao Lianshe　台北佛教蓮社
Taicang, Ven.　太滄法師
Taichung (city)　台中
Taidong (town) see Taitung
taiji　太極
Taiji Tu Shuo　太極圖説
taikong　太空
taima (Jpn)　大麻
Tainan (town)　台南
Taitung (town)　台東
Taiwan Bukkyō Chūgakurin (Jpn)
　台灣佛教中學林
Taiwan Fojiao Daoyou Hui　台灣佛教
　道友會
Taiwan Fojian Qingnian Hui　台灣佛
　教青年會
Taiwan Fojiao Qingnian Hui Da
　Jiangyan Hui　台灣佛教青年會大講
　演會
Taiwan Foxue Yuan　台灣佛學院
Taiwan Jilue　台灣紀略
Taiwan Kaiyuansi Shamen Liezhuan
　台灣開元寺沙門列傳
Taiwan Kangyō Kyōshinkai (Jpn)　台灣
　勸業共進會
Taiwan Sheng Fojiao Fenhui　台灣省
　佛教分會
Taiwan Sheng Fojiao Hui　台灣省佛
　教會
Taiwan Sheng Guoyou Tezhong
　Fangwu Dichan Qingjie Chuli Banfa
　台灣省國有特種房屋地產清結處理
　辦法
Taiwan Sheng Jieshou Riren Simiao

Caichan Qingjie Chuli Banfa
　台灣省接收日人寺廟財產清結
　處理辦法
Taiwan Tongshi　台灣通史
Taiwan Xinyue Longhua Fojiao
　Shengguoshan Baoan Tang　台灣新
　約龍華佛教聖國山保安堂
Taixu, Ven.　太虛法師
Taizhong see Taichung
Taizhong Fojiao Lianshe　台中佛教蓮社
Takabayashi Gentaka, Ven. (Jpn)　高林
　玄寶
Tamsui (town)　淡水
tang (hall)　堂
taochan　逃禪
tebie huiyuan　特別會員
Tendai-shū (Jpn)　天台宗
tiandao　天道
tianhua　天化
Tianliu Shilun, Miss　田劉世綸
Tianning Temple　天寧寺
Tianshang Shengmu　天上聖母
tianxia zhaitang　天下齋堂
Tian Zhen Gu Fo　天真古佛
tidu　剃度
tiechi　鐵尺
ting (administrative district)　廳
Tongshan She　同善社
tu sun　徒孫
tu zhi　徒姪
tudun　土遁

Waiguo Ji　外國記
waishu　外叔
Wang Jianchuan　王見川
Wang Jinyun (Ven. Zhengyan's lay
　name)　王錦雲
Wang Rixiu　王日休
Wang Zuotang　王佐塘
Wangmu Miao　王母廟
wangsheng jingtu　往生淨土
Wangsicheng　枉死城
Wangye　王爺
Wanquan Hall　萬全堂
Wanshan, Ven.　萬善法師
Weishi　唯識
Weixin Jingtu　唯心淨土

Weng Wenfeng 翁文峰
"wu zi zhen jing li" 無字真經理
wu jie 五戒
Wu Ziyang 吳紫洋
Wuchang (city) 武昌
Wuchang Foxue Yuan 武昌佛學院
wudun 五遁
Wufeng Bujiaosuo 霧峰佈教所
Wugu 五股
wuji 無極
Wuji Laomu 無極老母
Wuji Shengzu 無極聖祖
Wuji Tianzun 無極天尊
Wuji Zhengpai 無極正派
Wuming, Ven. 悟明法師
Wushang, Ven. 無上法師
Wusheng Laomu 無生老母
Wuyi, Ven. 悟一法師

Xia Daohong 夏道洪
xian (county) 縣
Xianggang Fojiao Lianhehui 香港佛教
聯合會
xiao 孝
xiao qidao 小祈禱
Xiaoyun, Ven. 曉雲法師
Xiamen (Amoy) 廈門
xiantan 顯壇
Xian Tian Dao Mu 先天道母
Xiantian Sect 先天派
Xifang Jingtu 西方淨土
Xigan Hall (Chengdu) 西乾堂
Xihua Hall 西華堂
Xilai An Shijian 西來庵事件
Xilian Jingyuan 西蓮淨苑
Xilian Wenyuan 西蓮文苑
Xindao, Ven. 心道法師
Xinde Hall 心德堂
Xinfeng Xiang 新豐鄉
Xingjin, Ven. 性進法師
Xingshan Hall 興善堂
Xingyun, Ven. 星雲法師
Xining South Road (Taipei) 西寧南路
Xinsheng Bao 新生報
Xinyuan, Ven. 心源法師
Xinyue Longhuajiao 新約龍華教
Xinzhu (town) see Hsinchu

Xiucan (Ven. Zhengyan's self-conferred
dharma-name) 修參
Xiudao, Ven. 修道法師
xiu shi 修士
Xizhi (town) see Hsi-chih
Xu Jinan 徐吉南
Xu Lin 許林
Xu, Mrs. (Ven. Zhengyan's sponsor)
許太太
Xu Wentong 許文通
Xuanhua, Ven. 玄化法師
Xuanjing, Ven. 玄精法師
Xuanshen, Ven. 玄深禪師
Xuepen Jing 血盆經
xue shi 學士
Xuming, Ven. 續明法師
Xuyun, Ven. 虛雲禪師

Yaguang (magazine) 亞光
Yang Huinan, Prof. 楊惠南
yangsheng 養生
Yang Shichun (Pubu's lay name)
楊時春
Yang Shouyi 楊守一
yangxi 養息
yanjiusuo 研究所
Yanpei, Ven. 演培法師
Yao Wenyu 姚文宇
Yaoshi Jiangjing Fahui 藥師講經法會
Yazhou renmin Fangong Tongmeng
亞洲人民反共同盟
yi (administrative unit) 邑
Ye Aming (Ven. Miaoguo's lay name)
葉阿銘
"yi shi zhi wei ji zhi, yi fo xin wei ji
xin" 以師志為己志, 以佛心為
己心
yibao 依報
Yicun, Ven. 義存法師
Yiguandao 一貫道
Yimin, Ven. 義敏法師
Yin Jinan 殷繼南
Yingjiang Temple 迎江寺
yinli shi 引禮師
Yinguang, Ven. 印光法師
Yinguang Fashi Jiayan Lu 印光法師嘉
言錄

Yinshun, Ven. 印順法師
Yishan Temple 一善寺
yishi 議事
Yishi Hall Branch (Yishi Tang Pai)
　一是堂派
Yitong Temple 一同寺
Yongding, Ven. 永定法師
Yongli, Ven. 永力法師
Yongming Yanshou 永明延壽
Yongquan Temple (Fujian) 湧泉寺
Youyuan Temple 有緣寺
youzhi (childish) 幼稚
youzhi (right branch) 右枝
Yu Qingfang 余清芳
Yuan Zhiqian 袁志謙
Yuanguang Temple (Chungli) 圓光寺
Yuanguang Temple (Lion's Head Mt.)
　元光寺
Yuanjing, Ven. 元精法師
Yuanming Dao 圓明道
Yuanying, Ven. 圓瑛法師
Yuemei Mountain 月眉山
Yuhuang Zhenjing 玉皇真經
Yunqi Zhuhong 雲棲袾宏

zaijia Fojiao 在家佛教
zaike Bukkyō (Jpn) 在家佛教
Zeng Puxin 曾普信
Zeng Yuhui 曾玉暉
zhai seng 齋僧
zhaijiao 齋教
zhaijie 齋戒
zhaitang 齋堂
zhai tian yi 齋天儀
Zhaixin She 齋心社
zhaiyou 齋友
Zhan Arui 詹阿瑞
Zhang (Ven. Ruxue's and Shengyan's lay
　surname) 張
Zhang Jiayi 張嘉義
Zhang Lang 張朗
Zhang Luqin (Ven. Yinshun's lay name)
　張鹿芹
Zhang Qiyun, Prof. 張其昀
Zhanghua (town) see Chang-hua
Zhangjia Living Buddha 章嘉活佛
zhanglao 長老

Zhao (Ven. Yinguang's lay surname) 趙
Zhao Puchu 趙樸初
Zhao Zhenpeng 趙桭鵬
Zhaoming, Ven. 照明法師
Zhenchang, Ven. 真常法師
Zheng Chenggong 鄭成功
zheng huiyuan 正會員
Zheng Jing 鄭經
Zheng Langsong 鄭郎松
Zheng Rongsheng 鄭榮生
Zheng Tianzhu 鄭天柱
Zheng Zhuoyun 鄭卓雲
zhengbao 正報
Zhengyan, Ven. 證嚴法師
zhengzhi seng 政治僧
Zhenhua, Ven. see Chen-hua
Zhiben (town) see Chih-pen
Zhiding, Ven. 智定法師
Zhiguang Temple 智光寺
Zhiguang, Ven. 智光法師
zhihui 支會
Zhikai, Ven. 志開法師
Zhimiao, Ven. 智妙法師
Zhiyu, Ven. 智諭法師
Zhongguo Fojiao Hui (BAROC) 中國
　佛教會
Zhongguo Fojiaohui Guoji Wenjiao
　Jiangxue Jijin Dongshihui 中國佛教
　會國際文教獎學基金董事會
Zhongguo Fojiao Sengqie Hui 中國佛
　教僧加會
Zhongguo Fojiao Xiehui 中國佛教
　協會
Zhongguo Fojiao Yuekan (magazine) 中國
　佛教月刊
Zhongguo Fosi Xiehui 中國佛寺協會
Zhongguo Minyi Ceyan Xiehui 中國
　民意測驗協會
Zhongguo Wenhua Xueyuan 中國文
　化學院
Zhonghua Fojiao Hui 中華佛教會
Zhonghua Fojiao Jushi Hui 中華佛教
　居士會
Zhonghua Fojiao Wenhuaguan 中華佛
　教文化館
Zhonghua Fojiao Zonghui 中華佛教
　總會

Zhonghua Fosi Xiehui 中華佛寺協會

Zhonghua Foxue Yanjiusuo 中華佛學研究所

Zhonghua Minguo Dacheng Zhi Sheng Xianshi Fengji Guanfu 中華民國大成至聖先師奉祀官付

Zhonghua Minguo Xiandai Fojiaoxue Hui 中華民國現代佛教學會

Zhonghua Minguo Zongjiao Jiaoyu Xiehui 中華民國宗教教育協會

Zhonghua Xueshu Yuan Foxue Yanjiusuo 中華學述院佛學研究所

Zhongliu Yuekan (periodical) 中流月刊

Zhongri Fojiao Wenhua Jiaoliu 中日佛教文化交流

Zhongxing Daxue *see* Chung Hsing University

zhongzhi 中枝

Zhou Chunmu 周春木

Zhou Dunyi 周敦頤

Zhou Pujing 周普經

Zhou Xuande 周宣德

zhu shen 主神

zhuangyan jingtu 莊嚴淨土

Zhujing Risong 諸經日誦

Zhunan (town) 竹南

Zhuxi Temple 竹溪寺

Zifu Temple 資福寺

zisun miao 子孫廟

Ziyou Shibao 自由時報

Ziyou Zhongguo Taiwan 自由中國台灣

zongchi 總敕

zongjiao 宗教

zongwu 總務

zuozhi 左枝

BIBLIOGRAPHY

Bartholomeusz, Tessa. 1994. *Women Under the Bo Tree: Buddhist Nuns in Sri Lanka.* Cambridge Studies in Religious Traditions, 5. Cambridge: Cambridge University Press.

Boorman, Howard L., ed. 1967. *Biographical Dictionary of the Republic of China.* New York: Columbia University Press.

Brook, Timothy. 1993. *Praying for Power: Buddhism and the Formation of Gentry Society in Late-Ming China.* Harvard-Yenching Institute Monograph Series, 38. Cambridge: Harvard Council on East Asian Studies.

Buddhism in Taiwan. n.d. Taichung: Bodhedrum Publications.

Buswell, Robert E., Jr. 1992. *The Zen Monastic Experience: Buddhist Practice in Contemporary Korea.* Princeton: Princeton University Press.

Cai Jintang. 1994. *Nihon Teikoku Shugika Taiwan no Shūkyō Seisaku (Religious Policies in Taiwan Under Japanese Nationalism).* Tokyo: Dōsei.

Chan, Wing-tsit. 1953. *Religious Trends in Modern China.* New York: Columbia University Press.

Chang, Winnie. 1994. "Finding a Place on the Intellectual Map." *Free China Review* 44 (2): 28–36.

Chanmen Risong (Daily Recitations for the Gate of Chan) [1900] 1988. Changzhou: Tianning Si; reprint, Taipei: Xinwenfeng.

Chen Huijian, ed. 1994. *Dangdai Fomen Renwu (Contemporary Buddhist Figures).* 3rd. rev. ed. Taipei: Dongda Tushu Gongsi.

Chen I-te. 1968. "Japanese Colonialism in Korea and Formosa: A Comparison of its Effects upon the Development of Nationalism." Ph.D. diss., University of Pennsylvania.

Ch'en, Kenneth. 1964. *Buddhism in China: a Historical Survey.* Princeton: Princeton University Press.

Chen Lingrong. 1992. *Riju Shiqi Shendao Tongzhixiade Taiwan Zongjiao Zhengce* (Religious Policies in Taiwan Under the Shinto System During the Period of the Japanese Occupation) Taipei: Zili Wanbao.

Chen, Meikuei. 1994. "Buddhism in Taiwan: The Interactive Relationship Between Buddhism and Social Change." M.A. Thesis, University of Oregon.

Chen Ruitang. 1974. *Taiwan Simiao Falü Guanxi zhi Yanjiu* (A Study of Laws Concerning Temples in Taiwan). Taipei: Sifa Xingzhengbu Mishushi.

Chen Xiaochong. 1991. "1937-1945 Nian Taiwan Huangminhua Yundong Shulun" (An Account and Discussion of the "Japanization Movement" in Taiwan, 1937–1945). In *Taiwan Yanjiu Shi Nian* (Ten Years of Research on Taiwan), ed. Chen Kongli. Taipei: Boyuan Chuban Youxian Gongsi.

Chen Zhengxiang. 1993. *Taiwan Diming Cidian* (A Geographical Dictionary of Taiwan) 2nd ed. Taipei: Nan Tian.

Chen-hua. 1992. *In Search of the Dharma*. Trans. Denis C. Mair, ed. Chun-fang Yü. SUNY Series in Buddhist Studies. Albany: State University of New York Press.

Chongxiu Fengshanxian Zhi (Revised Gazetteer of Fengshan County). [1764] 1983. n.p.: n.p.; reprint, 4 vols. Taipei: Chengwen Chubanshe.

Chongxiu Fujian Taiwan Fuzhi. (The Revised Gazetteer of the Government of Taiwan Prefecture, Fujian Province). [1743] 1983. n.p.: n.p., reprint, 4 vols. Taipei: Chengwen Chubanshe Youxian Gongsi.

Chu Ch'i-lin, ed. 1988. *Taiwan Fojiao Mingcha* (Famous Buddhist Monasteries in Taiwan). 2 vols. Taipei: China Cosmos Publishing House.

Chu Hai-yüan. 1988. "Taiwan Diqu Minzhongde Zongjiao Xinyang yu Zongjiao Taidu" (Religious Beliefs and Attitudes of the People of Taiwan). In *Bianqianzhongde Taiwan Shehui* (Taiwan Society in Transition). ed. Chu Hai-yüan and Yang Kuo-shu. Academia Sinica Ethnology Institute Zhuankan Yizhong, no. 20. 2 vols. Taipei: Academia Sinica.

———. 1990. "Zhonghua Minguo Youguan Zongjiao 'Faling' ji Falü Caoan Huibian" (A Compendium of Laws and [Unpassed] Bills Relating to Religion in the Republic of China). *Minzuxue Yanjiusuo Ziliao Huibian* 2:113–139.

Copper, John F. 1993. *Historical Dictionary of Taiwan*. Asian Historical Dictionaries, No.12. Metuchen: Scarecrow Press.

Da Zang Jing Zong Mulu (General Index of the Chinese Tripitaka). 1981. Taipei: Xinwenfeng Chuban Gongsi.

Daguang. 1991. "Guangfu Hou Taiwan Fojiao Nüxing Jiaosede Bianqian" (The Changing Role of Women in Taiwan Buddhism After Retrocession). *Fojiao Wenhua Yuekan* (Buddhist Culture Monthly) 15:12–17.

Dai Guohui and Ye Yunyun. 1992. *Aizeng 2,28 Shenhua yu Shishi: Jiekai Lishi zhi Mi* (Myth and Reality in Love and Hate of the 2/28 [Incident]: Unraveling a Historical Puzzle). Bentu yu Shijie, 12. Taipei: Yuanliu Chuban Shiye Gufen Youxian Gongsi.

Daoan. 1979. "1950 Niandai de Taiwan Fojiao: Minguo 38 Nian zhi 46 Nian" (Buddhism in Taiwan during the 1950s: From 1949 to 1957). In *Taiwan Fojiao Pian* (Buddhism in Taiwan), ed. Zhang Mantao. Xiandai Fojiao Xueshu Congcan, 87. Taipei: Dacheng Wenhua Chubanshe.

Davis, Winston. 1992. *Japanese Religion and Society*. Albany: State University of New York Press.

de Groot, J.J.M. 1970. *Sectarianism and Religious Persecution in China: A Page in the History of Religions.* 2 vols. Amsterdam: Miller, 1903–1904. Reprint. Taipei: Chengwen Publishing Company.

de Mallmann, Marie-Thérèse. 1967. *Introduction à l'Étude d'Avalokiteçvara.* Annales du Musée Guimet Bibliothèque d'Études, LVII. Paris: Presses Universitaires de France.

Dongchu. 1974. *Zhongguo Fojiao Jindaishi* (A History of Modern Chinese Buddhism). 2 vols. Taipei: Dongchu Chubanshe.

Dumoulin, Heinrich. 1988. *Zen Buddhism: A History.* Trans. James Heisig, Paul Knitter. 2 vols. New York: Macmillan.

E-tu Zen Sun, ed. and trans. 1961. *Ch'ing Administrative Terms: A Translation of the Terminology of the Six Boards with Explanatory Notes.* Cambridge: Harvard University Press.

Editorial Committee for the Complete Annals of the Longshan Temple. 1951. *Mengjia Longshansi Quanzhi.* (The Complete Record of the Longshan Temple, Mengjia), Taipei: The Committee.

Feuchtwang, Stephan. 1974. "City Temples in Taipei Under Three Regimes." In ed. Elvin and Skinner. *The Chinese City Between Two Worlds,* Stanford: Stanford University Press.

Fo Kuang Shan, Committee of Religious Affairs. 1991. *Our Report: What Has Fo Kuang Shan Achieved?* [Kaohsiung: The Committee].

———. 1979. *Wanfo Santan Dajie Tongjielu* (Ten Thousand Buddhas Triple Platform Ordination Yearbook). Kaohsiung: Xingyun.

Foguang Dacidian (Buddha's Light Dictionary). 1988. 8 vols. Kaohsiung: Foguang Chubanshe.

Foguangshan Wenjiao Jijinhui (Fo Kuang Shan Educational and Cultural Foundation). 1991. *Foguangshan Wenjiao Jijinhui Gongzuo Baogao* (Report on the Work of the Fo Kuang Shan Educational and Cultural Foundation). Kaohsiung County, Dashu Rural District: Foguang Chubanshe.

Foguangshan Zongwu Weiyuanhui (Foguangshan Religious Affairs Committee). 1994. *Women de Baogao: Foguangshan Zuole Xie Shemne?* (Our Report: What has Fo Kuang Shan Accomplished?). Kaohsiung: Foguangshan Zongwu Weiyuanhui.

Fomen Bibei Kesongben (Essential Recitations for the Buddha Gate). 1954. Rev. ed. Taipei: Fojiao Chubanshe.

Fu Chu-ying. 1997. *Handing Down the Light: The Biography of Venerable Master Hsing Yun.* Trans. Amy Lui-ma. Los Angeles: Hsi Lai University Press.

Fujiyoshi Jikai. 1968. "Inshun hōshi no 'Jōdo Shinron' ni tsuite—Gendai Chūgoku Jōdokyō no Ichidammen" (On Yinshun's "Jingtu Xin Lun"—a Phase of Pure Land Buddhism in Modern China). *Indogaku Bukkyōgaku Kenkyū* 16 (2): 737–744.

Gombrich, Richard, and Gananath Obeyesekere. 1988. *Buddhism Transformed: Religious Change in Sri Lanka.* Princeton: Princeton University Press.

Günzel, Marcus. 1994. *Die Morgen– und Abendliturgie der Chinesischen Buddhisten.* Veröffentlichungen des Seminars für Indologie und Buddhismuskunde der Universität Göttingen, 6. Göttingen: Seminar für Indologie und Buddhismuskunde.

Han'guk Pulgyo Ch'ongnam (A Comprehensive Handbook of Korean Buddhism). 1993. Seoul: Korean Buddhism Promotion Foundation.

Hardacre, Helen. 1989. *Shintō and the State, 1868–1988*. Princeton: Princeton University Press.

Harrel, Stevan, and Huang Chün-chieh, eds. 1994. *Cultural Change in Postwar Taiwan*. Boulder: Westview Press.

Henricks, Robert G. 1989. *Lao-Tzu Te-Tao Ching: A New Translation Based on the Recently Discovered Ma-Wang-Tui Texts*. New York: Ballantine Books.

Hsin Tao. 1992. *The Quality of Mercy*. Trans. G.B. Talovich. Fulien Village: Lingjiaosan Prajna Cultural and Educational Foundation.

Hsing Fu-chuan [Xing Fuquan]. 1981. "The General Development of Taiwanese Buddhism." In *Chinese Culture: A Quarterly Review* 22 (3): 79–84. See also Xing Fuquan.

———. 1983. *Taiwanese Buddhism and Buddhist Temples*. Taipei: Pacific Cultural Foundation.

Huang Mei. 1984. "Taiwan Bukkyō no Kindō-ha ni tsuite" (On the Chin-chuang Sect of Taiwan Buddhism). *Indogaku Bukkyōgaku Kenkyō* 32 (2): 747–749.

———. 1985. "Taiwan Bukkyō no Senten-ha ni tsuite" (On the Xiantian Sect of Taiwanese Buddhism). *Indogaku Bukkyōgaku Kenkyō* 33 (2): 615–617.

Huang Zhaotang. 1994. *Taiwan Zongdufu* (The [Japanese] Viceregal Government in Taiwan), Chinese trans. Huang Yingzhe. Taipei: Qian Wei Chubanshe.

Jiang Canteng. 1993–1994. "Chaofeng Si yu Dagangshan Pai" (The Chaofeng Temple and the Dagang Mountain Lineage). *Zhongguo Fojiao* 37 (12): 28–33; 38 (1): 30–34; 38 (2): 49–53; 38 (3): 30–33; 38 (4): 28–31; 38 (5): 30–33; 38 (6): 28–31; 38 (7): 32–35.

———. 1994. "Jieyanhou de Taiwan Fojiao yu Zhengzhi" (Taiwan Buddhism and the Government After Martial Law). Paper delivered at International Conference on Buddhism and Chinese Culture, July 24, Taipei.

———. 1988. "Taiwan Dangdai Jingtu Sixiang de Xin Dongxiang" (New Directions in Pure Land Thought in Taiwan). *Dangdai* 28:45–62.

———. 1996. *Taiwan Fojiao Bai Nian Shi zhi Yanjiu* (Studies in One Hundred Years of Taiwan Buddhist History, 1895–1995). Taipei: Nan Tian.

———. 1993a. *Taiwan Fojiao Wenhua de Xin Dongxiang* (New Directions in Taiwanese Buddhist Culture). Taipei: Dongda Chubanshe.

———. 1992. *Taiwan Fojiao yu Xiandai Shehui* (Taiwanese Buddhism and Contemporary Society). Taipei: Dongda Chubanshe.

———. 1990. *Xiandai Zhongguo Fojiao Sixiang Lunji* (Collected Essays on Contemporary Chinese Buddhist Thought). Vol. 1. Taipei: Xinwenfeng.

———. 1993b. "Xiandai Zhongguo Fojiao Yanjiu Fangfaxue de Fanxing" (Reflections on Methods in the Study of Modern Chinese Buddhism). *Dangdai* 84:36–41.

Jiang Canteng and Gong Pengcheng, eds. 1994. *Taiwan Fojiao de Lishi yu Wenhua* (The History and Culture of Buddhism in Taiwan). Taipei: Lingjiushan Banruo Wenjiao Jijinhui Guoji Foxue Yanjiu Zhongxin.

Jianzheng. 1989. *Yinguang Dashi de Shengping yu Sixiang* (The Life and Thought of the Great Master Yinguang). Dongchu Zhihui Hai, 15. Taipei: Dongchu Chubanshe.

Jingxin Da Fashi Wuzhi Huadan ji Pushan Guangdesi Shiwu Zhounian Jinian Zhanji (A Commemorative Volume for the Fiftieth Birthday of the Great Master Jingxin and the Fifteenth Anniversary of the Guangde Temple) 1978. N.p.: n.p.

Jones, Charles B. 1996. "Buddhism in Taiwan: A Historical Survey." Ph.D. diss., University of Virginia.

————. 1997. "Stages in the Religious Life of Lay Buddhists in Taiwan." *Journal of the International Association of Buddhist Studies* 20 (2): 113–139.

Kamata Shigeo. 1973. "Taiwan no Bukkyō Girei—Chōbōka Shō ni tsuite" (A Taiwanese Buddhist Ceremony—Morning and Evening Devotions). *Indogaku Bukkyōgaku Kenkyū* 20 (2): 598–601.

————. 1974. "Taiwan no Bukkyō Girei—Nembutsu Hōkai ni tsuite" (A Taiwanese Buddhist Ceremony—Concerning the Buddha-Recitation Dharma-Meeting). In *Indo Shisō to Bukkyō*, ed. Nakamura Hajime. Tokyo: Shunjōsha.

Kawamura Kōshō. 1980. "Chūka Minkoku Bukkyōshikō" (A Consideration of the History of Buddhism in the Republic of China). *Tōyōgaku Kenkyū* 15:27–43.

Kerr, George H. 1976. *Formosa Betrayed*. Boston: Houghton Mifflin, 1965; reprint: New York: Da Capo Press.

————. 1974. *Formosa: Licensed Revolution and the Home Rule Movement, 1895–1945*. Honolulu: University of Hawai'i Press.

Kogi Shingon-shū. [1940?] *Taiwan Kaikyō Keikaku-an* (Draft Plan for Propagating Religion in Taiwan). [Kōyasan]: Kogi Shingon-shū Kyōgakubu.

Kubo Noritada. 1984. "Taiwan Bukkyō to sono Seikaku" (The Character of Taiwanese Buddhism). *Tsurumi Daigaku Kiyō* 20 (3): 47–71.

Lan Jifu. 1993. *Dangdai Zhongguoren de Fojiao Yanjiu* (The Buddhist Research of Contemporary Chinese People). Shang Ding Foxue Mingzhu Xuankan, 1. Taipei: Shang Ding Wenhua Faxing.

————. 1993. "Dangdai Zhongguoren de Fojiao Yanjiu Qushi" (Trends in Contemporary Chinese Buddhist Research). *Dangdai* 84:42–51.

————. 1991. *Ershi Shijide Zhong Ri Fojiao* (Chinese and Japanese Buddhism in the Twentieth Century). Taipei: Xinwenfeng.

————. 1987. "Taiwan Fojiao Fazhan yu Qianjing" (A Look Back and a Look Ahead at the Development of Taiwan Buddhism). *Dangdai* 11:47–54.

Li Xiaofeng. 1991. *Taiwan Gemingseng Lin Qiuwu* (Taiwan's Revolutionary Monk Lin Qiuwu). Taiwan Bentu Xilie, 1st ser., no. 9. Taipei: Zili Wanbaoshe Wenhua Chubanshe.

Lian Heng. 1977. *Taiwan Tongshi* (General History of Taiwan). Taipei: Youshi Wenhua Shiye Gongsi.

Liang Xiangrun and Huang Hongjie, eds. 1993. *Taiwan Fojiaoshi Chugao* (A History of Buddhism in Taiwan: Preliminary Manuscript). Taipei: Xingmao Chubanshe.

Lin Delin. 1934. "Taiwan Fojiao Xin Yundong zhi Qianqu" (The Precursor to the New Buddhist Movement in Taiwan). *Nan'e Bukkyō* 13 (5):23–34.

Lin Hengdao. 1976. "Taiwan Simiao de Guoqu yu Xianzai" (The Past and Present of Taiwan's Temples). *Taiwan Wenxian* 27 (4): 41–49.

Lin Jindong, ed. 1958. *Zhongguo Fojiao Faling Huibian* (A Compendium of Chinese Buddhist Laws). Taichung: Guoji Fojiao Wenhua Chubanshe.

Lin Meirong and Zu Yunhui. 1994. "Zaijia Fojiao: Taiwan Zhanghua Chaotian Tang Suo Chuan de Longhua Pai Zhaijiao" (Lay Buddhism: The Longhua Sect of Zhaijiao as Transmitted by the Chaotian Hall in Chang-Hua). Unpublished paper.

Lin Wanchuan. 1984. *Xiantian Dao Yanjiu* (Studies in the Xiantian Sect). Tainan: Tianju Shuju.

Lingquansi Tongjie Lu. (A Record of Ordination-Mates at Lingquan Temple). 1955. n.p.: n.p.

Lu Huixin. 1994. "Fojiao Ciji Gongdo Hui 'Fei Simiao Zhongxin' de Xiandai Fojiao Texing" (The Special Characteristics of the Buddhist Compassion Tzu Chi Association's "Non-Temple Centered" Modern Buddhism). Paper delivered at the Center for Chinese Studies Conference on Temples and Popular Culture, March 18–20, Tainan.

————. 1992. "Taiwan Fojiao 'Ciji Gongde Hui' de Daode Yiyi" (The Moral Significance of Taiwan Buddhism's "Buddhist Compassion Relief Tzu Chi Association"). Paper delivered at the Shanxi University International Symposium on Chinese Buddhist Thought and Culture, July 12-18, Taiyuan City.

[Marui Keijirō, attrib.]. [1919]. *Taiwan Bukkyō* (Buddhism in Taiwan). n.p.: n.p.

————, ed. 1993. *Taiwan Shukyō Chōsa Hōkokushō* (Report of the Investigation into Religion in Taiwan). Vol. 1. Taihoku [Taipei]: Taiwan Sōtokufu, 1919; reprint: Taipei: Jieyou Chubanshe.

Masuda, Koh, ed. *Kenkyusha's New Japanese–English Dictionary.* 1974. 4th ed. Tokyo: Kenkyusha.

Matsunaga, Alicia and Daigan Matsunaga. 1976. *Foundation of Japanese Buddhism.* 2 vols. Los Angeles: Buddhist Books International.

Matsunaga Masayoshi, Liu Jinqing, Wakahayashi Masahiro, eds. 1993. *Taiwan Baike* (Taiwan Almanac). Taiwan Baike Congshu, no. 1. Taipei: Kening Chubanshe.

Mendel, Douglas. 1970. *The Politics of Formosan Nationalism.* Berkeley: University of California Press.

Miyamoto Nobuto. 1988. *Nihon Tōchi Jidai Taiwan ni okeru Jibyō Seiri Mondai* (The Problem of Temple Regulation in Taiwan During the Japanese Era). Tenri City: Tenrikyō Dōyūsha.

Mochizuki Shinkō. 1957. *Bukkyō Daijiten.* Rev. ed. 10 vols. Tokyo: Sekai Seiten Kankō Kyōkai.

Morohashi Tetsuji. 1984. *Dai Kanwa Jiten* (Great Chinese–Japanese Dictionary). 13 vols. Tokyo: Daishukan.

Mote, Frederick, and Denis Twitchett, eds. 1988. *The Cambridge History of China.* Cambridge: Cambridge University Press.

Mu Soeng. 1987. *Thousand Peaks: Korean Zen—Tradition and Teachers.* Berkeley: Parallax Press.

Murano Takaaki. 1934. "Zaike Bukkyō to shite no Saikyō" (Zhaijiao, a Form of Lay Buddhism). *Nan'e Bukkyō* 13 (8): 8–11.

Murray, Stephen O. and Keelung Hong. 1991. "American Anthropologists Looking Through Taiwanese Culture." *Dialectical Anthropology* 16:273–299.

Nakamura Hajime. 1981. *Bukkyōgo Daijiten* (Dictionary of Buddhist Terminology). Tokyo: Tōkyō Shōseki Kabushiki Shakai.

Nakamura Hajime, Kasawara Ichio, Kanaoka Hidetomo, eds. 1976. *Ajia Bukkyōshi, Chūgoku hen* (The History of Buddhism in Asia: China). Vol. 4: *Higashi Ajia Shochi-iki no Bukkyō* (Buddhism in all regions of East Asia) Tokyo: Kōsei Shuppansha.

Nanting. 1954. "Liu Nian Lai 'Zhongguo Fojiao Hui' zhi Chengjiu" (The Achievements of the BAROC over the Last Six Years). *Rensheng* 6 (11/12): 308–310.

Naquin, Susan. 1985. "The Transmission of White Lotus Sectarianism in Late Imperial China." In *Popular Culture in Late Imperial China,* eds. Johnson, Nathan, and Rawski, 255–291. Berkeley: University of California Press.

Nelson, Andrew N. 1961. *The Modern Reader's Japanese–English Character Dictionary.* 1st ed. Tokyo: Charles E. Tuttle Co.

O'Neill, P.G. 1972. *Japanese Names: A Comprehensive Index by Characters and Readings.* Tokyo: Weatherhill.

Ono Gemmyō. 1932–1936. *Busshō Kaisetsu Daijiten* (Encyclopedia of Buddhist Literature) 12 vols. Tokyo: Daitō Shuppansha.

Overmyer, Daniel L. 1978. "Boatmen and Buddhas: the Lo Chiao in Ming Dynasty China." *History of Religions* 17 (3/4): 284–302.

Overmyer, Daniel L., and David K. Jordan. 1986. *The Flying Phoenix: Aspects of Chinese Sectarianism in Taiwan.* Princeton: Princeton University Press.

Pittman, Don Alvin. 1987. "Mahayana and the Meaning of Morality: A Study of the Chinese Monk T'ai-Hsü and his Vision for a Modern Buddhism." Ph.D. diss., University of Chicago Divinity School.

Raguin, Yves. 1976. "Buddhism in Taiwan." In *Buddhism in the Modern World,* ed. Heinrich Dumoulin. New York: Macmillan Publishing Company.

———. 1971. "Lion Head Mountain and Buddhism in Taiwan." Trans. J. Maynard Murphy. *Journal of the China Society* 8:21–30.

Reed, Barbara. 1994. "Women and Chinese Religion in Contemporary Taiwan." In *Today's Woman in World Religions,* ed. Arvind Sharma. Albany: SUNY Press.

Reischauer, Edwin O. 1970. *Japan: The Story of a Nation.* New York: Alfred A. Knopf.

Republic of China. Government Information Office. *Republic of China Yearbook.* Annual.

Sakauchi Tatsuo. 1981. "Gendai Chūgoku Bukkyō" (Buddhism in Modern China). *Indogaku Bukkyōgaku Kenkyū* 29 (2): 747–750.

Satō Tatsugen. 1980. "Tōnan Ajia ni okeru Bukkyō no Jittai" (The Condition of Buddhism in Southeast Asia). *Komazawa Daigaku Bukkyō Gakubu Ronshū* 11:31–42.

Sengcan. 1981. "Shanhui Heshan zhi Shengpin ji qi Yigao" (The Life and Manuscripts of Ven. Shanhui). *Rensheng* 6 (11/12) 308–310.

Sharma, Arvind, ed. 1987. *Women in World Religions.* Albany: State University of New York Press.

Shepherd, John R. 1993. *Statecraft and Political Economy on the Taiwan Frontier, 1600–1800.* Stanford: Stanford University Press.

Shi Chanhui (Seck Zen-huei). 1981. *Jueli Chanshi Nianpu* (The Annals of Reverend Jywe-Lih), ed. Shi Ruxue. Miaoli: Fayun Chan Temple.

Shih Yung Kai. 1988. "Nuns of China: Part II—Taiwan." In *Sakyadhītā: Daughters of the Buddha.* 1988. ed. Karma Lekshe Tsomo. Ithaca: Snow Lion.

Shih Heng-ching. 1992. *The Syncretism of Ch'an and Pure Land Buddhism.* New York: Peter Lang.

Shijie Fojiao Tongxun Lu (World Directory of Buddhist Organizations), 1994 ed. Taipei: Falun Zazhi She.

Soothill, William E. and Lewis Hodous. 1977. *A Dictionary of Chinese Buddhist Terms.* London: Kegan Paul, Trench, Trubner & Co., 1937, reprint: Delhi: Motilal Banarsidass.

Sponberg, Alan. 1982. "A Report on Buddhism in the People's Republic of China." *Journal of the International Association of Buddhist Studies* 5 (1): 109–117.

Suzuki Seiichirō. 1989. *Taiwan Jiu Guanxi Su Xinyang* (Old Customs and Folk Beliefs of Taiwan). Rev. and enl. ed. Trans. Feng Zuomin. Taipei: Zhongwen Tushu Gongsi.

Taiwan Fuzhi (Annals of Taiwan Prefecture). [1696] 1983. n.p.: n.p.; reprint, 4 vols. Taipei: Chengwen Chubanshe Youxian Gongsi.

Taiwan Provincial Historical Commission. 1992. *Chongxiu Taiwan Sheng Tongzhi* (Revised General Gazetteer of Taiwan Province), Fasc. 3, *Annals of the People,* vol. 1: *Religion Section,* ed. Chu Hai-yüan. Nantou: The Committee.

———. 1971. *Taiwan Sheng Tongzhi* (General Gazetteer of Taiwan Province). Fasc. 1, *Annals of Folklife,* vol. 2: *Religion Section.* Taipei: The Committee.

Taiwan Sōtokufu Bunkyōkyoku. 1943. *Taiwan Jibyō Mondai: Kyūkan Shinkō Kaizen ni kan suru Chōsa Hōkoku Daishi* (The Problem of Temples and Shrines in Taiwan: The Fourth Report on the Investigation into the Improvement of the Old Customs and Beliefs). n.p.: Taiwan Sōtokufu Bunkyōkyoku.

Tang Xianqing. 1982. "Jushi Tuanti Yi Lishu Zhongguo Fojiao Hui" (Lay Organizations Ought to Submit to the BAROC). *Zhongfohui Kan* 17:4.

Thompson, Laurence G. 1964. "Notes on Religious Trends in Taiwan." *Monumenta Serica* 23:319–349.

Tien Hung-mao. 1989. *The Great Transition: Political and Social Change in the Republic of China.* Hoover Press Publications 378. Stanford: Hoover Institution Press.

Tien Po-yao. 1995. "A Modern Buddhist Reformer in China: the Life and Thought of Yin-shun." Ph.D. diss., California Institute of Integral Studies.

"Tongyi Sengqie Fuse Zhufang Yijian Jijin" (Miscellaneous Opinions from all over Regarding the Standardization of the Color of Monastic Robes). 1965. *Zhongguo Fojiao Yuekan* 9 (9): 10–28.

Tsung, Shiu-kuen. 1978. *Moms, Nuns, and Hookers: Extrafamilial Alternatives for Village Women in Taiwan.* Ph.D. diss., Department of Anthropology, University of California, San Diego.

Ui Hakuju. 1938. *Bukkyō Jiten* (Dictionary of Buddhism). Tokyo: Daitō Shuppansha.

Vuylsteke, Richard. 1994. "A Research Field Comes of Age." *Free China Review* 44 (2): 4–10.

Wang Jianchuan. 1993. "Taiwan Zhaijiao Yanjiu zhi Yi: Jinchuang Jiao Sanlun" (One Study Into Taiwan Zhaijiao: Three Essays on the Jinchuang sect). Paper delivered at Annual Symposium on Eastern Religion, October 2, Taichung.

Wang Shih-ch'ing. 1974. "Religious Organization in the History of a Taiwanese Town." In *Religion and Ritual in Chinese Society,* ed. Arthur Wolf. Stanford: Stanford University Press.

Welch, Holmes. 1967. *The Practice of Chinese Buddhism, 1900–1950.* Harvard East Asian Studies, 26. Cambridge: Harvard University Press.

———. 1968. *The Buddhist Revival in China.* Harvard East Asian Studies, 33. Cambridge: Harvard University Press.

Wilson, Bryan. 1982. *Religion in Sociological Perspective.* Oxford: Oxford University Press.

Wu Jiaqian et al., eds. 1984. *Riben Xingshi Renming Dacidian* (Great Dictionary of Japanese Surnames and Personal Names). Taipei: Mingshan Chubanshe.

Xing Fuquan [Hsing Fu-chuan]. 1981. *Taiwan de Fojiao yu Fosi* (Buddhism and Buddhist Temples in Taiwan). Taipei: Taiwan Shangwu Yinshuguan. *See also* Hsing Fu-chuan.

Xingyun. 1987. *How to Be a Fo Kuang Buddhist.* Vol. 1. Fo Kuang Dharma Propagation Series 7501. Kaohsiung County, Dashe Rural District: Foguang.

———. 1994. *Jie Da Huanxi* (Great Joy for All), Xingyun Baiyu, 2; Foguang Wenxuan Congshu, 5114. Kaohsiung: Foguang.

———. 1952. "Wo Weishenme Yao Ci 'Zhongguo Fojiao Hui' Changwu Lishi?" (Why do I want to Resign form the BAROC Standing Committee?). *Rensheng* 4 (10): 2–3.

Xu Jiaqiang. 1991. "Taiwan Zongjiao Xinyang de Rentong yu Shenfen: Yi ge Chutan" (Self-Identification of Religious Belief and Status in Taiwan: A Preliminary Investigation). M.A. thesis, Donghai University.

Xuxiu Taiwan Fuzhi (Continued Gazetteer of Taiwan Prefecture). [1774] 1984. n.p.: n.p.; reprint, 6 vols. Taipei: Chengwen Chubanshe Youxian Gongsi.

Yang C. K. 1994. *Religion in Chinese Society.* Berkeley: University of California Press, 1961; reprint Taipei: SMC Publications.

Yang Huinan. 1991. *Dangdai Fojiao Sixiang Zhanwang* (A Survey of Modern Buddhist Thought). Taipei: Dongda Tushu Gongsi.

———. 1993. "Taiwan Fojiao Xiandaihua de Xingsi" (Reflections on the Modernization of Buddhism in Taiwan). *Dangdai* 84:28–35.

Yao Lixiang. 1988. "Taiwan Diqu Guangfu Hou Fojiao Bianqian Chutan" (A Preliminary Investigation into Changes in Post-Retrocession Taiwan Buddhism). *Furen Xuezhi: Fa Guanli Xueyuan zhi Bu* 20:229–249.

Yinguang. 1991. *Yinguang Dashi Quanji* (The Complete Works of Great Master Yinguang). Rev. and expanded ed. Comp. and ed. Shi Guangding. 7 vols. Taipei: Fojiao Chubanshe.

Yinshun. 1971. *Fo Zai Renjian (The Buddha in the Human Realm)* Miaoyun Ji, 14. Taipei: Zhengwen Chubanshe.

———. 1992. *Jingtu yu Chan* (Pure Land and Chan). Rev. ed. Taipei: Zhengwen Chubanshe.

———. 1985. *Youxin Fahai Liushi Nian* (Sixty Years of Roaming the Mind in the Sea of Dharma). Taipei: Zhengwen Chubanshe.

Yoshioka Yoshitoyo. 1974. "Taiwan no shukyō no genjō" (The Present Situation of Religion in Taiwan). In *Gendai Chūgoku no Shōshukyō.* Ajia Bukkyōshi: Chūgoku hen, vol. 3, eds. Nakamura Hajime, Kasahara Kazuo, and Kanaoka Shuyo. Tokyo: Kōsei Shuppansha.

Zhang Fangjie, ed. 1992. *Far East Chinese–English Dictionary.* Taipei: Yuandong Tushu Gongsi.

Zhang Mantao, ed. 1978. *Jingtu Sixiang Lunji* (Collection of Essays on Pure Land Thought). Xiandai Fojiao Xueshu Congcan, 66. Jingtu Zong Zhuanji, 3. Taipei: Dacheng Wenhua Chubanshe.

———, ed. 1979a. *Jingtu Zong Gailun* (General Essays on the Pure Land School). Xiandai Fojiao Xueshu Congcan, 64. Jingtu Zong Zhuanji, 1. Taipei: Dacheng Wenhua Chubanshe.

———, ed. 1979b. *Taiwan Fojiao pian* (Buddhism in Taiwan). Xiandai Fojiao Xueshu Congcan, 87. Zhongguo Fojiao Shi Zhuan Shu, no. 8. Taipei: Dacheng Wenhua Chubanshe.

Zhang Shengyan. 1968. *Guicheng* (Homecoming). Taipei: Dongchu Chubanshe.

———. 1993. *Shengyan Fashi Xuesi Licheng* (The Course of my Education and Thought). Taipei: Zhengzhong Shuju.

Zheng Zhiming. 1990. *Taiwan de Zongjiao yu Mimi Zongpai* (The Religions and Secret Societies of Taiwan). Taipei: Taiyuan Chuban Gongsi.

———. 1984. *Taiwan Minjian Zongjiao Lunji* (Collected Essays on Taiwanese Folk Religion). Taipei: Taiwan Xuesheng Shuju.

———. 1989. *Xiantiandao yu Yiguandao* (The Way of the Prior Heavens and the Way of Great Unity). Banqiao: Zhengyi Shanshu Chubanshe.

Zhengyan. 1991. *Jingsiyu* (Still Thoughts by Dharma Master Cheng Yen). Ed. Gao Xinjiang; English trans. Lin Jiahui. Taipei: Xinyang Wenhua Jiaoyu Jijinhui.

Zhu Qichang, ed. 1977. *Taiwan Fojiao Siyuan An Tang Zonglu* (General Record of Buddhist Temples, Hermitages, and Halls in Taiwan). Kaohsiung: Foguang Chubanshe.

Zhuluo Xianzhi (Annals of Zhuluo County). [1724] 1983. N.p.: n.p. Reprint, 3 vols. Taipei: Chengwen Chubanshe Youxian Gongsi.

BUDDHIST PERIODICALS

Fojiao Wenhua (Buddhist Culture)

Haichaoyin (The Sound of Ocean Waves)

Nan'e Bukkyō (The South Seas Buddhist)

Pumen (Universal Gate)

Rensheng (Human Life)

Sengqie Zazhi (*Saṅgha* Magazine)

Taiwan Fojiao (Taiwan Buddhism)

Zhongfohui Kan (BAROC Newsletter)

Zhongguo Fojiao Yuekan (Chinese Buddhism Monthly)

INDEX

ABOUT THE AUTHOR

Charles B. Jones received his doctorate in religious studies in 1996 from the University of Virginia. He spent over three years living in Taiwan pursuing the research for this book and for journal articles about religion on the island. His current research focuses on late Chinese Pure Land thought and interreligious dialogue. Professor Jones is on the faculty of the Department of Religion and Religious Education at the Catholic University of America.